Rapid Agile Business System Analysis:
Fast, Agile, Measurable Results

By Trond Frantzen

Cataloguing-in-Publication Data

Copyright © 2015 by **Trond Frantzen**.

Rapid Agile Business System Analysis:
Fast, Agile Measurable Results

1. Business and system requirement analysis
2. Business and system requirement process modeling
3. Business and system analysis methodology
4. Business and system requirement Data and Information modeling

You can reach Trond Frantzen at the e-mail address below:

Trond.Frantzen@PowerstartGroup.com

The Subject Matter

Acknowledgements

There are a whole lot of people who have influenced my thinking about business and systems analysis, particularly about the differences between the two.

'Business analysis' is a study of <u>what</u> the business is supposed to do, while '<u>system analysis</u>' is a study of the systematic behavior of the business – hopefully, based on what it's supposed to do – with an emphasis on its methods and tools; in other words, <u>how</u> it does things. This has led me to the conclusion that pure <u>business analysis</u> is insufficient for just about any information technology project, while <u>system analysis</u> generally misses the foundation of the work required; and therefore the result becomes an almost insurmountable challenge for the analysts and software engineers who usually do the work.

My solution to this challenge – which I call **Event-based Business Analysis** – has been developed over several years of research and applying the foundations laid down by many other experts, and experience on real projects. The person who influenced me the most was my friend **Bob Proctor** (star of *The Secret*), who taught me the clear difference between **what** and **how** many years ago. From the technical side, the greatest influence has been the late **Matt Flavin** (who wrote the brilliant *Fundamental Concepts of Information Modeling*).

Other influences are **Tom DeMarco**, author or many wonderful books, including the original *Structured Analysis and System Specification*; and **Steve McMenamin**, (who coauthored *Essential Systems Analysis* with **John Palmer**) who introduced me to the early concept of event-based analysis.

While I am forever grateful for what I learned from all of them, the best teachers of all have been my corporate and government clients, and their challenging projects. The real life experience of working in the trenches – dealing with issues and problems and people – has made **Event-based Business Analysis** the solution it is today, which I offer to my colleagues as an open door to successful projects.

Trond Frantzen
Trond.Frantzen@PowerstartGroup.com

1. In the Beginning …

Contents

In the Beginning …

So, why do software projects have so many problems?

"Without knowing anything at all about your current project, I'll bet even money that you'll be late. After all, well over half of all projects deliver late or deliver less than was promised by the original deadline. … Project people seem disconcerted when I proclaim that I'm willing to bet against them. They try so hard to believe that they'll buck the odds. What usually happens is that everyone agrees that the deadline is very tight; everyone works very hard; and then, when people see that they won't make it, they are shocked, disappointed, and deeply dismayed."

Tim Lister in **Waltzing with Bears**

For many projects, the software development cycle simply takes too long, or it doesn't deliver what the business needs.

In **Waltzing with Bears:** Managing Risk on Software Projects, (Dorset House, New York, NY) Tom DeMarco and Tim Lister identify the five primary reasons why software projects have so many problems.

1. **Schedule Flaws:** Either an error in the original schedule or an error in the way the project is run can affect its timing.

2. **Requirements Inflation:** This happens when what is needed changes during development.

3. **Staff Turnover:** When key people leave during a project, it can have a serious impact on continuity and schedule.

4. **Specification Breakdown:** Anything less than complete agreement on specifications can be fatal.

5. **Underperformance:** Substandard work by anyone on the team will affect project quality.

OK, this book isn't about project management. It's about a really fast way to conduct business system analysis and how to uncover the requirements completely, accurately and quickly – right up front.

Therefore, we're not going to talk about flaws to a project's schedule (item # 1 above). Nor are we going to discuss Staff Turnover (item # 3), since that's a different kind of problem than the subject of this book. And we're not going to touch Underperformance (item # 5), since it's more fun to discuss a way that enables all team members to soar with eagles.

That leaves **Requirements Inflation** (item # 2) and **Specification Breakdown** (# 4).

Requirements Inflation, also known as "scope creep", is everywhere. It happens on virtually every project. It seems that we no sooner have agreement on a project's scope, and then it changes. The clients (or "users", as we used to call them) can't seem to make up their minds. They always want to change things. It's like pinning Jell-O to a wall. Every project seems to be a "moving target". Clearly, to eliminate scope creep we need a better and faster way to figure out the business requirements of a project. This book is about that way.

Specification Breakdown is the other area that causes a lot of concern. Anything less than complete agreement on the business requirements can be fatal to a project. Most project requirements are very technical (being based on the solution), or are so vague that the business experts simply can't agree with them. The general nature of most specifications – and the fact that most specifications are based on a predefined solution to the target system – leads invariably to disagreement, scope creep and disillusionment with the technical team. And this lack of clarity usually leads to revisiting many areas of the project to get a better understanding of the client's requirements. This often takes a lot of time and is done over and over again.

To eliminate the circle of revisiting, redefining, revising, and re-specifying business system requirements – the endless loop between specification breakdown and requirements inflation – there must be a better way. This book is about that better way.

What's this all about?

Whether you are a professional with twenty years of experience, or a new analyst, or a certified software engineer – and whether your projects are short two-week efforts or multi-million dollar corporate initiatives – the Event-based analysis approach covered in this book is for you.

This book is about "agile" business system analysis; and how to create a modern, useful business requirements specification <u>really fast</u>, without the tedious constraints of the past, and without the risk often associated with the term "agile".

"Agile" business system analysis is about how to find the exact, specific questions to ask your clients and users (subject-matter experts) – in the specific context of your project – and a way of doing the highest quality analysis in the fastest way possible, without chaos.

It's about business-based analysis suitable to building the complex integrated systems for the 21st century and beyond.

It's about you, and how to find and specify the business requirements for a project successfully. And fast.

This is **not** a book on program design, programming, web site design, database design or social media apps (although it's a prerequisite for all of these). It's not even about programming languages or other software tools. It's not a silver bullet nor is it a magic wand to wave over troubled legacy systems.

This is a book about getting the business requirements for a system specified fast and right the very first time – without engaging in an archaeological dig that takes forever.

"So, is this more of the Same Old Stuff," you might ask, *"but with different packaging?"*

No, this is not more of the Same Old Stuff (with – you guessed it – the Same Old Results). But, find out for yourself. Try the event-based analysis approach described in this book – and you tell me – you can find my email at the end of this chapter.

Admittedly, "agile" means a lot of different things to different people; but few have defined it as well as Scott Ambler. Do a Google search for his name and you'll find all kinds of information about Scott (a Canadian) and the Agile Alliance. My own definition of an agile environment can be found in the last Chapter of this book, since I want to lay down a good foundation before I expand the definition.

I also know there will be some who seek instant answers and instant tools. But the only tools that count in the area of business system analysis is your ability to ask the right questions of your subject-matter experts (clients and users), in the context of your specific project, and to properly document their responses – but without taking forever. This book will show you how to do it – with precision and accuracy.

Exactly what is Analysis?

So, what exactly do we mean by *analysis*? At www.YourDictionary.com, analysis is defined as, *"A separation or breaking up of any whole into its parts, especially with an examination of these parts to find out their nature, proportion, function, interrelationships, etc."* and *"Any detailed examination."*

Yet any system, by its very nature, is a synthesis of different elements *all brought together.* A database can be a system, and so can a garden hose. The importance of the analysis that we conduct is that it reduces the complexity of any system to bite-size pieces that can then be examined individually. In other words, we can minimize complexity by partitioning the effort. This is the essence of **Weinberg's Lump Law**, which we'll explore more throughout this book.

This event-based approach to business analysis provides a method by which the business process and data requirements for any business unit or organization can be determined rapidly.

But why is analysis so important? After all, there is a whole school of thought (yes, they really are out there) which believes that we simply spend too much time on analysis already, *"... so let's just get on with the real work of building the software."* And there's another school of modern-day Luddites that are being pulled into the 21st century against their will, shouting and screaming, *"... complete requirements analysis is impossible and can't be done, so let's just forget it and get on and build something!"*

The value of careful and complete analysis is that it enables us to know exactly where we are going and how complex the going will be. In other words, analysis enables us to create a clear and complete roadmap of the effort required to achieve our goals.

Accordingly, business requirements analysis provides the foundation for all subsequent work.

But it has to be fast, and visible, or it will be perceived as a waste of time.

Finding the Questions to Ask

You will find that a common thread throughout the event-based approach to requirements analysis requires that you ask a lot of questions, and these questions have to be not just "good" but the right questions in order to get at useful information.

Finding the right questions is the first step in analysis. And it's the toughest step, too. Asking questions in a "good" way that's clearly understandable to the client in a meaningful context requires a lot of skill. But "good questions" sounds more like an art than a science. How do we define "good"? What does it mean? Does it mean the same to everyone? All the time?

Good questions are precise and have definite limits that are clear to the listener. A good question indicates a clear context, which makes it more likely that it will get consistent answers from different people.

Naturally enough, not everyone agrees on what makes a "good" question. So, to avoid the complaint that analysis is an "art," this event-based approach to requirements analysis is based on a systematic approach and a language of structure.

The systematic approach in event-based analysis enables you to immediately find all the right questions – in the context of a specific business process – that you must ask the subject-matter experts, to quickly get at the answers.

The language of structure required by event-based analysis is a distinct method for asking good questions that are clear, concise, unambiguous, and understandable to the listener. The methodology underlying event-based analysis provides a solid framework by which you can gather detailed information and document business requirements in a clear and understandable way.

Delivering What the Client Wants, On Time

The most elegant software architecture in the world (a system that works right) isn't worth much if it doesn't do what it's supposed to do (the right system).

A cathedral may display a brilliant system of vaulting, yet it would make a terrible garage. Yes, it would work – but it's not a garage. If a garage is needed, then let's design a good garage. Similarly, a business system must serve the specific needs of its end users.

One of the worst things we, as analysts, can do is to force upon the client what we believe they need. While we might want to try to convince them of what we believe to be worthy, it is our responsibility to deliver to them exactly what they want if they remain unconvinced of the goodness of our view of their business.

With that objective in mind, we start a project. And when starting a project, most of us have been faced with the dreaded "Blank Page Syndrome".

It works something like this:

We get a new project – and all conscious thought immediately grinds to a halt.

After hours on end of staring at holes in space, wondering where to begin and what to do next, panic and frustration begin to set in. Eventually, however, we overcome that helpless, rudderless feeling, and we finally get started.

But getting started was a momentous task.

This event-based analysis approach gets things started really fast, while eliminating the frustrating *"Where do I begin?"* and *"What do I do next?"* questions – part of that "blank page syndrome". In a dramatic departure from the uncertainty of the past, this approach to business system analysis is very straightforward, making it easy to begin and finish.

1. Analysis begins immediately when the project starts. Immediately. The first activity is to find the **context** in which to ask specific questions of the subject-matter experts regarding the target system. Since almost all systems are stimulus/response based, then any system will have many different circumstances or conditions to deal with. These are the contexts, or what we call *business events*.

2. The second activity is to find the **subject** of questions to ask users. We must also recognize that the same subject can show up in different contexts.

3. The third activity is to **structure** the question about each *subject* in the right *context*. These "good" context-driven questions – each with a single specific subject and predicate – presented in precise, non-threatening language, lead to "good" answers virtually immediately. This, in turn, leads to rapid and visible progress. We'll explore how, with specific examples, further on in this book.

Finding subjects to ask questions about, and the context to ask the questions, is a central issue of business system analysis. While the above is not a specific structure as to how we do it (you have to read the whole book for that), I promise not to leave you with wonderfully esoteric abstractions like *"All you have to do is think it through carefully."* While that may sound wonderful, it's also pretty useless. The BUSINESS RULES TABLE (which we'll discuss a little later) will guide you directly to each relevant subject in the target system, and then clearly identify the question to ask in a very specific context.

With this approach to business analysis, you will learn how to identify *business events* or circumstances in the target system; how to find the subjects for context-specific questions; how to structure the questions to be asked; and how to organize and document the results – all without pain.

Business Development Teams

The most successful project teams consist of (a) business partners (i.e., clients and subject-matter experts), and (b) the analysts who documents the client's business requirements in a useful way. The business partners provide the business vision, and the analysts bring the questions to ask. This kind of cooperation allows for separation of biases, and enables a better focus on the business. These teams, consisting of business partners and analysts, enable a true partnership between the members of the teams.

Bringing business professionals – often called users or subject-matter experts – together with analysts in a JAD-like "requirements discovery session" is the cornerstone of the environment you will create when doing business requirements analysis. This environment creates a dynamic and a "user buy-in" rarely seen before. (JAD is an acronym for Joint Application Development; discovery sessions usually conducted in teams consisting of system developers and end users or subject-matter experts).

On the surface, the event-based approach to business system analysis described in this book will appear to be non-technical in its application. It was developed this way because there was no apparent reason to make business requirements analysis a technical exercise. Under the surface, however, there is a very technically precise blueprint that enables us to find context-specific questions to ask the business experts; document concise answers to those questions; and a method to generate a prescription for database design (if required) based directly on the business needs.

The First Principle of Analysis – Simplicity

Several years ago, Gerald M. (Jerry) Weinberg coined what he called **The Lump Law**, which stated: *"In order to understand anything, we shouldn't try to understand everything all at once."* In other words, if we want to understand anything at all, we should learn about it in tiny, understandable chunks, and synthesize it chunk by chunk. It's frustrating and self-defeating to try to understand everything all at once – to try to get the big picture right away – especially if the subject is complex or new. It only leads to information overload.

This same principle applies to business system analysis. That is, if we try to understand everything about the target business requirements all at once (i.e., linking all the stuff in a system), we'll suffer from serious brain sprain. And we certainly won't get the full set of requirements right the first time, because it will simply be too complex. This is usually what happens when we try to figure out the solution first and then try to extract the business requirements to fit that solution.

Accordingly, I have restructured Weinberg's *Lump Law* into **The First Principle of Analysis – Simplicity**, because it is so fundamental to the approach in this book:

Partition the effort to minimize complexity.

In the context of business system analysis, this can be stated as follows:

> **Break down the work required to produce the business requirements into small, non-redundant, manageable and understandable pieces.**

When doing business analysis you will apply this principle often, and we will revisit it many times, in context.

Source Material & Foundations

You may already have noticed that I have not included a bibliography. That's quite intentional. A bibliography, by definition, can only be frozen in the time capsule created by hardcopy publishing. Any bibliography is great stuff when something is first published – but undoubtedly more has been researched, experienced and written since that first publication date on the inside cover of any book.

The approach to business system analysis described in this book is not simply the Same Old Stuff, nor is it regurgitated from someone else's work. However, the foundations were established by others in years gone by; and it's their pioneering work that allowed me to put together this particular approach to business requirements analysis. And if you haven't read the foundation works by now, you probably won't, since so many of these fine old books are now out of date or out of print. Most recent works are spin-offs from the original foundation works.

And that other long list of loosely related methodology works that so many have come to expect as standard reference materials – well, there isn't much point in referring you to works that are well written but still don't address <u>how to find the questions</u> to ask in analysis. (After all, what's analysis all about?) So I won't.

But let's give credit to the pioneers who deserve it the most.

Modern business system analysis would not be possible without the brilliant foundations conceived by several leading thinkers and consultants. That list – and you'll find lots of information on these individuals with a good Internet search – must include the following:

- The event-based concepts of Steve McMenamin and John Palmer;

- The process modelling methods formulated by Tom DeMarco, James & Suzanne Robertson, and Chris Gane & Trish Sarson;

- The data modelling and normalization methods of Peter Chen, Matt Flavin, Edgar F. Codd, Ronald G. Ross, Charles W. Bachman and John Zachman;

- The information engineering philosophy and system thinking of Gerald M. Weinberg; and

- The object-oriented analysis approaches of Grady Booch, Peter Coad and Scott Ambler.

And most importantly, many enhancements to the approach described in this book have come from the in-field experience of the many clients I have had the honor to work with.

The New Business Revolution

Before we proceed to discuss business system analysis, it will be useful to review how we previously approached system analysis and design. Before we learn about something new, it's often helpful to know where we came from, how we used to do things, what was right with what we used to do, why we do what we do, and why we need to change our current approaches.

It's my belief that organizations, private and public, don't try very hard to change how they go about doing "business analysis" until they are so expert with their present paradigm that they become uncomfortable with it. Let me explain.

Organizations and their managers generally only accept that there is something new to learn about "business analysis" when they know there's something wrong with what they are presently doing. If they believe that what they are doing seems to be working just fine, then they are not unhappy with that situation and have no desire to complicate their lives by changing simply for the sake of change. However, as they become more familiar with their approach to business analysis and more expert at it, they also become more familiar with its problem areas – what they can't do, what doesn't work, and what's awkward and difficult. Eventually, these imperfections in their approach to business analysis become the catalyst for the desire to change. Like their experience with some aspects of yesterday's "structured analysis".

When they are sufficiently uncomfortable with their current approach to business analysis, that's when they seek change or improvement. That's when they are ready for it. In the world of software, that's when organizations switch from one product to another, even though they were initially quite happy with the original product. In the world of requirements analysis, that's when we are ready to switch from the old world of structured analysis and data modelling to a new paradigm.

And the need to change paradigms is now more urgent than ever before – because there is a revolution growing, a business revolution. As a result, business system analysis and design is dramatically changing forever. But to understand why we are where we are today, let's take a brief journey through history to review our pedigree.

Heritage

In the beginning, somewhere around 1955 anyway, the availability of commercially usable computers created a new area of specialization. We called it "data processing".

In those early days programmers wrestled with machine language, and even plug boards, to automate processes to help the number-crunchers in private business and government – mostly insurance companies, the banking industry and the military. Wonderful things were expected from this fledgling industry of ours, including a whole lot of magical answers to difficult questions.

Unfortunately, we didn't know the questions, much less the answers. That wasn't anyone's fault. It was a new and young profession and we were all struggling. Sadly, we learned in time, the computer was not the panacea we had so eagerly wished for. In fact, for some, it turned out to be a bit of a headache.

It quickly became evident that while computer systems and programs were static, business was not. The world just wouldn't stand still while we, coding feverishly in the back room, built the computer system.

The tools we had at the time – 2nd and 3rd generation technology and languages – wouldn't allow us to even consider the dynamic aspects of any business problem, so we built monoliths of code that required vast amounts of money and effort. There are some who are still doing it.

Sometimes these rigid system structures, incapable of responding to changes, didn't at all help companies grow and prosper. While smaller, more dynamic organizations were able to respond to needs of the market, the larger monolithic organizations with extensive rigid system structures lagged woefully behind when they had to address rapid and effective change.

Part of the problem was, of course, technology. The machinery we used (both hardware and software) wasn't capable of meeting the business demands placed on it from either the storage or processing points of view. Handling large volumes of data wasn't very practical, and processing was slow by comparison to the need.

Furthermore, programming was a new and hermetic trade that required highly specialized people. Programming languages were awkward and technically difficult.

These new technicians were to become the gurus of data processing.

Evolution

The problems associated with those early efforts at system building gave rise to the notion that since systems were made of code (an erroneous inference, I might add), then the way to fix them would be to improve the programming languages.

So we see the entry of Assembler, Autocoder, COBOL, and finally (sigh) RPG.

Well, this helped but there still seemed to be "users" who complained that the systems didn't do what they really wanted.

"Well," said the experts, *"we'll freeze the specifications. That will do the trick."*

And it sure did! It helped us apply rigor to the process of building systems. And you know what word usually follows 'rigor' … "freezing the spec" did just that.

Those same experts who said "freezing the spec" would solve the problem (we were calling them consultants by now) proceeded to propose another solution to the problem.

"Obviously," the experts said, *"the problem must be in the way the code is organized."*

That sounded reasonable, so we saw the entry of Modular Programming and Structured Programming – and everyone agreed these methods must be the answer!

And they were. To a point.

These wonderful new methods helped (but only on the technical side) to produce "neat code" which could then be corrected easier. Among other wonders of the modern world, we had GOTO-less programming and other techniques to reduce the maintenance effort. This certainly made it easier to fix the bugs that somehow always found their way into the computer system.

But it didn't help much with the original code. The users – the business people – they still complained. These new methods sure made programming easier, but it didn't help to accurately specify what the user wanted and what was to be programmed.

So the experts of the day spoke again:

"All right," they said, *"if the code is good and it's well organized – clearly, then, the problem must be in the design, right?"*

Well, yes, that was right. Of course it was.

So we advanced some more. The Structured Design concepts of Larry Constantine (American) helped considerably. But even this didn't solve the problems of systems that didn't quite do what the business people thought they wanted them to do. They weren't always entirely clear as to what that was, but they knew it was more than what they were getting.

What they were getting, they said, was so ... technical. And it should cost less. And, anyway, systems people should be able to do it faster.

But, they sometimes admitted, what they were getting was without a doubt far better than it ever was in the past. Constantine had brought about a quantum leap in computer system specification. Technical, but good.

So, by about 1975, the *"Structured Revolution"*, as we called it, was well underway. Nothing could stop us now. This appeared to be the answer to all our "system specification" problems.

In the subsequent years we learned all about Structured Programming from Edsger Dijkstra (Holland), and academics Corrado Böhm and Giuseppe Jacopini (Italy). We also experienced Chief Programmer Teams from Harlan Mills (American), Walkthroughs from Ed Yourdon (American) and Tom Gilb (American-Norwegian), Structured Design from Larry Constantine of course, and finally Structured Analysis from Tom DeMarco (American), with notational differences in the STRADIS version by Chris Gane and Trish Sarson (both American). A whole lot of "good structured stuff" was being practiced in hundreds of organizations across the United States, Canada and Europe.

We saw enthusiastic teams designing and implementing systems faster and better than ever before. It was like Camelot in some organizations! We were Knights of King Yourdon's Court, and the world was Structured. We were winning! We had come of age.

Yourdon, Inc. was the most prolific training organization of the day, based in New York, London and Toronto. The terms "structured analysis" became synonymous with Yourdon, although it was primarily Tom DeMarco who developed the methodology.

So between 1976 and 1986 hundreds of thousands of system professionals were trained in North America and Europe in the Structured Methods. The legacy lingers to this very day.

And, if we look carefully, we'll see that most of the legacy systems that we are now replacing were built during this early period of enthusiasm and passion for the new Structured Methods. It therefore follows that much of the maintenance work done on those legacy systems, and their documentation, also resulted from those efforts.

Nonetheless, we did make tremendous gains in both productivity and quality. But, the amount of maintenance we faced did not go down in a measurable, meaningful way. And our documentation was still a mess.

But why? We had good code (we fixed that one), and good design (we were mending that one too), so what could possibly be wrong?

Well, let's face it. Most programs still spring from truly wretched specifications. This is particularly true for "agile" projects. Throughout the development process, subject-matter experts, programmers and analysts are engaged in a kind of ritual dance of successive approximation of the target system. Structured Analysis didn't solve this issue at all, although the quality of work did improve. But not enough.

So, does this mean that we failed with the Structured Revolution? Could it really be that our analysis was faulty? Could all the goodness and light of structured analysis and design not have been the miracle weapon, the silver bullet, we had been expecting? And if structured analysis and design didn't help us much, could we fix it at all? After all, we were doing our work faster and better. Productivity was up, and so was quality. We knew that much. But, was there really any point in doing the wrong thing faster? No matter how well we did it?

While the best of these "Structured Methods", particularly Tom DeMarco's brilliant *"Structured Analysis and System Specification"* (Prentice Hall, Englewood Cliffs, NJ) became the *de facto* requirements specification for virtually all computer assisted software engineering (CASE) products on the market, not much was achieved in the "better-way-of-thinking" department. The industry virtually stood still, resting on its laurels, for an entire decade.

Driven by new technology, however, choices were starting to appear. But we still had to solve the nagging question of how to describe and organize the data; i.e., how to define what we needed to know about the *business* and what data was needed to support business *conditions* and *circumstances*.

So during the late 1970s and through the early 80s, on a second front, technology led the way again with the introduction of database management systems (DBMSs) and the need for data modelling. Unfortunately, as time and technological progress moved relentlessly on, new issues of data organization and integration became even bigger and tougher to resolve and understand.

So a whole new set of challenges came into being. The systems community leaped at promises of these new data tools, anticipating that "the answer" was in new ways of database design. So the experts spoke again. *"Organize the data,"* they said, *"and your problems will be over."*

And a great many latter-day experts went to work to explain the data side of "data processing," trying to understand and implement the earlier works of data gurus such as Dr. Edgar F. Codd (British-American).

Dr. Codd is considered to be the father of the relational data model by just about everyone. His seminal work is considered to be an article titled *A Relational Model of Data for Large Shared Data Banks* published in the Communication of the ACM (June 1970). However, this was actually preceded by release of his IBM Research Report (RJ599, August 19, 1969) on the subject titled *Derivability, Redundancy, and Consistency of Relations Stored in Large Data Banks*. Since his early work, Dr. Codd consistently expanded his definition of the relational model in many papers until his death in 2003. In some academic reports Dr. Codd is referred to as "Edward" or "Ted" Codd.

Following the works of Dr. Codd were two brilliant professionals, Hans Albrecht Schmid (Germany) and J. Richard Swenson (American), who published an early paper while they were with the University of Toronto – *On the Semantics of the Relational Data Model* – which they presented at the ACM Conference on the Management of Data (SIGMOD Conference) at San Jose, CA, in 1975. While this early entry in the field of theoretical relational data modeling – based primarily on the work of Dr. E. F. Codd – was well received in the world of academia, it was largely ignored by private enterprise.

However, Dr. Peter Pin-Shan Chen (Chinese-American) followed in 1976 with publication of *The Entity-Relationship Model – Toward a Unified View of Data*. Peter Chen's now famous work, which expanded on Schmid & Swenson's work of a year earlier, was first published in the ACM Transactions on Database Systems in March 1976. His seminal work is considered to be the foundation of the modern ER Model. (Dr. Chen's paper is still one of the most referenced technical papers in systems journals.)

Eventually there were a whole lot of others who either became recognized or joined the fray: people like Charles W. Bachman (American), Chris Date (British), and John Zachman (American), to mention a few. These experts, and many others, all had good technical answers to the organization and location of data. In other words, everyone agreed they introduced good, sound stuff.

So, while the Structured Analysis revolution was making extraordinary gains on the process side of system development, successes on the data-oriented side were also very impressive.

With the rise of data modelling whole data organizations were set up to design, build and administer databases that would contain all you ever wanted to know about the organization but were afraid to ask. Gargantuan projects were undertaken to define and specify requirements and to control access to corporate data. (Data modelling is also known as entity-modelling, entity-relationship modelling, object modelling, enterprise modelling and E-R diagramming; and sometimes even Information Engineering or IE.)

Unfortunately, while the theories were very convincing, only a small handful of these "big bang" projects were actually successful.

The introduction of database management systems placed the focus on "data" (a very good move) and away from "processing" (not so good). Sadly, while we got closer to relational databases, this selectivity of emphasis moved us even further away from the business.

The argument was that if data was organized internally to reflect the interests of the corporate structure, and the latest output technology was added at the user end, then everyone in the organization would have access to all the data they needed to manage the business better. All the information would be *"right there in the database."* All anyone had to do was to ask. So the experts said.

To design such a structure it was necessary to perform a variety of mysterious analytical tasks to reduce the data to its so-called simplest form. Part of this exercise was to create a model of the corporate data in *"normalized form"* suitable for database design. ("Normalization" is a method by which all forms or redundancy, and therefore potential inconsistency, is removed from the database. We'll talk more about this from a purely business perspective later in the book.) Database designers wrestled with the technical problem of developing a repository of *"normalized data of interest to the enterprise"* and dutifully ignored other business objectives in favor of focusing on logical and physical database designs.

To accomplish this, large departments sprang up, and these database designers wanted to implement a whole new world of data. While the motivation was right, the implementation clearly had a problem. We soon came to call some of these valiant efforts *"close encounters of the third normal form"*.

Most of these exercises took a long time and cost lots of money. And the problem of accurately and quickly specifying the solutions clients thought they wanted still hung on, despite the utopian environment offered by database experts.

Even after all this, the problem of creating an accurate specification, fast and in non-technical business terms, was still not solved.

Having said that, let's not misunderstand. There has been, and continues to be, very considerable evidence of success on the <u>data</u> side of the software engineering profession. The only point of contention is the selectivity and exclusion of process orientation by some of yesterday's and today's professionals.

In my view, the process-oriented data flow specialists – in their excitement and enthusiasm over the Structured Revolution – looked mainly at one side of the equation; while the data-oriented experts looked primarily at the other. And never the twain would meet. Yet the profession had always been called "data processing." There had to be a hint in those two words somewhere. In my opinion, there must be two sides to the business of building systems: the data side and the process side. Just like a coin, these are simply two sides of the same thing.

Data Modelling vs. Information Modelling

The late and brilliant Matt Flavin, now lost to all of us, authored a small, concise book describing a workable approach to defining organizational information needs. His wonderful book, ***Fundamental Concepts of Information Modeling***, was reprinted in

1986 by publisher Prentice-Hall. The book is neither well known nor well read. But it was well ahead of its time.

Incredible as it may seem, that book was written as long ago as the late 1970s, and then first published in 1981. In his book Matt proposed the use of Object-based entity-relationship diagrams to illustrate the organization of information based on the way a company conducts its business.

Matt's version of the entity-relationship diagram (ERD) was supported by descriptions, in business terms, of each Object's data and business policies. His work was largely ignored because most data processors of the day were too interested in the emerging technologies to pay attention to the esoteric art of business-based analysis, including data analysis, however valuable it might be.

The challenge in Matt's significant but complex work was that to understand it, you already had to understand its foundation and you had to have an open mind to be able to deal with new insights and a different paradigm. To a new reader – someone not yet introduced to the concepts of data modelling – this book would probably mean very little. And if you already knew something about data modelling, you would need a very open mind indeed. Matt's thinking was quite different from the accepted, convoluted thinking of the day.

There is nothing elementary about this book, as may be suggested by its title. It is not an easy read. While it does contain a clear description of what I have come to believe is the essential foundation for business data modelling, it's still quite a difficult read. It integrates concepts of Business Object Modelling (more commonly known as *conceptual data modelling* and *object modelling*) with database design and implementation concerns. It is detailed, concise, clear (if you can learn to love the pain of studying it) and quite unambiguous. But, it is deeply complex. It is not for a novice.

But it's nice to know who shone the first light on the path to Object-based business analysis. Matt's work was the first significant extension, in my opinion, to the standard works of the day. Matt treated it as a business modelling exercise, using Objects, which resulted in a database model.

We have certainly come a long way since Matt wrote his powerful book. His little book (one of the IT profession's best kept secrets) was a very personal, and significant, discovery for me. It became the primary foundation for the business systems analysis approach described in this book.

Meanwhile, the data-oriented schools of conventional beliefs were arguing and bickering as to the true meaning of the relational model and how this "true normal form" could solve all problems past, present, and future.

While all this was going on, equally interesting work was developing on another front.

Essential Business Models

The "Structured Analysis" camp, unfettered by internal bickering (mostly), continued to refine data flow diagramming, or process modeling as it was coming to be known, during the early 1980s.

Their ongoing work – felt to be old hat by some since it didn't focus on data modelling, and ridiculed as the "same old stuff" by those who were out of the loop and didn't understand it – was intended to solve another problem: How to not use the entire budget documenting the current system, only to throw the documentation away when done or, at best, to archive it in the darkest dungeon of documentation. And, worse, the conventional approach to structured analysis – whether it was called top down or bottom up – didn't seem to give analysts a better understanding of the business requirement even after they had used structured analysis on a project.

So, how did all this come about? Well, through the "structured revolution" between 1976 and 1986, many of us were weaned on a litany of ...

Current Physical → Current Logical → New Logical → New Physical

This became our shorthand version of a system analysis methodology. Let me refresh your memory as to how this worked:

1. First – we uncovered the **"Current Physical"** system; that is, we documented the existing system in all its finery as best we could. This took a long time and never delivered anything new. But we certainly knew a lot about the system in place. (This is sometimes known as the "AS IS" system.)

2. Second – we distilled the **"Current Logical"** system from the *Current Physical*; that is, we tried to remove all traces of implementation in the existing system, so we wouldn't have a technological bias when developing the new system. Most system designers had a lot of trouble with this.

3. Third – we added new "logical" business requirements to the *Current Logical* model to arrive at the **"New Logical"** system model; that is, we added new business requirements without reference to *how* it would be implemented (the system solution), but rather *what* would be added. Keeping a solution bias out of this proved again to be very difficult for most system designers.

4. Fourth – to the *New Logical Model* we eventually added hardware, software, manual procedures and constraints, finally delivering the **"New Physical"** system model – or, a specification for all seasons. This was more fun than the other three. (This is sometimes known as the "TO BE" system.)

Current Physical → Current Logical → New Logical → New Physical. **Whew!**

But for those of us who understood it (or thought we did), this was still a whole lot faster and better than the more conventional method of creating a system specification. After all, a picture was worth a thousand words. Accordingly, the hundreds of pictures we produced were worth ... Well, you get the idea.

Two things, however, were wrong with this otherwise excellent process:

Problem # 1: The method almost forced system developers, by default, to build the same system again, with the same ways of doing business. The major differences in the "new" system would be better application of technology and perhaps better, more reliable code. But certainly not much was achieved in the "better business methods" department. And while we all agreed that systems consist of software, manual procedures and people, very few developers actually looked beyond the code.

Problem # 2: Re-creating the existing system's documentation (that was the *Current Physical* model) was certainly an admission that the "current" documentation either wasn't there or couldn't be trusted. While our users were impressed by our ability to re-create some of the documentation, they were less impressed by the fact that – after a great deal of time – we were no closer to specifying their new system.

Interestingly enough, this exercise of creating the *Current Physical*, or documenting the existing system – full of its biases and older ways of doing business – was one of the most time consuming and unproductive undertakings imaginable. Trying to figure out the intricacies and culture of the existing system often became an archaeological dig of mammoth proportions.

But let's face it: The user didn't ask for the current system; they asked for a new one.

When we were done (and most will admit that we were never really done), we were sure a whole lot wiser about the existing system, but we were not a whole lot wiser about the requirements for the new system! It took a long time to do this *Current Physical* model, and the resulting documentation was usually filed away in some dark recess to never be looked at again. But we did it because it was the then-current industry wisdom. And, it was a lot better than what we had before.

No wonder clients and users got a bit frustrated when told that a team of highly paid computer professionals were documenting the system some other highly paid computer professionals designed and documented a few years ago. *Why*, they wondered, *do we need a blueprint of the old building*, functional as it is, *to be able to build a new one?* The new building would have different architecture, different and expanded functionality, different dimensions, and different patterns of data and traffic flows. Why did we need a blueprint of the old building to be able to create a blueprint for the new building?

The first theory (told to us by the experts) was, of course, that we had to know where we had been to be able to figure out where we were going; otherwise we might stumble along the way.

This is interesting, but...

The other theory (we were told by those same experts of the day) was that it was far too difficult to get our users to accurately tell us about their requirements. After all, we were told, they didn't really understand the complexities of the business, and in any event they would only tell us about the old system with a few changes. They were just users after all.

We now know that those popular theories were based on some imagined fantasy. Our users already knew where they were, and where they had been. That's why they wanted new systems. And they knew it wasn't just a matter of regurgitating the old system with a few new wrinkles. They knew that they wanted changes to the current system because they were dissatisfied with the status quo. And they wanted to improve the business methods as well as the application of technology. They wanted to re-engineer the systems and, if possible, the business.

And, yes, they could tell us all about it – if we had a common language with which to communicate effectively, to ask questions, and to document the results. If we only knew how to ask the questions, then we would be able to get at the answers our users had.

I have come to believe that a *Current Physical* model of a system (or an "AS IS" model) was – and still is, in many cases – documented primarily because analysts didn't know how to find the specific questions to ask users. Therefore, it becomes easier to document what already existed and then use that foundation as a starting point. (*"It's the same, but different…"*)

In the past, it made a lot of sense to document answers from the existing system (based on code and output) when we had no idea what the questions should be, and we didn't have a common language with which to communicate with users. It made a lot of sense – but it didn't make a new system, with new functionality, or new opportunities for business or process re-engineering. It only gave us the old stuff, with old business methods, and it took much too long – simply because we didn't know how to find the questions to ask them.

And that's the way almost everyone has been doing it since the beginning of time, when wheels were square. And just about everyone knows it doesn't work very well.

But since we did have to go through the exercise of the archaeological dig to create the *Current Physical* model, it's little wonder that it took almost forever doing analysis. And to make matters worse, our users were rarely involved in this front-end dig to uncover the existing system.

Now if this wasn't enough, the difficulty encountered in extricating a *Current Logical* model from the *Physical* one proved to not be for the faint-of-heart. Senior analysts suffered serious trauma attempting to extract the logical processes and their associated data, piece by tiny, unyielding piece. The resulting models were woefully lacking in accuracy and acceptability, and the work done was often far less productive and less understandable than the experts had predicted.

So, what was the problem?

The tools introduced by Tom DeMarco (data flow diagrams) were clearly more than adequate for illustrating data movement, memory, and external interfaces, as well as for specifying the processes. But there was something missing. It wasn't the tools (they seemed to work quite well). And there wasn't much point in throwing away a good set of tools with which we seemed to be able to communicate some things quite effectively. Clearly, we needed to find new ways of using those good tools.

On the other side of the street (some said there was more light there), the methods advocated by Codd, Chen, Date, Bachman and others (entity-relationship diagrams) were also more than adequate to define and understand the data from a database design perspective. But there was something missing there too. Again, it didn't appear to be the tools. Once again there wasn't much point in throwing away a perfectly good set of tools. Equally clearly, we needed to find new ways of using these data modelling tools – and perhaps to consolidate or integrate them with the other tool, the data flow diagram.

All of this research and experience on both sides of the "data processing" coin was of great value. We were finally realizing that we were a maturing industry, and we had to use some of this "good stuff" from both schools of thought to address business concerns and not just data and technology.

And then it happened – the first few tentative steps towards using all the great good from the preceding 20 years of systems analysis experience and applying it to real business needs. In 1981, Stephen McMenamin and John Palmer publicly introduced the concept of "events." That was the same year Matt Flavin first published *Fundamental Concepts of Information Modeling*. And in 1982, Steve McMenamin and I met at a seminar he delivered in Toronto and discussed the event-partitioning concept at length. It was in the early stages, without a doubt.

McMenamin and Palmer later followed with their groundbreaking book, *Essential Systems Analysis*, first published by Prentice-Hall in 1986 and reissued in 1994.

In my opinion, this was the first significant early work on event-partitioned analysis. Among other interesting items, their book showed how to avoid the laborious step of creating a model of the *Current Physical* system. This allowed analysts to start at the "logical" model rather than *Current Physical* level and thereby avoid the painful process of "logicalization". The word "essential" was used to describe the processes and the data that had to exist regardless of the technology applied to the target system. These models were said to be technologically neutral.

All of this predated **Use Case** modelling by several years, which was introduced by Ivar Jacobson, Magnus Christerson, Patrick Jonsson and Gunnar Overgaard (all Swedish) when they published *Object-Oriented Software Engineering*: *A Use-Case Driven Approach* in 1992 (Addison-Wesley, Wokingham, England).

McMenamin and Palmer's work replaced the *Logical Model* defined by Tom DeMarco in name only. The new "event-based model" resulted directly in what was previously known as the *Logical Model*. Event models also provided a basis for modelling the entire business requirement rather than just the computer system.

In theory (but certainly not in practice) the *Current Physical Model* disappeared (thank goodness) and along with it the arduous task of logicalization – sometimes known as *"work in the impossible region."* Clearly the focus was now on the business and not its machinery, in contrast to the earlier notions that concentrated exclusively on the technology and the software systems.

In my own earlier book on a complete system development methodology, *A Game Plan for Systems Development* (Prentice Hall, Englewood Cliffs, NJ, 1988), co-authored by Ken McEvoy, I devoted a section to expanding McMenamin & Palmer's event-partitioning concepts. However, my first book was primarily on a project-based methodology and did not deal in depth with the concept of event-partitioned Object-based analysis – nor did it do justice to McMenamin & Palmer's seminal work. As you can imagine, many advances have occurred since then.

A New Business System Analysis

So what came out of all of this history?

Well, quietly but surely, a new revolution has been growing since the first days of the Structured Methods – a revolution from within the business community and from outside systems departments. The legacy of the Structured Revolution is business and user-centered systems development.

With the earlier introduction of walkthroughs we involved users in looking carefully at their systems. Now, after years of participating in walkthroughs, these users are looking for better business methods to analyze and specify their requirements, and new ways of applying technology to their business systems. Accordingly, many organizations are unwilling to continue supporting technological solutions that are not understood, developed or even supported by the user community.

The tolerance level from the business community for "neat" technical solutions is at its lowest ever. They are now demanding – and for the first time with real teeth, since they can now engage in a technological end-run on the systems department – real productivity in analyzing, design and specifying their target systems. And some of them won't settle for anything less than achieving real productivity immediately.

I'm sure we can all agree that to survive and prosper in these early years of the 21st century we need fast, accurate ways to specify business requirements – much faster and better than the original methods of the Structured Revolution.

The data flow diagrams from the School of Structured Analysis and entity-relationship diagrams from the opposing School of Data Modelling are both still invaluable in their usefulness to graphically represent business needs and the supporting data. And any technology that makes getting the picture easier as well as faster is going to be around for a long time. So let's not totally discount those good, old tools. But they are *tools*, not methods. Methods (such as the event-based approach defined in this book) use those tools, and will survive the test of time.

Those vibrant, graphic tools – modified to suit newer methods – enable us to uncover and document useful business and system requirements virtually immediately. But to do this effectively, we must also liberate ourselves from an exclusive data modelling or an exclusive process modelling mindset. After freeing ourselves from the old-school code-oriented monolithic mindset of yesteryear, we will find it is much easier to accept the notion that we need only describe the client's information requirements in business terms, and in complete yet sufficient detail to move on to the next step – the solution design and implementation of a commercially usable system.

Combining the methods in this book with a highly client-interactive "discovery" approach, my experience indicates that business and system requirements analysis can be effectively implemented in virtually any size or type of organization, given motivated individuals.

And, yes, the business partners (users) can tell us all about their needs – they can answer our questions, clearly and concisely – when we use a common language with which to find the precise questions to ask and to document the results. When we know how to find the exact questions to ask, then we can get the answers they have.

Conclusion

None of what I have said is intended to treat cavalierly or invalidate any previous work in Structured Analysis, Structured Design, Data Modelling or Object-oriented Analysis. Those were the foundations, and they were very good. The foundations we have so far discussed have enabled the development of the discipline of integrated data modelling and process modelling to respond to new business challenges – the challenges of greater understandability, faster results, and truly significant productivity gains.

The target of analysis and design has always been to understand the exact needs of the client and their business, and to create a specification of the target system so we can acquire it or build it and implement it. While we were often successful at creating a generalized requirements document, we have also often failed to document a clear and unambiguous functional specification – quickly. That's because, until now, we really haven't had an appropriate, user-oriented, non-technical approach to finding the exact questions that would enable us to understand and specify the client's target business system. With today's technology, we can implement anything that we can specify. The challenge, then, is to know how to specify – clearly, concisely, completely and accurately – and in business terms.

As with any profession, this is best accomplished by understanding the concepts developed in the past and by adapting these to our current environment – and to avoid dogmatic application of old rules. The best professionals do not persist in using methods from the past, just because the methods were wonderful – in the past. To paraphrase Albert Einstein, *"To keep doing the same thing over and over again, and to expect different results, is madness."*

Commercially, we have only a little more than five decades of history with the business of computerized systems. Compared to other industries, that's not a lot of time. But during those five decades, we developed a whole lot of "good stuff." And in the methodology underlying this approach to business system requirements analysis, we keep much of that "good old stuff". I'm a firm believer that it isn't useful to throw everything out every time someone discovers a new mousetrap.

By the time you first apply this event-based analysis approach on a project I am confident you will agree that this is a really fast and effective way of going about it, built on a solid foundation of practical methods. You will see that specifying the essence of a business system well doesn't have to take forever. And the process doesn't have to be alien to the business folks either. Not any more.

But to accomplish all of this we must be prepared to use modern methods suitable to today's business environment and to the technologies that can catapult businesses successfully forward through the competitive 21st century.

And we must always remember – **_form_** (the shape or implementation a system takes) **_follows_** **_function_** (the condition that needs to be supported). Understanding this fundamental concept is essential to developing great systems.

To accomplish all of this we must also have a passionate belief that the most effective way to reduce the system maintenance problem is to get it right the first time. And "getting it right the first time," above all else, is about knowing how to find the precise questions to ask our business partners and system users.

And, to comment about that ever-present rush to get the job done faster, one thing is for certain: If we haven't got time to do it right, we sure won't have time to do it wrong.

Many important people have suggested that good system analysis is really a matter of art rather than science. I completely disagree. If that was really true, then most people would be excluded from being "good" analysts. The quality of a system requirements specification is not a question of "goodness", but rather an issue of whether the requirements have been specified completely and accurately. Completeness and accuracy are the only measures of goodness.

It is now time to stop calling analysis an "art" (which disqualifies just about everybody, since so few of us are artists) and call it by its proper name – a precise discipline that everyone can learn. Let's call it simply *business system analysis*.

Getting Started

With that discussion of our history and pedigree, you have begun a marvellous journey – a journey with a powerful approach to business system requirements analysis. Let's move ahead through these pages together and learn how to uncover, determine, specify, and integrate information technology with today's business requirements. Let's explore fascinating and powerful methods of good business-oriented communication, and a different and proven way of doing top-quality work in the fastest way possible.

And let's turn the profession of business requirements analysis into an agile and responsive discipline, where the work can be done quickly. I know you will never look back.

Trond Frantzen
Trond.Frantzen@PowerstartGroup.com

2. Foundation & Introduction

Contents

2.1 The Professional's Success Code

2.2 Pitfalls with Conventional Analysis Methods

2.3 Advantages of the Event-based Approach to Business Requirements Analysis

2.4 Is this only for 'Business' Systems?

2.5 What Will I Learn from this Book?

2.6 The Business Requirements Document

2.7 The 6 Steps of Business System Analysis

Never before in the history of information technology has the business community – our clients and users – been so outspoken in their demands, and so determined in their claims to have technologically creative business solutions that are delivered quickly, on time, and at the right price.

And if they can't get it from us, they are quite prepared to make a technological end-run around the IT professionals who they perceive to stand in their way.

It's a tough world these days. And if we don't respond quickly to their demands with real business solutions, using the best of technology available to us, then they <u>will</u> press ahead on their own.

Yes, right or wrong, good or bad, the new breed of business professional is determined to get what they want. So make no mistake about it – they <u>can</u> do it, and they <u>will</u> do it. The Internet revolution has made it all possible. For the first time ever, the business community has the ability to go it on its own.

Today, the business community just isn't willing to patiently wait as they did in the past, while someone tries to solve their system needs at yesterday's snail speed. And because of that impatience, they are growing their own revolution. Many are now engaging in an end-run around those IT departments they see to be slow, inert and expensive.

Clearly, the answer is improved and advanced methods – system requirement and project management methods that complement our advanced technologies. Today, it's no longer just a matter of charting the path – it's also knowing which buttons to push, how hard to push them, and when. It means knowing what the questions are **when we start**, not after system testing.

This means developing expert people, as well as systems – and doing so quickly.

And that is exactly what the Event-based approach to business system analysis helps you to do: Develop yourself as an expert in business systems analysis **and** deliver the immediate results that your clients want and expect.

2.1 The Professional's Success Code

To be successful on the projects we take on we must not only have a good system acquisition methodology – one that supports agility and responsiveness without chaos and risk – we must have an agile approach to business requirements analysis that is predictable and repeatable as well. What I mean by this is that every analyst who applies the methodology should apply it more or less the same way. It also means that if different analysts do the same work, the result should be the same too. If the result is the same, then the methodology has a strong scientific foundation, rather than results being based on best efforts by the most available person.

Every professional must have a foundation that guides all system acquisition or development work. I believe the foundation can be best described as follows:

- **Be on budget, on time, no problems.**

The project manager or team leader must be committed to ensuring that the project is problem-free, on budget, and all deadlines are met. Since what is done up front determines all subsequent results, the approach to business system analysis described in this book helps make this objective possible.

- **Foster teamwork and client participation.**

The best relationship you can have with your clients is one of partnership, teamwork and active participation. The best results come when you work directly and visibly with your clients. Never work in isolation from them. This approach to business system analysis helps make the partnership possible.

- **Apply hands-on modern management methods.**
- **Encourage on-project coaching and mentoring.**
- **Get management commitment to the project.**

Every project should be guided directly by a practicing expert in the tools, techniques and methodologies to be used on the project. It's a lot easier to advance when everyone is on board and understands how the work is actually done, rather than relying on theory passed on from an absentee practitioner or methodologist.

Management commitment and sponsorship is also enormously necessary to a project's success, as is a well-defined and developed professional development program for the business analysts and system developers. This approach to business system analysis helps to make all of this possible.

- **Be highly visible.**

My experience is that an informed and involved client will usually make the best decisions. We have found that visibility – contrary to popular myth – eliminates fear, uncertainty and doubt by the business community. Visibility always results in interaction and ownership. Don't hide from sight or work in isolation from the client. Have pride in your work. Success is the only option. The nature of the "discovery" sessions that make up part of the Event-based approach to business system analysis also helps to make this possible.

- **Use best practices.**

Always use the best and most modern methods. This always results in faster results, less money being spent, and the highest quality. Always look for better ways. Avoid the *'Not Invented Here (NIH)'* syndrome. Look outside your organization. Be devoted to finding the best methods available. And then measure satisfaction by your client community. The approach detailed in this book also helps to make this possible.

- **Apply the best methodologies.**

Use the most effective and pragmatic methodologies that you can find. Don't use them because they are popular, or the *solution du jour*; use them because they have an excellent track-record <u>according to your clients and subject-matter experts</u>. While I naturally suggest you apply the Event-based business system analysis approach described in this book on all projects, big or small, <u>adapt</u> it as required to your organization, your industry, and your personal style of working. This will help you get the best results.

- **Use common sense – and a coach and mentor.**

A popular old saying is, "*common sense just isn't very common.*" But I think it is. The first step is to get yourself a personal coach and mentor, and ask that person for some help whenever it's needed. Take a practical, common sense approach to all projects. Every situation is unique and each has different needs. The analysis approach described in this book helps to make this possible too.

2.2 Pitfalls with Conventional Analysis Methods

Conventional analysis methodologies range from really awful to pretty good. So let's only focus on those in the "pretty good" category. These include most methods that fall under the structured analysis and data modeling schools of thought. Unfortunately, virtually all of these conventional analysis methodologies have similar problems.

Client expectations are hard to manage.

Business system analysts are expected to know all about their client's business – what it is, how it works, and all the finite details. The analyst is also expected to have all the solutions to the problems, whether these have been identified or not. This appears to include reading the client's mind about the future.

Analysts need more time to become intimately familiar with the client's business.

There is general agreement by corporate management that the analyst needs to become familiar with the details of the client's business when a project first starts. But, the time needed to ramp up is almost always perceived to delay the project and increase costs.

This contradiction creates conflict, so many managers simply reduce the amount of time budgeted for business requirements analysis. The resulting lack of time to properly understand the client's business often leads to the necessary risk of *approximating* the true requirements. Also, the resulting lack of time to ramp up often results in a system that doesn't address all the client's requirements.

The client is often disappointed with the results, stating one of the following reasons:

1) Since the client usually perceives that the team will create (or interpolate) the business requirements as part of the technical solution, there is an expectation that knowing the technical solution also means completely understanding the business requirements – an analyst's paradox.

2) The time from business requirements to solution delivery is too long, and the installed system no longer meets the client's current business needs.

3) The system does what the client asked for, but not what was needed. It was expected that a professional business analyst would bridge that gap.

4) The business requirement specification was not clear, leading to ambiguity and problems down the line, especially during testing.

5) The system has to be revised over and over again, before the client accepts it.

2.3 Advantages of the Event-based Approach to Business Requirements Analysis

With all of the challenges of conventional approaches to business requirements analysis, including process and data modeling, and Use Case scenarios, there's no doubt the issues identified above must be resolved. The approach to system requirements analysis described in this book helps in all of the following ways.

1) It enables better management of client expectations – because the client is directly and actively involved in specifying the business requirements right up front. Since their involvement in producing the requirements is direct, and not just as "approvers" of the resulting document, they take ownership of the product based on the idea that most people don't disagree with themselves. (We'll discuss client-interactive "discovery" sessions later in the book, and how these sessions create the buy-in and ownership needed.)

2) It enables effective and efficient transfer of business knowledge from the client to the business analyst – again, because of the client's direct involvement. The approach to business requirements analysis described in this book uses a knowledge engine (a matrix) that generates context-specific questions for the subject-matter expert, which they are able to answer more directly. (In a later section of the book, we'll detail how this matrix with its *language of structure* drives out the real answers to succinct questions.)

3) The event-based approach to business requirements analysis enables identification of important business *conditions, situations* or *circumstances* not previously mentioned or recognized by the client. These 'events' that were not previously recognized as within the scope of the project, are discovered from answers to specific questions generated from the **BUSINESS RULES TABLE**. These discoveries can include new opportunities for business revitalization not previously expected by the client. (We'll discuss the power of this table later in the book.)

4) This approach to business system analysis facilitates client 'buy-in' since they are directly involved in the discovery process of establishing the essential business processes, the data required to support those processes, and key business rules that govern the required behavior of the system. (We'll discuss client-interactive "discovery" sessions, and the role of the subject-matter expert in these sessions, later in the book.)

5) The client-interactive "discovery" sessions conducted when using an event-based approach to business system analysis dramatically reduces the amount of time spent on identifying key business requirements. (We'll discuss client-interactive "discovery" sessions, and use of the **BUSINESS RULES TABLE** to speed up the process later in the book.)

6) The **BUSINESS REQUIREMENTS DOCUMENT** (BRD) you produce will consist of a clear, concise, and complete business document that communicates relevant requirements information to both the client and system developers. For the client there is a brief but concise business document (the BRD), in their own business language, stating all the business rules, relationships and essential processes that were uncovered in a series of "discovery" sessions. For the system development team – there are technology notes, an Object list and definitions, data attributes for all the Objects, foreign keys[1], Object cardinality and multiplicity[2], and a prescription for the database design[3] based on the business requirements. (The amount of detail may be more or less, depending on software acquisition or development strategy.) All the information – for both client and technical team – is contained in a single document (the **BUSINESS REQUIREMENTS DOCUMENT**), but the technical items remain transparent to the client. (We'll discuss the BRD and its composition later in the book.)

---

[1] A "foreign key" is a way of pointing from one distinct group of data (an Object) to another distinct group of data (another Object), so that redundancies can be eliminated and integrity can be maintained in the database.

[2] "Cardinality" and "multiplicity" are data analysis terms that have to do with the permitted ratio of occurrences between two Objects; e.g., 1 to 1, or 1 to many, etc.

[3] This Rx for database design based on business requirements is the foundation of what database analysts call the 'Conceptual Data Model'.

7) As an added benefit of using an event-based approach to business systems analysis, the technical team automatically gets all the information they need to produce a fully normalized[4] conceptual data model (if they need one) – based entirely on the business requirements – yet this technical side is transparent to the business client. (This may not sound much like business system analysis – but it is; it's the "system" part of business <u>system</u> analysis. We'll briefly discuss this "conceptual data model" later in the book, and how database analysts derive it directly from the business analyst's business requirements.)

8) This approach to business requirements analysis reduces acquisition, development and implementation time considerably by removing ambiguity and ensuring fewer revisions (caused by omission) to the final system. In other words, it's faster when we get all the information right the first time. That's really what "agile" should mean, isn't it? (We'll discuss "time to market" implications of fast and accurate requirements analysis later in the book.)

9) An event-based approach to business system analysis is essentially a **single-iteration approach**. What this means is that after one fast "discovery" session with subject-matter experts for each 'event' in the target system (we'll discuss 'events' later) the BUSINESS REQUIREMENTS DOCUMENT will be complete – within the framework of the 80/20 Rule[5]. No further revisiting, reiteration, rediscovery or redefinition of business requirements is necessary. A single-iteration (once through) approach to business system requirements means your analysis efforts are as fast as possible. This truly is the definition of "agile" within a no-risk paradigm.

2.4 Is this only for 'Business' Systems?

No, using an event-based approach to business system analysis is not limited to "business" in the conventional sense. This highly versatile approach to business requirements analysis can be used in many ways, including the following:

- E-business and B2B[6] or B2C[7] projects.
- Conventional business system requirements.
- Business Area models.
- Data warehouse projects.
- GIS[8] projects.
- Departmental business and system models.
- Corporate information models.
- Manual (non-automated) business process definitions.
- Mapping new requirements onto *legacy* systems and databases.

[4] "Normalized" or "normalization" means all data redundancies and inconsistencies have been removed.
[5] Also known as the **Pareto Principle**: 80% of the results can come from 20% of the effort.
[6] B2B = Businesses that sell products or provide services to other businesses.
[7] B2C = Businesses that sell products or provide services to consumers.
[8] GIS = Geographical information systems, with spatial views, such as maps and municipal grids.

- Business process innovation and re-engineering projects.
- Conceptual data models.
- Feasibility studies.
- Gap analysis.
- Business requirements documents issued as an RFI, RFP or RFQ[9] to consulting companies and 3rd party software solution vendors.

2.5 What Will I Learn from this Book?

While this book has many secondary objectives, its primary objectives are as follows:

1) Understand the **process of determining and defining** business system requirements by using an 'event partitioning' approach.

2) Know what is included in the Business Requirements Document.

3) Know how to define and find **business events** (i.e., conditions and circumstances that must be handled by the business area or system) that are part of a project's scope.

> **Erewhon Registrations Inc.**
>
> Vendor Registry
> Business Requirements
> Document
>
> July 10

4) Know **what questions to ask** the project's subject-matter experts in order to build their required Business Processes.

5) Know how to identify, define and partition Business Objects.

6) Know and understand The 5 Rules of Business Data and why and how to eliminate data redundancy, starting with the business requirements.

7) Know how to write a clear, concise and complete **task-based process narratives** for a project's Business Processes, in understandable business language.

8) Using the Business Rules Table, know how to **find the precise questions** (in project context) to ask the project's subject-matter experts.

9) Know how to conduct a successful and interactive "discovery" session with your clients and subject-matter experts.

10) Understand how a prescription for database design (an initial Conceptual Data Model) can be created directly from the business requirements.

---

[9] RFI = Request for Information. RFP = Request for Proposal. RFQ = Request for Quotation.

The objective of all of this, of course, is to deliver a BUSINESS REQUIREMENTS DOCUMENT that has all the information we need to understand the client's business requirements, and delivered in such a way that it doesn't have to be rewritten for the technical team. It has to contain everything the business needs in a system, without biasing the eventual technical solution. But, it must also contain everything about process and data that's needed to acquire or build a suitable solution.

Let's look (below) at the BUSINESS REQUIREMENTS DOCUMENT and what it consists of.

2.6 The Business Requirements Document

Project Business Event List

(from the *Project Scope Blitz*)

- List of project **business events** from the *Project Scope Blitz*, including business area ownership and involvement, and requirement priority.

For each Event (*n* occurrences)

- A **Business Process Diagram** that support the **business event**.
- A task-based narrative for the business process.
- References or links to Object definitions.
- A list of Business Areas affected by the business process
- A Business Rules Table for Objects supporting the business process.
- Any Implementation (design solution) considerations.

For each Object (*n* occurrences)

- Definition of the Object.
- Business Rules for the Object.
- Data attributes for the Object.

The Business Rules Table (BRT)

- Matrix of intersecting Objects.
- Cardinality (0,1,N) for each Object.

SALES AND PROCUREMENT PROJECT
AIR Telecom Inc.

List of Potential Events	SALES	MARKETING	PURCHASING	ACCOUNTING	Priority (1, 2, 3)
1 A Customer Buys a Product	★	★		★	1
2 A Customer Requests an Unavailable Product	★	★			1
3 A Product is Returned by a Customer	★	★		★	1
4 It is Time to Determine a Salesperson's Commissions	★			★	2
5 It is Time to Order a Product from a Supplier	★	★	★	★	1
6 It is Time to Pay a Supplier for Product Delivered	★	★	★	★	1

Total Number of Events = 6
Pilot & Copilot: Days to BRD = 2.7
Pilot Only: Days to BRD = 4.4

Fig. 2-1: Example of a Project Business Event List

**Erewhon
Registrations
Inc.**

Vendor Registry
Business Requirements
Document

July 10

BRT	customer	product	payment
1 customer		1,N,0	1,N,0
1 product	1,N,0		1,N,0
1 payment	1	1,N	

Fig. 2-2: Example of a Business Rules Table

Some of the components of the B‍USINESS R‍EQUIREMENTS D‍OCUMENT can be treated as separate and discrete units – such as the data and process components – but I really don't recommend that since each is inexorably linked to the other.

Since we live in a serial world – and you will probably read this book sequentially – these components (data and process) are the product of the progression we go through to create the B‍USINESS R‍EQUIREMENTS D‍OCUMENT. While we do gather information from subject-matter experts serially (but only for one Business Process at a time), we actually build the requirements specification in a non-serial fashion, more like component assembly. But since we know the ingredients that are required to complete the B‍USINESS R‍EQUIREMENTS D‍OCUMENT, we know exactly where to put the information so we can have a complete picture when we're done. It's those components we're going to step through in this book.

The B‍USINESS R‍EQUIREMENTS D‍OCUMENT ultimately consists of all of the items listed on the preceding page. This sometimes gets expanded into a full system requirement, which is a technical specification of the system solution, including (if required) database components.

Before getting into the details of how to find, document and organize these components to create the B‍USINESS R‍EQUIREMENTS D‍OCUMENT, let's briefly review the parts.

The List of Project Business Events

Everything is based on what we call a *business event*. This is an essential business circumstance, state or condition that the affected business area or target system must respond to and deal with. The business condition itself (the *business event*) is determined by a decision, a situation, time or a third party need.

More on this later.

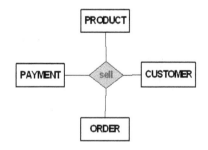

Fig. 2-3: Example of a Project Business Event List

The Business Objects

For each individual *business event* there must be either an **Object-Relationship Diagram** (Fig. 2-4) or a **Business Process Diagram** (Fig. 2-6). While some professionals still produce both kinds of diagrams, it is unnecessary to do this when conducting business system analysis. As you will see, it is redundant to produce both. However, this vintage approach is still taught extensively in colleges and universities almost everywhere.

Fig. 2-4: Example of an Object-Relationship Diagram

Several Business Objects may be needed, in association, to support a *business event*. In Fig. 2-4 several Objects are shown as "joined" in the **Object-Relationship Diagram**. This stipulates that they are all required to support a single *business event*.

An **Object** or *entity* is a noun (i.e., person, place, thing, or concept). It is some*thing* that is *essential* in order to conduct business. Each Object contains information about the business, like business rules that govern the behavior of the business involving that Object in a specific business process, and unique data about the Object.

Objects participate in relationships to support *business events*. If a required Object is not present in a relationship to support a *business event*, its absence will prevent us from conducting business in the manner desired.

Business Objects must have two or more data attributes to exist, and each Object is described by *business rules*. Objects are subject to THE **5** RULES OF BUSINESS DATA (which are described later in this book) in order to be properly attributed with data without redundancy. We'll discuss this in detail later, too.

CUSTOMER

Someone who requests or buys product from the company.

Unique Identifier
Customer-ID

Business Rules
- May purchase several PRODUCTs.
- May never buy a PRODUCT (but must have requested something that was unavailable).
- May make several PAYMENTs for PRODUCTs purchased.
- May place one or more PRODUCT ORDERs for products.
- May never make a PAYMENT for a PRODUCT (e.g., didn't buy anything; or returned a defective product).

Data Attributes
customer name
customer address
phone number
...

Pointers to Related Objects
Product-ID (mv)
Payment-ID (mv)
Order-ID (mv)

Fig. 2-5: Example of a Business Object definition

The Business Processes

The **Business Process Diagram** shows the process, the data that supports the process, any planned responses, and what is recorded for a specific business circumstance, or *business event*. A single **Business Process Diagram** may support more than one *business event*. In addition to the diagram there must be a precise narrative text. For each Business Object that appears on a diagram, it must eventually have all the business rules and data attributes that are required.

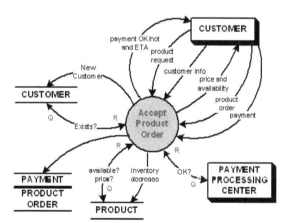

Fig. 2-6: Example of a Business Process Diagram

The Business Rules Table

The BUSINESS RULES TABLE is a matrix created from Business Objects that participate in a **Business Process Diagram** or an **Object-Relationship Diagram**. Based on a formal *language of structure* used to ask questions of

BRT	customer	product	payment
1 customer		1,N,0	1,N,0
1 product	1,N,0		1,N,0
1 payment	1	1,N	

Fig. 2-7: Example of a Business Rules Table

subject-matter experts, each Object's cardinality is entered in the appropriate cell. Cardinality is the number of instances of an Object – or how many records of an Object, such as **CUSTOMER** – that can exist, in the context of a specific business process. The Object's cardinality is indicated by "0", "1", or "N" (numerous). The cardinality (or *ratio of occurrences*) translates into declarative business rules that are specific to a business process, and identify the behavioral rules of the process based on the participating Business Objects. These business rules are then documented in plain language, as illustrated under the Object **CUSTOMER** (Fig. 2-5).

The Business Interfaces Diagram

The Business Interfaces Diagram identifies the interface communications needed between the target system and its outside world, without the specific application of technology. This diagram shows the net flow of data received from every outside source of information (i.e., outside the target system) and the destination of data to some area or someone outside the target system. This is derived from **Business Process Diagrams**.

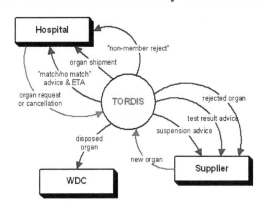

Fig. 2-8: Example of a Business Interfaces Diagram

2.7 The 6 Steps of Business System Analysis

Now that we have briefly discussed the components of event-based business system analysis, we can start looking at the details. The illustrations on the following pages show the steps we need to go through. The business analysis processes you will go through include:

1. Conduct a Project Scope Blitz
2. Plan Discovery Sessions
3. Develop a Business Process
4. Identify Business Objects
5. Query a Business Rules Table
6. Issue the Business Requirements Document

1. Conduct Project Scope Blitz

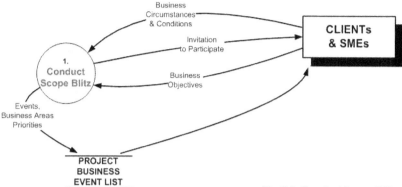

Fig. 2-9: Conduct Scope Blitz

Project Business Event List Description:

A list of **business events** (i.e., conditions, circumstances and states) client business areas must be able to recognize, deal with and respond to in a planned manner. Each **business event** identifies a part of the scope of the project. Each **business event** also identifies the business area(s) responsible for managing the **process** that supports the **business event**, and – in the context of the project – the priority of the implementation of the supporting business process and data.

Business Rules:

There must be only one in-scope **Project Business Event List** for a specific project.

Data:

* Business event statement
* Business Area responsible for the Process that supports the event (mv)
* Priority of implementation of the supporting Process and Data
* Date of Scope Blitz
* Location of Scope Blitz
* Participants at Scope Blitz (names, titles)
* Business objectives of the project
* Events determined to be out-of-scope

The Process:

* Determine the best time to conduct a *Project Scope Blitz*.

* Issue a Scope Blitz Discovery Invitation to all clients and prospective subject-matter experts.

* At the scheduled time, conduct the *Project Scope Blitz* with clients and subject-matter experts.

* During the *Project Scope Blitz* with clients and SMEs, determine *events* that are in-scope (as many as possible, but apply the 80/20 Rule, since other *events* will be found during the detailed Discovery sessions).

* Record *events* that are mentioned but are out-of-scope.

* Issue the **Project Business Event List** to all participants as soon as practical after the *Project Scope Blitz*.

2. Plan Discovery Sessions

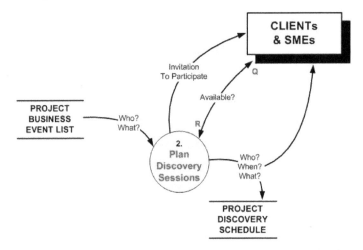

Fig. 2-10: Plan Discovery Sessions

Project Discovery Schedule Description:

A project's schedule for detailed business requirements Discovery sessions, partitioned by event, including who will participate, when and where.

Business Rules:

- For any specific project, there must be one or more **Project Discovery Schedule**s for a single **Project Business Event List**.
- For a single **Project Discovery Schedule** there must be a **Project Business Event List**.

Data:

- Date of Discovery
- Location of Discovery
- Time of day
- Duration of Discovery
- What *business event* will be analyzed (mv)
- Who will participate (mv)
- Discovery session Pilot
- Discovery session Co-pilot (can be the same as Pilot)

The Process:

- Based on the **Project Business Event List** produced from the *Project Scope Blitz*, determine the availability of clients and subject-matter experts to participate in detailed client-interactive Discovery sessions for the project.
- Create a **Project Discovery Schedule**, with participants and dates, for each event on the **Project Business Event List**.
- When the schedule is complete, issue the **Project Discovery Schedule** and a formal "Invitation to Participate" in the Discovery sessions to affected clients and SMEs.
- Follow up with the clients and SMEs for scheduling and participation.

3. Develop a Business Process <u>and</u>
4. Identify Business Objects

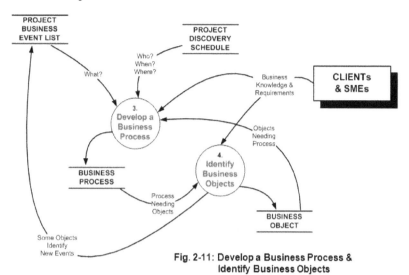

Fig. 2-11: Develop a Business Process &
Identify Business Objects

Business Process Description:

An activity that is carried out to support or deal with a specific business condition or circumstance (***business event***), resulting in a planned response and keeping track of (recording) what activity was carried out.

Business Rules:

- A specific **Business Process** must support one or more ***business events*** from the **Project Business Event List**.
- A single **Business Process** must be developed during one or more Discovery sessions identified on the **Project Discovery Schedule**.
- A single **Business Process** can result in one or more **Business Objects** to support it.

Data:

- Business Process diagram
- Narrative description
- Business area affected by the process

Business Object Description:

An entity that describes a person, place or thing that is essential to a business system, which the subject system needs to keep track of.

Business Rules:

- For a single, specific **Business Object,** it must support one or more ***business events*** on the **Project Business Event List**.
- A single **Business Object** will support one or more **Business Processes**
- A single, specific **Business Object** may or may not lead to the discovery of one or more other **Business Objects**.

Data:

- Business Object definition
- Data attributes
- Business rules

The Process:

- Periodically, based on the **Project Discovery Schedule**, meet with subject-matter experts to develop business requirements for the target area.

- For each ***business event*** on the **Project Business Event List**, develop the supporting **Business Process**, based on discovery dialogue with subject-matter experts.

- By dialogue with business subject-matter experts, determine the **Business Object**s that are required to support the **Business Process**.

- At a high level (apply the 80/20 Rule), attribute data to **Business Object**s according to the 5 Rules of Business Data.

- For those Objects and data items that identify the need for additional ***business events***, add those ***business events*** to the **Project Business Event List**.

- For those Objects that identify the need for additional **Business Process**es, develop those additional **Business Process**es.

5. Query a Business Rules Table

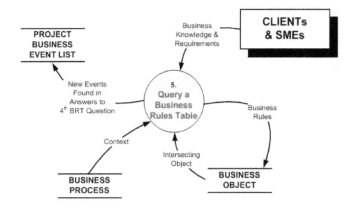

Fig. 2-12: Query a Business Rules Table

Business Object Description:

An entity that describes a person, place or thing that is essential to a business system, which the subject system needs to keep track of.

Business Rules:

- For a single, specific **Business Object,** it must support one or more *business events* on the **Project Business Event List.**

- A single **Business Object** will support one or more **Business Processes**

- A single, specific **Business Object** may or may not lead to the discovery of one or more other **Business Objects.**

Data:

- Business Object definition
- Data attributes
- Business rules

The Process:

NOTE: This is not a separate process. Querying the BUSINESS RULES TABLE is done immediately after each **Business Process Diagram** is finished, before proceeding to another business process.

- For two intersecting **Business Objects** specific to a **Business Process**, determine the Business Rules in the context of the **Business Process** by asking the 'BRT Questions'.

- For each Business Rule determined, attribute the Rule to the **Business Object** that forms the anchor (subject) of the 'BRT Question'.

- In the Business Rules Table, annotate the Rules (1, N and/or 0) in the intersection cell of the two queried **Business Objects.**

- Write each Business Rule in plain language under the **Business Object** to which the Rule has been attributed.

The 'BRT Questions" will be detailed later in the book.

6. Issue the Business Requirements Document

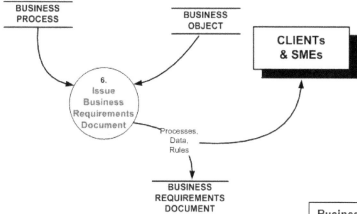

Fig. 2-13: Issue the Business Requirements Document

The Process:

- For each **Business Process** that has been completely defined, include it as part of the **Business Requirements Document**.

- When done, issue the **Business Requirements Document** to clients and subject-matter experts, as required.

  NOTE: Issuing the **Business Requirements Document** does not have to wait until it includes all business processes. Based on the project strategy, it can be issued incrementally to clients for approval, one *business event* at a time. This approach is more responsive and agile, and has proven to be faster and more productive.

  If it is issued one *business event* at a time, individual business processes may have to be updated as more is learned while developing the business processes for other events; which may require re-issue and approval for the changes.

Business Requirements Document Description:
A document (electronic or not) that contains the description of client business requirements for a system, specific to different business areas, with minimum reference to how those requirements could be implemented.

Business Rules:

- A single **Business Requirements Document** (BRD) will contain descriptions of one or more **Business Processes**.
- A single BRD will contain definitions of several **Business Objects**.
- A single **Business Process** will be documented in one or more BRDs.
- A single **Business Process** that is documented in a BRD will be supported by one or more documented **Business Objects**.
- A single **Business Object** will be documented in one or more BRDs.
- A single **Business Object** that is documented in a BRD will support one or more **Business Processes**.

Data:

- Project Business Event List
- Business Process diagrams to support each business event.
- Narrative description of each Business Process.
- Business Objects that support each Business Process.
- Data Attributes for each Business Object.
- Business Rules for each Business Object, written in the context of the Business Process in which the Business Objects participate.

The 6 Processes of Event-based Business System Analysis – Composite Diagram

Below is a composite diagram of the six processes of the event-based approach to business system analysis. It's a good overview diagram, which you can use as a "cheatsheet".

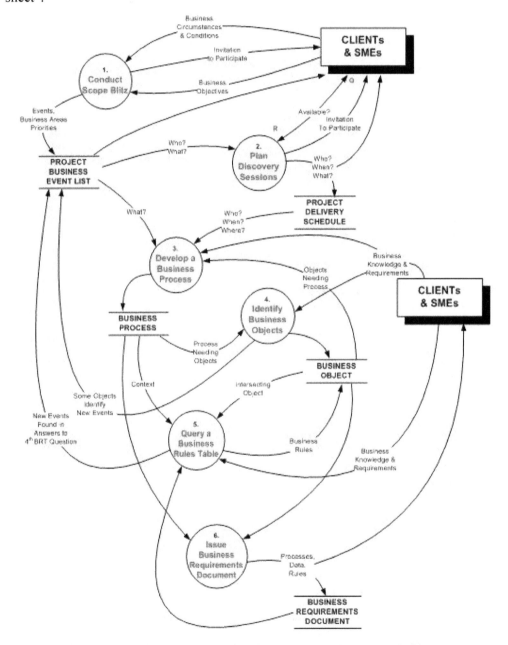

Fig. 2-14: The Event-based Business System Analysis Approach – Composite Diagram

3. The Business Event – The Foundation of a System

Contents

Since we live in a serial world we tend to do things in chronological order. However, gathering information and synthesizing it into knowledge is definitely not a sequential process. When assimilating information we constantly jump in and out of different "states" of knowledge and put the information we gather into one context or another based on the *situations, conditions* and *circumstances* that give the information meaning. Primarily, this is because our work (in the world of analysis) consists of contextual knowledge rather than the serial assembly of things.

Our knowledge repository – our brain – is like a neural network consisting of nodes with access paths that are busy (strong) or not so busy (weak). This neural network becomes our 'organized memory' with keys to join bits and pieces of data to form cohesive information (we hope), and blocks of information from which we can extrapolate knowledge.

In terms of functionality, data storage and desired results, computerized systems are not much different from the human brain. Computerized systems – as is also true for non-automated systems – must store data (i.e., *remember things*) to support various *conditions* and *circumstances* they have to deal with. In the context of business system analysis, these are called **business events**.

3.1 What is a Business Event?

A *business event* is an essential business condition, a state, circumstance, situation or requirement that exists – which the target system must respond to or deal with in order to carry on operations to successfully support its key business objectives, goals, mission, direction and vision. A *business event* transcends time and technology; i.e., it does not reflect **how** something is done; it represents **what** must be done without regard to a particular technology.

To summarize, a *business event* is:

1) a state, condition, circumstance, situation or requirement that exists;

2) essential (critical) to the business; and

3) based on time, a decision, situation or third party need.

3.2 The Four Types of Business Events

Business events come in four flavors:

1) **Situation Business Event** – non-controlled
   "The Customer Buys a Product"
   "The Customer Has Exceeded Their Credit Limit"

2) **External Business Event** – based on third party need
   "The Customer Requests a Higher Credit Limit"

3) **Temporal Business Event** – based on time
   "The Customer's Credit Card Expires"
   "It is Time to Increase the Customer's Credit Limit"

4) **Internal Business Event** – based on a decision
   "The Company Decides to Cancel the Customer's Credit Card"

Note that a *business event* **never** starts with a verb. That's because a *business event* is not a process. A *business event* is a condition, state, situation or circumstance that must be supported by a process. (A process, which we'll discuss later, does start with a verb and can support one or more *business events*.)

When a *business event* is identified we don't need to label it as one of the four kinds of *business events* listed above. We leave it unlabeled because, to a client or anyone else who is reading the documentation, a *business event* is simply a *business event*. It's a business circumstance. So why do we have labels (*situation, external, temporal, internal*) for the four different kinds of *business events* then? Because it gives the analyst an opportunity to think about what kind of situation or circumstance – *business event* – we are really dealing with.

For example, what's the difference between **"The Company Decides to Pay a Supplier"** and **"It is Time to Pay a Supplier"**?

The first one (an internal *business event* based on a decision) suggests that there is a decision point, and this decision must be reflected in the requirements document. The second one (an internal *business event* based on time) suggests that there is no decision involved, it's just time to pay the supplier – perhaps the goods ordered have been received, and it is therefore time to pay the supplier. Whatever the time criteria, this too must be reflected in the requirements document.

By assessing the type of *business event*, the analyst is able to think through the ramifications on the business requirements.

The most common type of *business event* used by those who are new to this kind of analysis is the temporal *business event* that starts with **"It is Time to ..."**. While this truly is a common type of *business event*, it is also the most common error, mostly because it is so easy to identify a *business event* as **"It is Time to ... (something)"**. For example, I have often seen *business events* such as **"It is Time to Receive a Product Shipment from a Supplier"** when it clearly should be **"Product Shipment Arrives from a Supplier"**. The arrival of the shipment from the supplier, while expected, is somewhat out of our control, therefore it is an external *business event*. To state **"It is Time to Receive a Product Shipment from a Supplier"** seems a bit awkward and certainly doesn't have the same meaning as **"Product Shipment Arrives from a Supplier"**. On the other hand, a *business event* such as, **"It is Time for a Product Shipment from a Supplier to Arrive"** is something else again. This kind of *business event* is within our control, and we must have a planned response for it.

Thinking through the type of *business event* we're dealing with is therefore helpful in stating it well.

3.3 The Different Diagramming Conventions

Business events that are identified to be part of a project's scope are supported by processes and data. In other words, the *business event* is the identified <u>circumstance</u> or <u>condition</u> that the system has to deal with. How the business system "deals with" a *business event* is described, partially, by a diagram that illustrates the supporting business process and data.

It's interesting to note that three distinct notational standards have developed to illustrate a system's processes and data. We explored the evolution of the foundations of diagramming conventions in detail in Chapter 1.

The most commonly used and most popular diagramming convention is *Use Case* notation. Developed by Ivar Jacobson (Swedish) in 1986 and first published in 1992, (***Object-Oriented Software Engineering:*** *A Use-Case Driven Approach*), *Use Cases* were originally intended to specify software systems, not business systems. More recently, *Business Use Cases* have been introduced. However, from a business point-of-view – in my opinion – this hasn't been too successful (although many technical analysts claim it's very successful) since most practitioners are using *Use Cases* to specify business requirements with a lot of "how" (the solution architecture) built in. While *Use Cases* theoretically see the target system as a "black box" (i.e., no implementation details or "how" things are done), the fact is this is rarely the case. The other issue, in my opinion, is that the use of *Use Cases* simply takes too long and the documentation is not very business-friendly. Jacobson himself appears to agree with this, as he has developed the **Essential Unified Process for Software Development**, which integrates principles from the unified process, agile and process improvement camps.

But, importantly, *Use Cases* and the Unified Process and most other analysis methodologies have been developed to assist with software development, not for business development, enhancement or improvement. On the other hand, the event-based business analysis approach has as its singular focus the identification and improvement of business processes, regardless of the technology (or lack thereof) that is applied to turn those processes into a "system". While the event-based business analysis approach recognized that most "systems" are supported extensively by software, this element is separated from the actual business requirements discovery, as you will see in this book.

In any event, *Use Case* usage is well documented, with hundreds of books available. The fact remains that *Use Cases* are derived from the foundations that came from data modeling and process modeling, discussed earlier, and clearly defined as such in Jacobson's book, **Object-Oriented Software Engineering:** *A Use-Case Driven Approach.* That being the case, I'm going to discuss event-based business analysis around the foundations of process and data modeling, since both are vendor neutral, and they enable us to be clearly non-physical in our approach to business system requirements analysis.

Recognizing that most analysts have either a data bias or a process bias (although some of us have a business bias), which of these diagramming conventions would be most helpful to you as an analyst?

It really depends on the kind of project you are working on. If you are working on a **data warehouse** type of project (e.g., statistical or actuarial systems) or **geographical information systems** (GIS), you should probably consider using **Object-Relationship Diagrams**. These diagrams tell you about the relationship between Objects in the context of individual *business events*.

On the other hand, if you are working on a project that's more process based (such as a financial system, distribution or relationship management) then it's probably best to use **Business Process Diagrams**, such as the one illustrated in Fig. 3.1. This kind of diagram shows the data that's needed to support a specific circumstance (*business event*), as well as where the data comes from and what you do with it (i.e., the data flow).

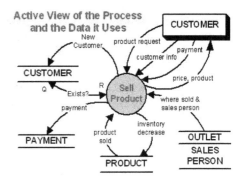

Fig. 3-1: Business Process Diagram

While **Object-Relationship Diagrams** are commonly used by database analysts and designers, these diagrams are limited to showing a static view of the data that's needed to support a *business event*, but they do not show the activity of the process that supports the *business event*. The reason for this is that **Object-Relationship Diagrams** are thought to be data-centric and, therefore, an activity description is not immediately required. However, the set of rules that come from the 'joining' of Objects that participate in a relationship (i.e., the *business event*) – through the 'diamond' in the diagram – are mandatory. These are the business and behavioral rules that define Objects and their relationships, which we will visit later when discussing the BUSINESS RULES TABLE.

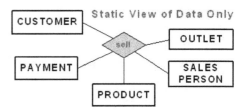

Fig. 3-2: Object-Relationship diagram

The **Business Process Diagram** (Fig. 3.1), on the other hand, shows both the activity in the process and the data that's needed to support that activity.

In the end, the diagramming style that you choose should be based on the type of project you are working on. Regardless of the diagramming style you use, everything you need will be there when properly documented (i.e., both diagramming types end up with the necessary information), but the **Object-Relationship Diagram** itself does not communicate the process as well as the **Business Process Diagram**. Although it works fine from a data centric view, it's simply not very business-friendly; therefore, it is contrary to the principles of agile analysis.

This, too, we will discuss in considerable detail throughout the book.

3.4 Work-through of a Business Event – Simplified

Before we go on to the details of how to derive the business requirements, let's look at a small, isolated example that's based on a single *business event*.

The *business event*: **A Customer Buys a Product**

The customer enters a shoe store, finds the right shoes (for example, lime green loafers, size 13), and buys them. The customer pays for the shoes. The sales person asks the customer for their phone number and name, and determines if they are already in the store's system. If they are not in the system, the sales person asks the customer for information (such as name, address, phone number, etc.) and enters it in the system. When the customer buys the shoes, and the payment is recorded, the store inventory for 'Lime Green Loafers, Size 13' is reduced by the quantity bought by the customer.

We also need to track the outlet where the customer bought the shoes (so we can have store sales statistics); and we need to know which sales person served the customer (so we can figure out commissions).

That's the scenario. Now, how does the business requirements "specification" for this look? There are two views, one for data warehouse type of projects and another for process-based projects. Each one is described below.

For Data Warehouse Projects

If this was a data warehouse type of system, we would ask the following question to get us started with the diagram:

> What do we need to *know about* or *remember* in order to support the condition (*business event*) **"A Customer Buys a Product"**?

We start by just drawing an unlabelled diamond to represent the joining point – the relationship – that binds the different Objects (or groups of related data) that are needed to support the *business event* **"A Customer Buys a Product"**.

Fig. 3-3(a): Object-Relationship diagram - Sell

Clearly, we need to know who the **CUSTOMER** is: we do keep track of customers. So we attach **CUSTOMER** to our diamond.

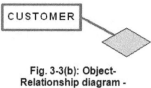

Fig. 3-3(b): Object-Relationship diagram - Sell

We also have to keep track of the shoes we sell (lime green loafers, size 13) so we can (a) find it in our inventory, and (b) reduce the inventory when we sell some. Let's call this **PRODUCT** and join it, too, to our diamond.

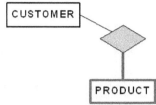

Fig. 3-3(c): Object-Relationship diagram - Sell

Because we need to gather statistics to determine store sales, we need to know the store in which the shoes were sold; and (for commission calculations) we need to remember the salesperson who served the customer. We can call these two Objects **OUTLET** and **SALESPERSON**, and attach them to the diamond too.

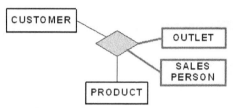

Fig. 3-3(d): Object-Relationship diagram - Sell

Finally, we need to remember the payment we got from the customer. Let's call it **PAYMENT** (that was easy) and attach it, too, to the diamond.

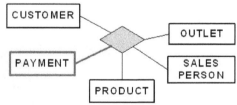

Fig. 3-3(e): Object-Relationship diagram - Sell

That seems to be all the things we need to *know about* or *remember* as part of the process to support the *event* **"A Customer Buys a Product"**. However, we do need to label the diamond, which represents the relationship connecting the Objects – and we have to

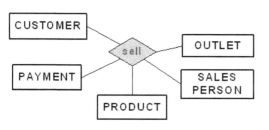

Fig. 3-3(f): Object-Relationship diagram - Sell

label it with a single verb. So, what's the relationship? While I'm sure you can think of several possibilities, I'll suggest that the relationship these Objects share is the *selling of shoes*; therefore, I'm going to label the diamond sell.

The reason we join all of these Objects to the diamond is because there are one or more relationships (i.e., business rules) that require the Objects to be connected. Once we have linked (or joined) all the Objects, then we can locate or find the different information (data) that is specific to the *business event* **"A Customer Buys a Product"**.

For example, if we know who the **CUSTOMER** is who bought a product in our store (e.g., Buster Brown), we can then find out what kind of **PRODUCT** he bought (lime green loafers, size 13); and the **PAYMENT** he made for that **PRODUCT**; which **SALESPERSON** served the **CUSTOMER**; and in which **OUTLET** (store) he was served.

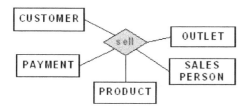

Fig. 3-4: Object-Relationship diagram - Sell

If, on the other hand, we only know the kind of **PRODUCT** we sold (lime green loafers, size 13), we can then locate or find all the **CUSTOMER**s who bought this **PRODUCT**, where they bought it (in which **OUTLET**), who served them (the **SALESPERSON**), and the **PAYMENT**s they made. All of this can be done because these Objects share the relationship of *selling shoes*.

As we develop this Object-Relationship Diagram, we progressively discover the need for each of the Objects. As each one is discovered, we also need to record some information about the Object. For the Object **CUSTOMER**, for example, we know we need to have their name, address and phone number.

CUSTOMER
Someone who requests or buys product or service from the company.
Data Attributes
• customer name
• customer address
• e mail address
• phone number

Fig. 3-5: Partial Customer Object

Each Object, such as **CUSTOMER**, also needs to have the "business rules" that affect their existence. The table in Fig. 3-6 is populated based on the Objects that participate in a relationship. In this example, we have **SALESPERSON**, **CUSTOMER**, **OUTLET**, **PRODUCT** and **PAYMENT**; all of which are used to populate this particular BUSINESS RULES TABLE.

BRT	Salesperson	Customer	Outlet	Product	Payment
1 Salesperson		N	1,N	N	N
1 Customer	1,N,0		1,N	1,N,0	1,N,0
1 Outlet	N	N		N	N
1 Product	1,N,0	1,N,0	1,N		1,N,0
1 Payment	1,N	1	1	1,N	

Fig. 3-6: Business Rules Table – "Sell"

Specific questions are derived from the BUSINESS RULES TABLE, and those questions are directed to the project's subject-matter experts using a specific syntax. Don't be concerned about how this table is generated. It's very straightforward, and we'll cover it in detail later.

This table, as we work through it, will generate the business rules specifically applicable to the individual Objects. **CUSTOMER** business rules, for example, would look like the example in Fig. 3-7.

Each of the other Objects in the BUSINESS RULES TABLE also generates rules applicable to those Objects. (Since this is a simplified example, I won't show the descriptions of the other Objects.)

After all the Objects have been defined, and data items attributed to each of them, all the rules that describe the relationship between the five Objects will have been completed.

CUSTOMER

Someone who requests or buys product or service from the company.

Business Rules

- may be served by one or more **salespersons**
- may never be served by a **salesperson** (e.g., the customer never buys anything)
- must have been in one or more **outlets**
- may buy one or more **products**
- may never buy a **product** (but must have requested something that was unavailable)
- may make several **payments** for **products** purchased
- may never make a **payment** for a **product** (e.g., didn't buy anything; or returned a defective product)

Data Attributes

- customer name
- customer address
- phone number

Fig. 3-7: Object Description – "Customer"

For Process-based Projects

There is a somewhat different perspective to consider if the project you're working on is a process-based business system, which most systems are. Process diagrams, as distinct from data warehouse type of diagrams, show the data that's needed to support a specific circumstance (*business event*), as well as where the data comes from and what you do with it. Accordingly, we ask the following question to get us started with the diagram:

1. How do I know that a **"A Customer Buys a Product"**?

This is followed by two follow-on questions:

2. What do I want to do about it?
3. What do I need to remember or record?

We start by just drawing an unlabelled circle (a bubble) to represent the process that's going to support the *business event* **"A Customer Buys a Product"**.

Fig. 3-8(a): Business Process Diagram: Sell Product

The answer to the initial question, *"How do I know that ... a Customer buys a product?"* is that a customer shows up in the store and asks for the lime green loafers, size 13. We can draw this in this manner:

(Just follow along for now. We're going to discuss the details of this process later in the book.)

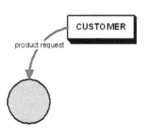

Fig. 3-8(b): Business Process Diagram: Sell Product

The next question, *"What do I want to do about it?"* requires that you think through all the things you need to do: check if the customer is already in our database; find the lime green loafers, size 13, in inventory and give them to the customer; get a payment for the purchase; record the store in which the transaction took place, and remember which sales person served the customer.

Let's start with determining if the customer is already on file with us, with the following diagram:

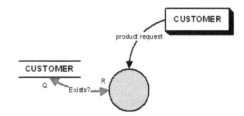

Fig. 3-8(c): Business Process Diagram: Sell Product

If they are not already recorded, get the customer's information and record it.

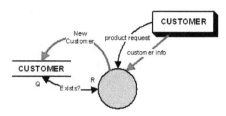

Fig. 3-8(d): Business Process
Diagram: Sell Product

Get the lime green loafers from inventory, and give the shoes and the price to the customer.

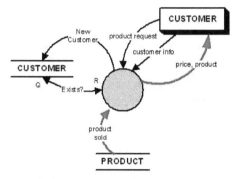

Fig. 3-8(e): Business Process Diagram:
Sell Product

Decrease the shoe inventory.

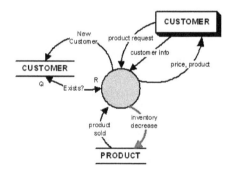

Fig. 3-8(f): Business-Process
Diagram: Sell Product

Receive the payment from the customer, and record it.

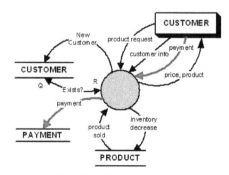

Fig. 3-8(g): Business Process
Diagram: Sell Product

Record the store where the transaction took place, and the salesperson who served the customer.

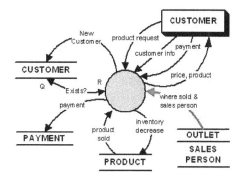

Fig. 3-8(h): Business Process Diagram: Sell Product

There's the whole diagram. Now we just need to label it, inside the bubble, with a strong and pointy name to define what this process actually does. Again, I'm going to just label it *sell product*.

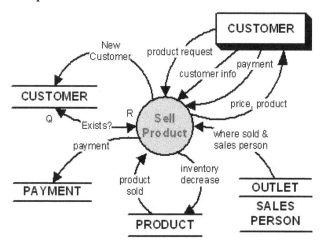

Fig. 3-9: Business Process Diagram: Sell Product

A picture might be worth a thousand words, but we can't leave the understanding of this diagram to chance or someone's intuition, so we still have to write the narrative – which could read as follows:

For each request for a product from the customer:
- Find out if the **customer** exists in our system
- Find the **product** sold
- If it is available, give the **product** to the **customer** with the price
- Accept the **payment** from the **customer**
- Remember the **payment**
- Remember the **salesperson** who served the **customer**, and in which **outlet**
- Reduce inventory by the quantity of **product** sold
- If it is a new **customer**, get the customer information from the **customer**.
- Remember the new **customer** information.

There's a specific way of determining the narrative, which we'll discuss in detail later. It certainly isn't some kind of stream of consciousness narrative. How we determine the process narrative is very precise.

As you are going through this process of drawing the diagram and writing the narrative, you also progressively identify the Objects (CUSTOMER, PAYMENT, PRODUCT, OUTLET, and SALESPERSON), defining and attributing data to them, such as CUSTOMER in Fig. 3-10.

CUSTOMER

Someone who requests or buys product or service from the company.

Business Rules
- may be served by one or more **salesperson**s
- may never be served by a **salesperson** (e.g., the customer never buys anything)
- must have been in one or more **outlet**s
- may buy one or more **product**s
- may never buy a **product** (but must have requested something that was unavailable)
- may make several **payment**s for **product**s purchased
- may never make a **payment** for a **product** (e.g., didn't buy anything; or returned a defective product)

Data Attributes
- customer name
- customer address
- phone number

Fig. 3-10: Object Description – "Customer"

Once this is done you build the BUSINESS RULES TABLE by allocating the business rules to the individual Objects.

BRT		Salesperson	Customer	Outlet	Product	Payment
1	**Salesperson**		N	1,N	N	N
1	**Customer**	1,N,0		1,N	1,N,0	1,N,0
1	**Outlet**	N	N		N	N
1	**Product**	1,N,0	1,N,0	1,N		1,N,0
1	**Payment**	1,N	1	1	1,N	

Fig. 3-11: Business Rules Table – "Sell Product" Business Process

I'll explain everything about the BUSINESS RULES TABLE later.

In my opinion, **Business Process Diagrams** are much more useful and business-friendly when describing a business process. Of course, underlying these diagrams is a whole methodology regarding the solicitation and discovery of the business processes the client needs.

4. The Business Object – Things to Remember in a Business System

Contents

The first step in business system analysis is not to find out **how** the system will function – the first step is to find *what we need to **know*** in order to support the conditions or circumstances that the business will encounter. In other words, we can't just say, "*what do you want the system to do?*" We first have to determine the circumstances the business has to support, and then we'll figure out how it's going to support those circumstances or conditions.

Figuring out <u>what</u> the business must support is called "analysis". Arriving at a solution as to <u>how</u> the system will do it is called "design" or "architecture". Determining what is needed must always come <u>before</u> determining how to accomplish it – ***"form follows function,"*** as the great architect Louis H. Sullivan wrote.

System design is by definition a solution; and a system solution (*how* the system does what it's supposed to do) is very physical. Business analysis, on the other hand, is obtaining knowledge and therefore not at all physical … at least, not yet. Analysis uncovers **what we need to know** about a planned approach to a business situation or circumstance, in all its composite pieces; but it is not about how the system will behave. Our analysis, therefore, must be completely free of any implementation bias, or we start trying to mix apples with sheep. What I mean by this is that clarity of thought (without an implementation bias) will always help us get the <u>business requirements</u> done faster and better. And "faster and better" should be the foundation for any "agile" approach to business requirements analysis. The best way I know of maintaining clear and focused thought is to not mix the complexities of a potential design solution with the essential business requirements. How to do this will become clear as we progress.

4.1 How to Base the Business Analysis on an Event

We have traditionally called the result of analysis the *system specification* – because, we presume, it should be specific. The problem, however, is that it has too often been a *generalization* – and much too focused on the *system*; i.e., a statement of the physical environment with general system behavior added. Well, that's been a problem.

To discover the real and complete needs of an organizational unit or a business initiative, all questions and the resulting specification must be put in a specific business context to be understandable. This context, in my opinion, should be a *business event*.

A *business event* is an essential <u>condition</u>, a <u>circumstance</u>, a <u>state</u>, a <u>situation</u> or an <u>external requirement</u> that exists which the business must respond to or deal with in order to carry on operations to successfully meet its key business objectives, goals, mission, direction and vision. A *business event* does not consider technology or specific time; i.e., it does not reflect **how** something is done; it exclusively focuses on **what** must be done without regard to a particular technology or implementation.

In summary, a *business event* is:

1)   a state, circumstance, condition, situation or external requirement that exists;
2)   essential (critical) to the business; and
3)   based on time, a decision, situation or third party need.

All *business events* have a specific structure. To reflect this structure, they come in four different flavors. These are:

Situation Business Event – non-controlled
> **"The Customer Buys a Product"**
> **"The Customer Has Exceeded Their Credit Limit"**

External Business Event – based on third party need
> **"The Customer Requests a Higher Credit Limit"**

Temporal Business Event – based on time
> **"The Customer's Credit Card Expires"**
> **"It is Time to Increase the Customer's Credit Limit"**

Internal Business Event – based on a decision
> **"The Company Decides to Cancel the Customer's Credit Card"**

Our first analysis objective on a project is to find just a few *business events* to start with. Although finding as many *business events* as possible is desirable, we don't need to find more than a handful. Once a few have been found, all others will follow. We'll discuss this concept in more detail when we look at the Business Rules Table.

Some other examples of *business events* are:

- **A Customer _buys_ a Product**
- **It is Time to _order_ a Product from a Supplier**
- **The Product _arrives_ from the Supplier**
- **An Employment Application _arrives_**
- **The Company _closes_ the Customer's Account**

Business event statements consist of nouns and verbs. The nouns usually become Objects, while the verb indicates the context of the process that supports the *business event*.

Note in the examples above that a *business event* <u>never</u> starts with a verb. That's because a *business event* is not a process. A *business event* is a <u>circumstance</u>, <u>condition</u>, <u>state</u> or <u>external requirement</u> that must be supported by a process.

Why the four different flavors of *business events*?

When a *business event* is identified we don't need to label it as this or that kind of *business event* – whether it is Situation, External, Temporal or Internal. Why not? Because, to the organization you are working with, a *business event* is simply a *business event*. It doesn't need labeling. So why do we have names for the four different kinds of *business events* then? Because it gives the analyst an opportunity to think about what kind of *business event* we are really dealing with; and it allows me (in writing this book) to refer to each of the four different kinds of *business events* by a distinct name. But our clients (the business folks and stakeholders) don't care, so it's unnecessary to label them in any documentation that you produce.

But there are distinct differences between the different kinds of *business events* (and that's why I've given them different labels); therefore, it's important to phrase the *business event* correctly.

For example, there's a clear difference between **"The Company Decides to Pay the Supplier"** and **"It is Time to Pay the Supplier"**. The first one (an Internal *business event*) suggests that there is a decision point, and this decision point must be reflected in the business specification. The second one (a Temporal *business event*) suggests that there is no decision point, it's just <u>time</u> to pay the supplier – perhaps the time criteria is 30 days after receiving goods from the supplier; perhaps it is upon receipt of the goods; or it's "time" to do so immediately after receipt of goods from the supplier. Whatever the time criteria, this too must be reflected in the business specification. By identifying the type of *business event* the analyst is able to more clearly think through the ramifications on the specification.

Create a short list of potential *business events* for the project

For most projects, it's usually helpful to start with a list of *business events* longer than just a couple. This will give a project a *kick-start* to get it off the ground. To arrive at a potential list of *business events* you need to do some brainstorming, applying a lot of imagination. Your general knowledge about the subject area or target business area will be a great help. One way of brainstorming a project's potential *business events* is to look at your history of *business events* from previous projects. (Yes, you should keep a **Master Business Events List** for your organization.) If you have a Master Business Events List, review each of the *business events* on that list and see how many of them might fit your project. For each *business event* on your master list, change the nouns to fit your project. If you think you have a *business event* that's within the scope of your project include it on your list of potential *business events*. Don't worry about finding all the *business events* for your project, or even if they are the right ones. Just add the ones you find to your list of potential *business events* for review with your clients and subject-matter experts in an interactive discovery session – they will tell you if a *business event* is within the scope of their planned work or not. Then eliminate those *business events* on your list that your clients or subject-matter experts have determined to be outside the scope of the project and keep the others. Remember that your list of potential *business events* can be quite long or very short in the beginning – but just a few *business events* is enough to start.

After a list of potential *business events* has been created, pick one *business event* to start with and, for that *business event*, ask your clients or subject-matter experts the following question:

"What do we need to <u>know about</u> or <u>remember</u> in order to support this business condition or circumstance?"

When you ask, "*What do we need to **know about**?*" you are looking for input information. When you ask, "*What do we need to **remember**?*" you are looking for what to record or keep track of. This question implies that you are <u>not</u> looking for the process. Your objective is to discover <u>what</u> (data) is needed to support the *business event*, not how things are to be <u>done</u> (the process).

When you ask these questions, your project subject-matter experts will respond with information that could be at the highest level of abstraction (pretty high level stuff) or at the lowest level of detail (right at the desktop level). It is the analyst's challenge to decipher what they have said and to determine what an Object is and what's a data attribute. More on how to do that later.

4.2 How to Find the Data You Need

For each *business event* identified as part of the project's scope, we need to identify and illustrate all the data that's required to support the *business event*. We do this by joining all the required Objects together that we have found to be needed to support the *business event*. The type of diagram in Fig. 4-1 (diamond in the middle, surrounded by boxed Objects) is called an **Object-Relationship Diagram**. It's good for data warehouse type of projects, geographical information systems, or research projects based heavily on repositories of data.

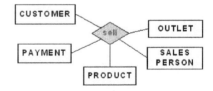

Fig. 4-1: Object-Relationship diagram:
A Customer Buys a Product

The relationship between Objects can also be illustrated as part of a **Business Process Diagram**, like Fig. 4.2 (bubble in the middle, surrounded by Objects between parallel lines). This kind of diagram is usually used when it's desirable to illustrate the business process, such as for marketing or accounting or justice systems.

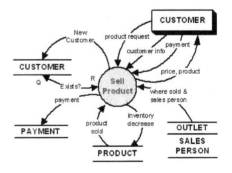

Fig. 4-2: Business Process Diagram: A
Customer Buys a Product

There isn't much difference between the two types of diagrams, except the conventions established over the past three decades. There's no rule that says you have to use one or the other of these diagrams – although there are some conventions. But, conventions are often the result of habit, and should sometimes be broken, especially when our knowledge changes. So, use any diagramming method you want. Use the one that you're more comfortable with, and the one that helps you communicate better in your environment. Since there are two schools of thought when it comes to the use of diagrams – data and process – I'm going to use both the **Object-Relationship Diagram** (Fig. 4-1) and the **Business Process Diagram** (Fig. 4-2) to discuss and illustrate each point in this section. Then I'll stop and only go with one of them.

What is an Object?

An Object or *entity* is a noun (i.e., a person, place, thing or concept). It is something that is *essential* or absolutely necessary in order to support the business process or data warehouse that in turn support the business condition or circumstance (*business event*) found to be in-scope.

An Object contains essential data and information about the business, including rules that govern the behavior of the business under specific circumstances (*business events*). Each Object is a distinct and unique collection of related data about something specific.

An Object must have lots of information to describe it. It must have a <u>description</u>, so everyone can understand what the Object is (and isn't). It must have <u>substance</u> – that is, it must consist of at least two data attributes. Each Object must also include <u>all the rules</u> that govern the business under specific circumstances (i.e., when the Object participates in various business processes with other Objects).

CUSTOMER
Someone who requests or buys product or service from the company.

Business Rules
- must be served by one or more **salesperson**s
- may never be served by **salesperson** (e.g., the customer never buys anything)
- must have been in one or more **outlet**s
- may buy one or more **product**s
- may never buy a **product** (but must have requested something that was unavailable)
- may make several **payment**s for **product**s purchased
- may never make a **payment** for a **product** (e.g., didn't buy anything; or returned a defective product)

Data Attributes
- customer name
- customer address
- phone number

Unique Identifier
- customer-ID

Fig. 4-3: Object Description – "Customer"

Find Objects by asking the Tracking Question

Now that we know what an Object is and what it's composed of, we can go on to the next step in gathering information from a client (or subject-matter expert), as well as how to define the Object and how to draw a picture – we'll use both styles of diagram (Fig. 4-1 and Fig. 4-2) – to illustrate that each Object participates in a 'relationship' with other Objects to support a *business event*.

After a list of potential *business events* is created for the target business system, select just one *business event* (and only ever do one at a time) for which you will develop a requirements specification. For example, you may want to start with the *business event* **"A Customer Buys a Product"**. Start by asking a project client or subject matter-expert (SME) the question *"What do we need to <u>know about</u> or <u>remember</u> in order to support this business circumstance?"* This is the Tracking Question. It must be specific to a *business event*. While your clients will be able to answer the question, perhaps with a little bit of prompting, be aware that they won't rush into answering this question until they are completely comfortable with what you are doing – which takes about a day of interactive 'discovery' sessions.

Also, remember that most systems only do one thing: they keep track of stuff. To keep track of stuff, the system has to record data. One of the main objectives of any business process is to remember what has been done. Remembering what has been done means recording data; and data recorded is data which is kept track of. This, in turn, enables a system to find the things we need to know.

Look and listen for nouns

The way to help your clients or SMEs move along quickly is to look for Objects in obvious places. The best place to start is in the *business event* statement itself. Every *business event* consists of at least a verb and a noun or two. The nouns in the *business event* statement are usually Objects, as long as they consist of two or more data items. Let's look at some examples.

"A Customer Buys a Product".
The noun **CUSTOMER** is an Object – if we can find more than one data item that belongs to it. Well, that doesn't seem too difficult – *name*, *address*, and *phone number*. That's three items (which have to be verified with a SME), so it qualifies as an Object.

CUSTOMER
Data Attributes
• customer name
• customer address
• phone number

The noun **PRODUCT** is also an Object, if we can attribute more than one data item to it. Once again, pretty easy – *product description*, *size*, and *color*. Again, with more than one data item, it qualifies as an Object.

PRODUCT
Data Attributes
• product description
• size
• color

"The Company Decides to Acquire an Asset".
The noun **ASSET** is an Object, if we can attribute more than one data item to it.

ASSET
Data Attributes
• asset description
• asset value
• date acquired

"The Client Opens an Account".
The nouns **CLIENT** and **ACCOUNT** are both Objects, since we can attribute more than one data item to each.

CLIENT
Data Attributes
• client legal name
• client operating name
• client address

ACCOUNT
Data Attributes
• account type
• account number
• minimum amount

"The Company Decides to Issue a Debit Card to a Customer".
The nouns **CUSTOMER** and **DEBIT CARD** are both Objects, since we can attribute more than one data item to each to describe them.

While **DEBIT CARD** is used here as an example, it is just a little bit physical – it represents the design solution to an Object which would be more correctly known as either **PRODUCT** or **ACCOUNT** – but, with the intent of communicating effectively with the client, I would consider it to be sufficiently useful to be included as a business Object.

What we call something conjures up specific images, and a specific image can turn into a perception (bias) of "a certain way of doing things", or an implementation bias. The word "fax" is a good example. Most of us get a certain image of a fax when we hear the word, usually involving a piece of paper that curls and falls behind the desk; whereas, the unbiased view of the technology would simply be an image or reproduction of the item. For the sake of clear analysis, it's best to stay away from words that create a specific technological image.

"It is Time to Deposit the Customer Payment to a Bank Account".
The nouns **CUSTOMER**, **PAYMENT** and **BANK ACCOUNT** are all Objects, since we can attribute more than one data item to each of them.

By helping the client discover Objects in this way you will find that they will soon get the hang of it and start contributing their own.

CUSTOMER
Data Attributes
- customer name
- customer address
- phone number

DEBIT CARD
Data Attributes
- transaction amount
- transaction date
- secret PIN number

CUSTOMER
Data Attributes
- customer name
- customer address
- phone number

BANK ACCOUNT
Data Attributes
- transaction amount
- transaction date
- transaction type (DR or CR)

PAYMENT
Data Attributes
- payment amount
- payment date
- method of payment

For the *business event* "**A Customer Buys a Product**" you will find that you need information about the **PRODUCT** we sold, who we sold it to (the **CUSTOMER**), where we sold it (the **OUTLET**), who served the customer (the **SALESPERSON**), and the **PAYMENT** the customer gave us. All of these Objects can be joined together in either type of diagram. The diamond in Fig. 4-4 is usually referred to as a "relationship"; and the bubble in Fig. 4-5 is usually called a "process". Both represent the same thing – a situation (**"A Customer Buys a Product"**) that needs data and a process to deal with it. Later, we'll devote a chapter to discussing how to construct a **Business Process Diagram**.

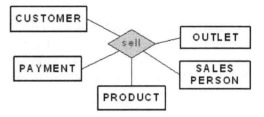

Fig. 4-4: Object-Relationship diagram:
A Customer Buys a Product

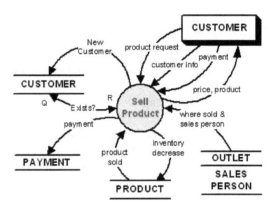

Fig. 4-5: Business Process diagram:
A Customer Buys a Product

Listen for nouns with "substance".

In a business model every Object must have two or more data items to have "substance". Anything less than this is just another data attribute. So when your client is answering your question – *"What do we need to know about or remember in order to support the business event* '**A Customer Buys a Product**'*?"* – listen very carefully for nouns "with substance". How do you find nouns "with substance"? Ask yourself (*shhh*, quietly, in your inside voice) whether the noun you heard can be decomposed into more than one data element. For example, when we hear the noun **CUSTOMER** can we imagine that we need several data items to describe it? Would we need to know the customer's name, address, phone number, etc? If so – and there are two or more such attributes and characteristics – then we have an Object. If not, then we just have a data item that belongs to some other Object.

It follows that not all nouns are Objects. Some are just data items that belong to and describe Objects. To determine the difference you must ask yourself if the identified noun can be further decomposed – if you can break it down even more. If you can, it's an Object.

Objects are things that we need to <u>know about</u> or <u>remember</u>. To ***know about*** means we get information from an Object (as some kind of input); and we ***remember*** things (for future knowledge) by recording items about an Object.

Identify data attributes by listening for nouns that are not Objects.

When a client or SME answers our basic question, *"What do we need to know about or remember in order to support the business event 'A Customer Buys a Product'?"* – and we expand the discussion with them – they will probably tell us all about the many data items that are not Objects. For example, a client may tell us they need to know the *customer name* – you know immediately that this is an item that belongs to the Object **CUSTOMER**, so we attribute it to that Object.

???
Data Attributes
• customer name
• customer address
• phone number

But sometimes we just don't know where a data item belongs. When a client tells us about a series of nouns that are data items and not Objects, but are also clearly related – such as *customer name*, *address*, *phone number* – then we must "roll up" a group of related data items to form a new Object.

CUSTOMER
Data Attributes
• customer name
• customer address
• phone number

It's quite common to find a data item first, before identifying the Object to which it belongs. This means keeping track of stray data items, and when two or more of them seem to belong to an Object that has not yet been identified, that's the time to create the new Object and attribute these data items to it.

Ask the Inclusion Question (for Objects).

Often when discussing with a subject-matter expert the process that supports a *business event*, different Objects are mentioned, but it becomes difficult to determine if we really need to include certain Objects to support a specific business process. How can we tell? One way to determine if an Object should be included is to ask the following question:

"If we know about {the OBJECT} what will it enable us to do that we could not do if we didn't know about it?"

Let's look at an example using the *business event* **"It is Time to Deposit the Customer Payment to a Bank Account"**.

First of all, are there any nouns "with substance" in the preceding *business event* statement? Reasonable candidates include the nouns **CUSTOMER**, **PAYMENT** and **BANK ACCOUNT**, since we can imagine more than one data item for each of them.

Our subject-matter expert (SME) for this example tells us that we need to keep track of the **PAYMENT**s that are **DEPOSIT**ed. We also need to know into which **BANK ACCOUNT** the payments are deposited.

As we listen to our SME we are able to identify each of these as proper Objects (they all are nouns, with substance), which we recognized to consist of two or more data attributes, or *things we want to know* about the Objects. But we aren't sure about the Object **DEPOSIT**. The word 'deposit' sounds like a verb, but if we want to *remember* the deposit then it certainly becomes a noun. So, is this really an Object, or is it what we do with the payments? How can we tell? Do we want to remember the payments deposited to the bank account? If so, does the Object **DEPOSIT** have two or more data attributes that don't appear elsewhere? What might these be? What about *date of deposit* and *name of depositor*? Do we want to remember these two items? (Our SME says yes.) Remember that a collection of two or more related data items makes a unique Object.

We also want to remember (record) the *amount of deposit*, but we can determine this by taking the total of the **PAYMENT**s deposited (*payment amount*), so it would be redundant as part of **DEPOSIT**. We can't have redundancy.

What else do we need to know about the **DEPOSIT**? Although it now has two elements of data that we want to remember about it, might there be something else we want to know about it? Clearly, we need to know the **PAYMENT**s that make up the **DEPOSIT** and the **BANK ACCOUNT** the payments are deposited into. We need to remember all of this.

CUSTOMER
Data Attributes
• customer name
• customer address
• phone number

PAYMENT
Data Attributes
• payment amount
• payment date
• method of payment

BANK ACCOUNT
Data Attributes
• transaction amount
• transaction date
• transaction type (DR or CR)

DEPOSIT
Data Attributes
• date of deposit
• name of depositor
• ~~amount of deposit~~

To verify the real need for an Object (such as **DEPOSIT**) we ask the question **"If we know about the DEPOSIT, what will it _enable_ us to do that we could not do if we didn't know about it?"** In this example it clearly enables us to know about all the things we stated above – i.e., who deposited what, where and when. By asking our subject-matter expert the *Inclusion Question (for Objects)* it enables us to determine if an Object, and its data, is really needed to support a process.

Here are two diagrams to illustrate the data that's needed to support the "deposit" process: the **Object-Relationship Diagram** (Fig. 4-6), and the **Business Process Diagram** (Fig. 4-7).

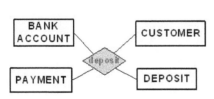

Fig. 4-6: Object-Relationship diagram:
It is Time to Deposit Customer
Payment to a Bank Account

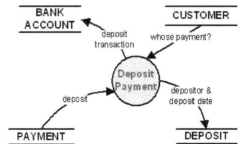

Fig. 4-7: Business Process diagram:
It is Time to Deposit Customer
Payment to a Bank Account

Ask the <u>Exclusion</u> Question (for Objects).

This is the other side of the mirror of the *Inclusion Question (for Objects)*. It's another way of determining if an Object and its data are needed to support a process.

The *Exclusion Question (for Objects)* determines the consequences of not having available a specific Object, and its data, to support a business process. How can we determine the downside of not having available the information represented by an Object? One way to determine if an Object and its data are needed is to ask the following question:

"If we <u>do not know</u> about {the OBJECT} what will it *prevent* us from doing that we must be able to do?"

Let's look at the same example as before, **"It is Time to Deposit the Customer Payment to a Bank Account"**.

As we discussed in the previous example, we know we need to keep track of **PAYMENTs** that are deposited. We also need to know to which **BANK ACCOUNT** they are deposited. We recognize each of these nouns as Objects since they all have two or more data attributes. Just like in our previous example, however, we aren't sure about **DEPOSIT**, even though it does have the legitimate structure of an Object (i.e., it has at least two data attributes).

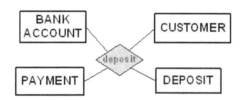

Fig. 4-8: Object-Relationship diagram: It is Time to Deposit Customer Payment to a Bank Account

Also, the **DEPOSIT** Object is "joined" by *foreign keys* to one or more instances of the **PAYMENT** Object – so we can know which specific **PAYMENTs** make up the deposit; and to a single instance of the **BANK ACCOUNT** Object – so we can know where the **PAYMENT** was deposited; and to the **CUSTOMER** Object – so we can know to which customer the deposited payment belongs. But, still, do we really need it, the **DEPOSIT** Object? How can we be sure? To find out let's use the *Exclusion Question (for Objects)*.

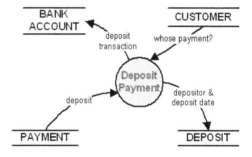

Fig. 4-9: Business Process diagram: It is Time to Deposit Customer Payment to a Bank Account

"If we <u>do not know</u> about the DEPOSIT, what will it *prevent* us from doing that we must be able to do?"

If the **DEPOSIT** Object didn't exist – if the information wasn't available – we wouldn't know about the *date of deposit* and the *name of depositor*. Do we need this? I would suspect so. Without the **DEPOSIT** Object we would still be able to know that certain **PAYMENTs** are associated with specific **BANK ACCOUNTs** and **CUSTOMERs**, but we wouldn't know *by whom* the payments were deposited. Is this key information? If your subject-matter expert says they need to know this, then the Object **DEPOSIT** must be part of the process or data relationship. Therefore, we can't exclude the Object **DEPOSIT** from participating in process that supports the *business event* **"It Is Time to Deposit the Customer Payment to a Bank Account"**.

Below are examples of the Objects (with data only) that are needed to support the relationship "deposit" (shown in the **Object-Relationship Diagram**, Fig. 4-10), or the process "Deposit Payment" (shown in the **Business Process Diagram**, Fig. 4-11).

CUSTOMER

Data Attributes

- customer name
- customer address
- phone number

PAYMENT

Data Attributes

- payment amount
- payment date
- method of payment

BANK ACCOUNT

Data Attributes

- transaction amount
- transaction date
- transaction type (DR or CR)

DEPOSIT

Data Attributes

- date of deposit
- name of depositor
- ~~amount of deposit~~

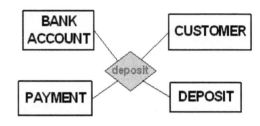

Fig. 4-10: Object-Relationship diagram:
It is Time to Deposit Customer Payment
to a Bank Account

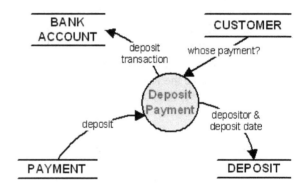

Fig. 4-11: Business Process diagram:
It is Time to Deposit Customer
Payment to a Bank Account

The Symbiotic Relationship between Objects and Processes.

A "process" is inseparable from a "data relationship" – they have a genuine symbiotic relationship. In other words, each *business event* (i.e., circumstance or condition) that needs to be supported by the target business area must be <u>dealt with by that target business area in some manner</u> (a specific process). This always requires <u>the use of data</u> (Objects) – either to retrieve some data or to record some data. It's impossible to have a process that doesn't involve retrieving, viewing or recording of data. It's equally redundant to have data that isn't ever involved in some kind of process – something has to happen to it, otherwise why do we bother recording it? Given this to be true, then it only makes sense to use just one diagram type – the **Business Process Diagram** – to illustrate process and its required data.

When we include an Object in any kind of diagram that supports a *business event,* it represents <u>all the instances</u> of that Object – its history. What distinguishes one occurrence of an Object from another may simply be a *date*.

In the **Business Process Diagram** in Fig. 4-12, for example, the Object **PAYMENT** can be seen as one or more instances of **PAYMENT**s; we can therefore see it as a <u>list</u> of all the payments (i.e., all its occurrences).

Equally, the **CUSTOMER** and **PRODUCT** Objects can be seen as <u>lists</u> of all the customers that we have done business with and all the products that we have sold to those customers.

Objects are always named and documented in the singular since we always view them as *one or more instances* of an Object and, as we will learn later, we always ask questions about an Object as if there was only a single instance of that Object.

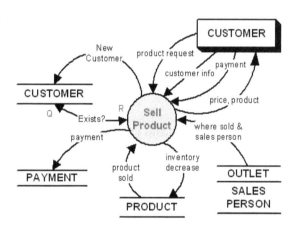

Fig. 4-12: Business Process diagram: Sell Product

Summary of How to Find Events and Objects

1. **Create a short list of potential *business events* for the project.** Don't worry about finding all the *business events* that are in-scope – just start with a few. You only need a few *business events* to find all the others.

    After an initial list of potential *business events* has been created, pick one *business event* to start with and ask the project subject-matter experts (the ones who have knowledge in the context of the chosen *business event*) the following question:

    "What do we need to <u>know about</u> or <u>remember</u> in order to support this business condition or circumstance?"

    The purpose of this question is to discover what data is needed to support the *business event*. To then find the data, you need to do the following:

2. **Look and listen for nouns.** Start by looking in the *business event* statement itself. It will consist of at least a verb and a noun or more. The nouns in the *business event* statement are usually Objects, as long as they consist of two or more data items.

3. **Listen for nouns with "substance".** An Object in a business data model must consist of at least two data items. Less is just a data attribute. For example, would the noun **CUSTOMER** need several data items to describe it? Would we need to know the *customer's name*, *address*, *phone number*, etc? If so – and if there are at least two such attributes and characteristics – then we have an Object. If not, then we just have an attribute that belongs to some other Object.

   It follows that all nouns are not Objects. Some are just data attributes that belong to and describe Objects. Others are full Objects. To know the difference you must determine if the piece of data, the noun, can be further decomposed. If you can't further decompose it, it's a data attribute. If you can, it's an Object.

4. **Identify data attributes by listening for nouns that are not Objects.**
   Sometimes we just don't know where a data item belongs, mainly because we haven't yet attributed enough data to create a suitable target Object. When a client mentions a series of nouns that are clearly data items and not Objects, but are also undoubtedly related – such as *customer name*, *address*, *phone number* – then we "roll up" a group of related data items to form an Object that hasn't yet been formed.

???

   Data Attributes
   - customer name
   - customer address
   - phone number

5. **Ask the Inclusion Question (for Objects).** For every Object that participates in a *business event* ask the following question:

   > "If I know about {the OBJECT} what will it enable us to do that we could not do if we didn't know about it?"

6. **Ask the Exclusion Question (for Objects).** For every Object in a *business event* ask the following question:

   > "If we do not know about {the OBJECT} what will it prevent us from doing that we must be able to do?"

It's also important to recognize that, so far, we have dealt with the issue of populating an Object with data (data attribution) only at the intuitive level. We have not yet dealt at all with the principles of normalization and data attribution; i.e., how to find the right home (in an Object) for data items, and how do we do so without redundancy? So, we'll look at that now, with an eye to ease of understanding and simplicity.

4.3 What is Normalization Anyway, and why do I Care?

During business systems analysis, information that is relevant to the project must be identified, organized and documented. This process of data discovery, data allocation and organization is called *data normalization*. Contrary to popular opinion, this does have to be done to ensure complete and accurate business requirements. But, also contrary to popular opinion, this doesn't have to take forever in the context of business requirements analysis. Nor does it have to be a technical exercise.

Normalization – what is it?

The purpose of normalization is to structure data in such a way as to eliminate all forms of redundancy and, ultimately, to allow the processing of the data – in a database structure – without inconsistencies or errors. This means that we have to make sure that any single data item (*customer name*, for example) is maintained in one place only, while being available everywhere it is needed.

Normalization, in its conventional packaging, is presented as being a progression of successively improved stages of data purity:

1. **First Normal Form (1NF)** – removes multi-valued data attributes and repeated groups from Objects.
2. **Second Normal Form (2NF)** – removes data attributes from Objects that are dependent on some of the other data attributes.
3. **Third Normal Form (3NF)** – removes data attributes from Objects that are not directly dependent on the Object.
4. **Fourth Normal Form (4NF)** – removes multi-valued dependencies within Objects.
5. **Fifth Normal Form (5NF)** – removes other remaining anomalies.

This is all very interesting, but what does *data normalization* have to do with business system requirements analysis, as I have suggested? And why would we care?

Many technical specialists would argue that you shouldn't care; that worrying about data and its *normalization* is the job of database designers. They would argue that you, as a business system analyst, don't need to know a thing about database design (and they are right); nor do you need to know anything about data modeling (again, in the technical sense, they're right). They will tell you that all the technical aspects of data belong in the domain of the database experts. And, of course, they are right.

So, why do you care?

When data is properly attributed to their Objects, and redundancies eliminated, you will then be able to ask highly focused, non-abstract questions of your clients and subject-matter experts. All the questions that you need to ask about their business requirements come <u>from the data</u> (after all, it is data that gives them the information they need from their systems). If the data is just a collection of 'stuff', then it is very difficult to ask meaningful questions. On the other hand, if the data is well organized and non-redundant, you will be able to ask the SMEs very specific and in-context questions about their business requirements, based on the data they need. To be able to find the data, you have to know how to identify it and attribute it properly to Objects. That's *data attribution*. You also have to eliminate the redundancies and data that are hiding behind aliases. That's *data normalization*.

When you allocate data items to Objects, and those Objects are partitioned well, you will achieve the level of detail necessary for good, precise questions for your SMEs, rather than vaguer questions that come from general knowledge. That old saying, *"the devil's in the details"* can be put to rest because proper data attribution and data normalization take the devilish complexity out of finding the questions to ask your clients and SMEs.

A full study of *data normalization* could be an academic endeavor that makes all your other studies pale by comparison. It is not for the weak-of-heart. Tomes have been written about this subject, mostly incomprehensible. Nor would such a study be all that productive. As a practicing business analyst, you need to be able to do it, but you don't necessarily need to explain to everyone what it is and how it works in all its theoretical finery. Accordingly, I have prescribed a set of five simple rules that – if you follow all of them all the time – will enable you to achieve sufficiently normalized data attribution and well-partitioned Objects, as part of your business requirements analysis, no less. What this means to you is (a) really good attribution of data to Objects; (b) no redundancy; and, (c) Objects that are ready for inclusion in the **BUSINESS RULES TABLE** so you can find and ask the detailed questions you have to ask your SMEs. (The BRT will be explored in detail in the next Chapter.)

4.4 The 5 Rules of Business Data

No redundancy whatsoever is the key to success with data. Follow these rules and you will never look back.

Business Data Rule # 1

- **Attribute the data item to the Object it describes best, and to no other Object.**

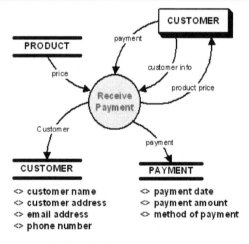

Fig. 4-13: Business Process diagram: With data attributes

When we speak with our clients and subject-matter experts to determine their business requirements, we hear all kinds of nouns to describe the business. Some of these nouns are Objects, which in turn consist of *other nouns* to describe an Object's content.

Those other nouns that describe an Object's content are data items that must be properly attributed to the right Objects. We call this *finding a home for the data –* or attributing data to an Object. But we don't attribute data items to just any old Object. Each data item must be attributed to the Object *it best describes*. And, of course, each data item can only be attributed to one Object.

But sometimes we hear 'stuff' from our clients, and we just don't know where a data item belongs – most likely because we haven't yet set up a named Object to which we can attribute the data we hear. The solution to this situation is to collect seemingly stray data items until we reach critical mass – until a pattern develops. When we have enough data items that are clearly related – such as *customer name*, *address* and *phone number* – then we "roll up" a group of related data items to form a new Object. This is not usually a big challenge since it only takes two data items to make a distinct Object.

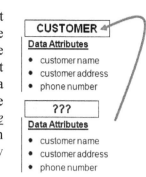

Object: An Object or *entity* is a person, place or thing that a business area or target system needs to know about or remember something about.

While an Object is always a noun, it is distinct from other nouns that are simple data attributes because a business Object:

(1) consists of at least two data attributes, to give it substance;

(2) is essential to the successful operation of the target business area or system (i.e., the Object and its data must be present or the business processes will not be able to do what they are supposed to do); and

(3) is defined by specific **business rules** in specific circumstances.

CUSTOMER

Someone who requests or buys product from the company.

Business Rules
- may purchase several **products**
- may never buy a **product** (but must have requested something that was unavailable)
- may make several **payments** for **products** purchased
- may never make a **payment** for a **product** (e.g., didn't buy anything; returned a defective product)

Data Attributes
customer name
customer address
phone number

Fig. 4-14: Customer Object

While it's true that all business Objects must consist of at least two data items to be considered an Object, these Objects can be 'decomposed' to just a single data attribute when designing the database. However, such decomposition comes much later and is not part of business analysis.

Data Attribute: A data attribute is an element of data that is a property of the Object to which it is assigned. A data attribute is defined by a name and description, and eventually represented by a set of values, which may include image and sound. In addition to the business rules that come from the BUSINESS RULES TABLE (which we will review in the next Chapter) data attributes are required to define what must be remembered or known about each Object. Fig. 4-14 is an abbreviated example of an Object description (CUSTOMER), with governing business rules and data attributes.

Totals and Flags: Totals and 'flags' <u>should</u> not be attributed to Objects, even though it may seem attractive at the time. Neither totals nor 'flags' are real data items; they are the convenient representation of something else. A total can be summed from other data items; therefore it is redundant. A 'flag' is really a status of some kind, which can usually be determined from some other data attribute such as *time* or *amount*, particularly when the *absence* of data will usually represent a specific status. Flags and totals are therefore redundant and are signs of an early design bias, or a pre-design way of keeping track of something. Flags and totals are usually used to improve database access efficiency. It is best to wait until database design is done to "denormalize" with flags and totals, when all the facts about volumes, data throughput and access requirements have been considered. However ... on real-life project, clients and SMEs often tell me they need this and that 'total' to keep track of accumulations. As an analyst, it's counterproductive to start telling them why we shouldn't do this. Accordingly, I do record their need for these totals (you need to be seen to be communicating effectively, after all), but I make sure the software engineering team understands they aren't really there, so they can design the appropriate way of determining totals.

Business Data Rule # 2

- **Each Object must have a unique identifier. The unique identifier must not be used as "data".**

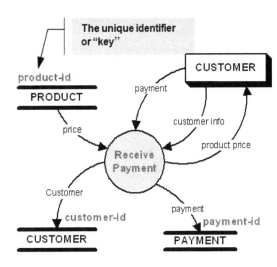

Fig. 4-15: Business Process diagram:
With unique identifiers for Objects

Objects are "joined" to support a business process, in such a way that there is no duplication of data. (**Business Data Rule # 1** eliminates redundancy; therefore data items only appear in one place.)

The data items that are needed to fulfill a business process often belong to different Objects. For example, data like *product description* belongs to the Object **PRODUCT**, while data such as *customer name* belongs to the Object **CUSTOMER**.

Unique Identifier: A unique identifier is an ID that is unique to a specific instance or occurrence of an Object. An Object's 'unique identifier' is also used as a pointer or link to other Objects that participate in a business process to support a *business event*.

An Object's 'unique identifier' is not to be used as data; that's a design choice (a 'how to'), and not a very good one, in my opinion. It is simply a 'unique identifier' or key.

So, why is it important when dealing with business Objects to discuss *unique identifiers* and *keys*? Well, it's so we can all have the same understanding of how

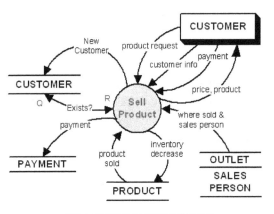

Fig. 4-16: Business Process diagram:
Sell Product

If a business process needs to be supported by several different Objects, then all the Objects that are needed must be shown as part of the **Business Process Diagram**.

Additionally, each Object must be non-redundant with respect to data. In other words, a specific data item can appear in one and only one Object, and only once, regardless of the name it uses. This means that a specific Object can only contain information about the subject of that Object, and about no other Object. (See **Business Data Rule #1**.)

This, in turn, means that to get information about one or more of the **PAYMENTs** received from a specific **CUSTOMER**, we need to know who the specific **CUSTOMER** is; and the **CUSTOMER** record (Object) must have a pointer or link of some kind that *joins* it to all the **PAYMENTs** we've received from that **CUSTOMER**. (Each **PAYMENT** is distinguished from the other **PAYMENTs** either by the *date of the payment* or by some other data attribute.) Equally true, then, is that if we know the ID of a specific **PAYMENT**, we will be able to find the **CUSTOMER** to whom it belongs.

So when an Object is shown as being part of a business process, it means that all other Objects (and their data) with which it shares the process can be individually *joined*, based on a pointer or key that connects one Object with another. For example, in Fig. 4-18, if we know who the **CUSTOMER** is, we can find all the **PAYMENTs** they made; and, if we know the **PRODUCT**, we can find all the **CUSTOMERs** who have bought this **PRODUCT**. Since a unique identifier joins each Object with the right data, we don't have to duplicate information in any Object.

CUSTOMER
Someone who requests or buys product from the company.
Business Rules
• may purchase several **products**
• may never buy a **product** (but must have requested something that was unavailable)
• may make several **payments** for **products** purchased
• may never make a **payment** for a **product** (e.g., didn't buy anything; returned a defective product)
Data Attributes
• customer name
• customer address
• phone number
Unique Identifier
• Customer-ID
Pointers to Related Objects
• Salesperson-ID (mv)
• Outlet-ID (mv)
• Product-ID (mv)
• Payment-ID (mv)

Fig. 4-17: Object description

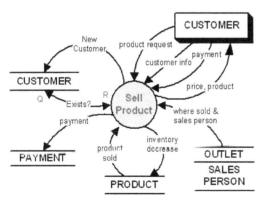

Fig. 4-18: Business Process diagram:
Sell Product

Pointers to Related Objects: A 'Pointer to a Related Object' is an Object's unique identifier contained within another Object. It is often called a "foreign key", meaning it is the key (unique identifier) of an external Object. The "foreign key" provides the ability to find data from other Objects to support the information needs of a specified business process.

The "joining" of Objects in this manner eliminates the need for data repetition or redundancy. "Foreign keys" can be single-valued (i.e., point to just one occurrence of another Object); or they can be multi-valued (i.e., point to several instances of another Object, using the qualifier "**mv**", which means multi-valued or a variable number of instances of the referenced Object). This ratio of occurrences between Objects is determined from the BUSINESS RULES TABLE, which in turn specifies the foreign keys needed for the Conceptual Data Model (the prescription for database design), both of which will be addressed later.

It is implicit in each **Business Process Diagram** – such as the one in Fig. 4-18 – that a "relationship" exists between each of the participating Objects. To find the related Objects and data, then, requires that each Object will have a unique identifier and that their respective unique identifiers connect all related Objects.

Business Data Rule # 3

- **Each Object must have two or more data attributes, other than the unique identifier.**

  (Data items can be part of an Object's data set; and can come from the process that supports the relationship.)

All business Objects must consist of at least two data items for the Object to have substance and therefore exist. If an Object does not have two or more data attributes there will be no way to distinguish an Object – *representing a collection of related data about something specific* – from any other noun that happens to be a single data item. This is the business view. From a database modeling perspective, an Object can be *normalized* to a single data item. But this is not the business view.

We sometimes have Objects that appear to be full of redundancy. Let's look at a typical **PURCHASE ORDER** Object as an example. Theoretically, the purchase order

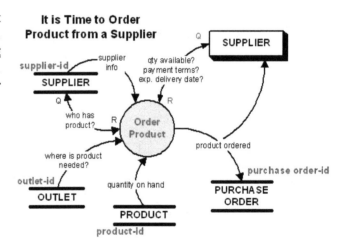

It is Time to Order Product from a Supplier

Fig. 4-19: Business Process diagram:
Object Relationships

PURCHASE ORDER

An agreement to purchase product from an accredited supplier, with specific payment and delivery terms prearranged.

Business Rules
- is issued to one **supplier** only
- may be for one or many **products**
- may be based on many customer **orders**

Unique Identifier
- purchase order-ID

Data Attributes
- quantity ordered
- payment terms (mv)
- currency type
- expected delivery date
- ...
- ...
- ...

Pointers to Related Objects
- supplier-ID
- product-ID
- outlet-ID (mv)

Fig. 4-20: Object description:
Foreign Keys and Data

should, in addition to the data that's specified in Fig. 4-20 under Data Attributes, also include information such as *product description*, *product cost*, and *supplier name* and *address*.

Of course, the **PURCHASE ORDER** Object doesn't have any of this because all of this data is already found in other Objects. In accordance with our **Business Data Rule # 1**, *product description* and *product cost* have already been attributed to the Object **PRODUCT**, and *supplier name* and *address* find their home in **SUPPLIER**. If we attributed this data again to **PURCHASE ORDER** then we would be in violation of **Business Data Rule # 1**; that is, we would have attributed data to more than one Object. And we can't do that.

We can't do that because we already have access to this data by way of *foreign keys* or *pointers to related Objects*. You'll remember that each Object must have a unique identifier (**Business Data Rule # 2**). The identifier for **PURCHASE ORDER** in the diagram above is purchase order-id. You will also recall that a *foreign key* is one Object's unique identifier contained within another Object, as a link. This means that if **PURCHASE ORDER** needs some information that is part of **SUPPLIER**, then **PURCHASE ORDER** will have the unique identifier of **SUPPLIER** as a *foreign key* or link. The same **PURCHASE ORDER** Object (Fig. 4-20) shows the *Pointers to Related Objects* (foreign keys) it needs to have access to data in the Objects **SUPPLIER** (supplier-id), **PRODUCT** (product-id), and **OUTLET** (outlet-id). Also notice that the **PURCHASE ORDER** may refer to several **OUTLET** records, and it does this by using the convention "mv", meaning multi-valued.

Data often arises from the process that supports a relationship – and that data must be attributed to an Object.

So, what does this mean?

An Object can have data attributed to it that's discovered as part of a supporting process; or, if you like, the data can *arise* out of the process that supports the *business event*. An Object that gets some of its data in this way cannot exist without being dependent on one or more of the other Objects that participate in the relationship. In other words, as shown in Fig. 4-21, if the **SUPPLIER** Object didn't exist in that process then **PURCHASE ORDER** could not exist either. Why not? Because **PURCHASE ORDER** is dependent on the existence of a **SUPPLIER** record to be able to know the *supplier name* and *address*. Equally, if the **PRODUCT** Object went away so would **PURCHASE ORDER** disappear.

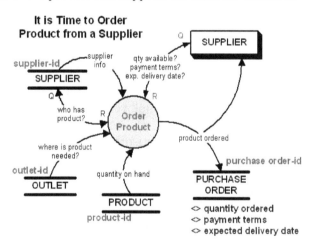

Fig. 4-21: Business Process Diagram – Order Product: Illustrating use of Foreign Keys

The **PURCHASE ORDER** also needs to know what *product* and its *cost* that make up the PO. This means that the **PURCHASE ORDER** is dependent on a specific record (occurrence) of the **PRODUCT** Object.

In the example (Fig. 4-21), the supporting process generates data such as *quantity ordered*, *payment terms*, *currency type* and *expected delivery date*. None of these data items, required by the **PURCHASE ORDER**, could be found in any other Objects, so they were generated by the supporting business process; which could have been done by a person on the phone, or by some kind of automated process, or a combination of both. How it's done is a solution design issue (we don't have to figure it out now). What is needed (the data attributes) is an essential business requirement, which does have to be determined now.

An Object that is dependent on other Objects and gets attributed with data in this way is called an *Associative Object*. Most Objects that sound somewhat physical are Associative Objects (such as **PURCHASE ORDER**, **CONTRACT**, **POLICY**, **LICENSE**, **PERMIT**). It's really not important what it's called (since we never label the type of Object in the documentation anyway) but it is important to know how it got its data. All required data that cannot be found in other Objects that participate in the same process (using *foreign keys*) must *arise from the process* that is being defined, and be attributed to the Associative Object.

Business Data Rule # 4

- **Any data item that is common to all subtypes of an Object must be attributed to that Object's supertype.**

- **Any data item that is attributed to one subtype Object cannot be attributed to any other subtype Object (See Business Data Rules # 1).**

There are times when we need to refer to something globally, and other times when we need to refer to a distinct part of something. For example, an organization with three different kinds of employees (full-time, part-time and contract employees) may refer to all of their employees (i.e., all three different kinds) under one circumstance, or just to one kind of employee (e.g., full-time) under another circumstance. The individual types of employees – **FULL-TIME EMPLOYEE**, **PART-TIME EMPLOYEE** and **CONTRACT EMPLOYEE** – will each have data that is unique only to them. This type of Object is called a *Subtype Object*. The general reference to an "**EMPLOYEE**" will have data that is common to the three different kinds of employees. This type of Object is called a *Supertype Object*.

Subtypes (such as **FULL-TIME EMPLOYEE**) depend on their supertype for existence because each supertype contains data that is common to all of its subtypes, and is necessary to completely describe those subtypes. Subtypes, however, can be dealt with independently of their supertype. It is usually more precise (and productive) to ask questions of clients and subject-matter experts about the subtype than about the more abstract supertype. For example, when we ask a question about the supertype Object **EMPLOYEE**,

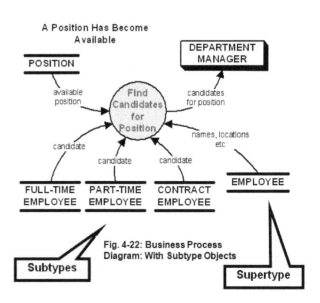

Fig. 4-22: Business Process Diagram: With Subtype Objects

we're implying that we include all the different kinds of employees in our questions. On the other hand, when we ask about the subtype Object **FULL-TIME EMPLOYEE**, it's a very specific question that excludes **PART-TIME EMPLOYEEs** and **CONTRACT EMPLOYEEs**. Questions at the subtype level lead to more specific answers than questions at the supertype Object level.

A subtype Object can also be a supertype to its own subtype.

Creating subtype Objects has a singular business objective: It permits you to ask your clients better, more focused and specific questions.

Business Data Rule # 5

- **When a repeating group of related data (multi-valued data items) is found in a previously defined Object, create a new Object from the multi-valued data items found.**

Sometimes we bury information inside an Object without realizing it. Using the example in Fig. 4-25 we will see how **Business Data Rule # 5** helps us find Objects within Objects. This, in turn, enables us to ask better questions of our clients, which we will see when we review the **BUSINESS RULES TABLE**. Let's look at an example of discovering "characteristic" Objects using the Object **CUSTOMER**.

To apply this rule we first determine if there are any data attributes in the Object that are multi-valued (mv), and seem to be part of a common group. In the process

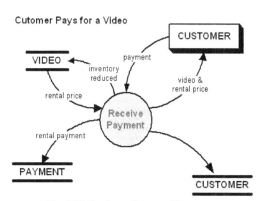

Cutomer Pays for a Video

Fig. 4-23: Business Process Diagram: Receive Payment

CUSTOMER

Someone who requests or buys product from the company.

Governing Business Rules
- may purchase several **products**
- may never buy a **product** (but must have requested something that was unavailable)
- may make several **payments** for **products** purchased
- may never make a **payment** for a **product** (e.g., didn't buy anything; returned a defective product)

Data Attributes
- customer name
- customer email address
- customer account #
- credit card type (mv)
- credit card # (mv)
- card expiry date (mv)

Unique Identifier
Customer-ID

Pointers to Related Objects
Payment-ID (mv)
Video-ID (mv)

Fig. 4-24: Object Description: Customer

"Receive Payment" (Fig. 4-23) we find that a customer can pay for a video, potentially at different times. Since we must track how each payment is made, we must include the data attributes *credit card type*, *credit card #* and *card expiry date*, and each must be multi-valued (mv) to support the different credit cards the customer uses.

To apply Business Data Rule # 5, the multi-valued items found in **CUSTOMER** that belong to a common group (*credit card type*, *credit card #* and *card expiry date*) are removed from the Parent Object (**CUSTOMER**) to establish a new Object (**CREDIT CARD**) that is characteristic of its Parent.

By taking repeating groups of data out of an Object (such as the above *credit card type*, *credit card #* and *card expiry date*, which are all multi-valued) and creating a new Object with the data, we are able to ask the client more precise and better focused questions (which we'll look at in detail when we get to the BUSINESS RULES TABLE, in the next Chapter). In this example (Fig. 4-25), we are now able to ask the client questions about the specific type of payment made by the customer (the credit card), not just the payment in general. This increased granularity gives us better knowledge about the process of paying for the video, and how that payment is made.

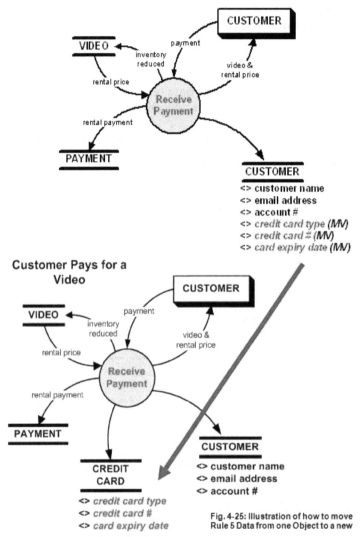

Fig. 4-25: Illustration of how to move Rule 5 Data from one Object to a new

Note that the data items we moved from **CUSTOMER** to create the Object **CREDIT CARD** – *credit card type*, *credit card #* and *card expiry date* – are no longer multi-valued when they are used to create the **CREDIT CARD** Object. That's because each Object is seen as a single instance or occurrence of the thing it represents; i.e., it is a single **CREDIT CARD** record. In other words, each **PAYMENT** is made with a single, specific **CREDIT CARD** by the **CUSTOMER**.

Once you have internalized the **5 Business Data Rules** you will find yourself automatically removing multi-valued groups of data to form new Characteristic Objects. You will find that you can do this literally as you speak with your clients and first determine the need for the Object (**CREDIT CARD** in this case) and as you discuss the need to know about the customer's payments at different times. Once you have had sufficient practice with this approach to business systems analysis you won't spend a lot of time thinking about it, you'll just do it. But you will also miss a few when you're working directly with the client. So, we suggest you carefully review each Object when

the client is not around. Then just look for any multi-valued ("mv") group of data that can be pulled out to make a new Characteristic Object. It's that easy. And remember, a group must consist of at least two data attributes (Business Data Rule # 3).

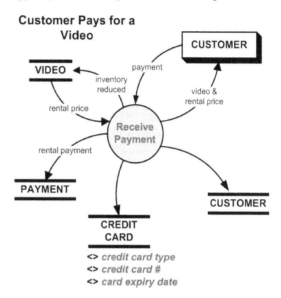

Fig. 4-26: Illustration of Rule 5 Data in a new Object being single valued.

Summary of the Business Data Rules

- **Business Data Rule # 1.** Attribute the data item to the Object it describes best, and to no other Object.

- **Business Data Rule # 2.** Each Object must have a unique identifier. The unique identifier must not be used as "data".

- **Business Data Rule # 3.** Each Object must have two or more data attributes, other than the unique identifier.

- **Business Data Rule # 4.** Any data item that is common to all subtypes of an Object must be attributed to that Object's supertype. Any data item that is attributed to one subtype Object cannot be attributed to another subtype Object.

- **Business Data Rule # 5.** When a repeating group of related data (multi-valued items) is found in a previously defined Object, create a new Object from the multi-valued data items found.

4.5 How to Determine if You Really Need a Data Item

As we discover Objects that are needed to support different business processes, we also find the nouns that are single data items, and we need to find a home for them. We attribute these data items to the right Objects by following the 5 Business Data Rules. But, data shouldn't be automatically accepted as necessary to support a business area or process just because someone mentions the data. In many cases data is included – just because it has always been there. The data item could be the legacy of a legacy system, but how do we find out if we still need the data that clients and subject-matter experts sometimes talk about?

Previously, we discussed how to apply the *Inclusion* and *Exclusion Questions (for Objects)*. We can do exactly the same thing with data items.

Ask the <u>Inclusion</u> Question (for Data).

Often when discussing a business process, different data items are mentioned by the client, but it's sometimes difficult to tell if all those data items are really necessary. How can we tell? One way to determine if a data item should be included is to ask the following question:

"If we know about {the data item} what will it <u>enable</u> us to do that we could not do if we didn't know about it?"

Let's look at an example using the *business event* **"It is Time to Deposit a Customer Payment to a Bank Account"**.

Our subject-matter experts tell us that we need to keep track of the **PAYMENTs** that are **DEPOSITed**. We also need to know into which **BANK ACCOUNT** the payments are deposited; and, since there are many customers from coast-to-coast, we must know which **CUSTOMER** the deposited payment belongs to so we have a proper audit trail.

DEPOSIT

Data Attributes

- date of deposit
- name of depositor

As we listen to our client we are able to identify each of these as proper Objects (they all are nouns) which we recognized to consist of two or more data attributes … things we want to know about them. One of the data attributes belonging to the Object **DEPOSIT** is *date of deposit*. If we weren't sure this item was really needed, the first question would be, *is this really a necessary data item*? How can we tell? To find out let's restate the "Data Inclusion" question.

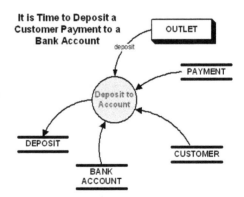

Fig. 4-27: Business Process Diagram: Deposit to Account.

"If we know about {the date of deposit} what will it <u>enable</u> us to do that we could not do if we didn't know about it?"

In this example, *date of deposit* will allow us to reconcile our deposits against statements provided by the bank. Of course, that begs the question *do we want to reconcile deposits?* Is it within the scope of the project? Only our client knows for sure. If the answer is... *yes, reconciliation is within the scope of the project...* then we definitely need to know about the *date of deposit.*

DEPOSIT

Data Attributes

- date of deposit
- name of depositor

Also, if reconciliation is within the scope of the project we must ask the question, *have we identified a business event for reconciliation yet?* If not, then we must add a new *business event*, **"It is Time to Reconcile Bank Statement"**.

Ask the <u>Exclusion</u> Question (for Data).

There is another side of the 'Data Inclusion' question. Sometimes it makes more sense to try to take something away than to imagine it being added. This is the same as the 'Data Inclusion' test, but we're just coming at it from the other direction. In this case, the question we ask is stated as follows:

"If we <u>do not</u> know about {the data item} what will it <u>prevent</u> us from doing that we must be able to do?"

Let's use the same example as before, **"It is Time to Deposit Customer Payment to a Bank Account"**.

"If we <u>do not</u> know about {the date of deposit} what will it <u>prevent</u> us from doing that we must be able to do?"

In this example (as in the previous one) it will prevent us from reconciling our deposits against statements received from the bank. Once again we have the same questions, *do we want to reconcile deposits?* Is it within the scope of the project? If the answer is... *yes, reconciliation is within the scope of the project...* then we must have the *date of deposit.*

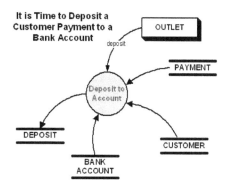

As with the 'Data Inclusion' test, we must add a new *business event* to be able to deal with **"It is Time to Reconcile Bank Statement"**.

Fig. 4-28: Business Process Diagram: Deposit to Account.

People have different views of things. That's why we have developed the 'Inclusion' and 'Exclusion' tests, so your clients will have the opportunity of seeing the subject from their own point of view – whether something is enabled, or it is prevented – which helps to make the questions clear to them; not just to the analysts, but to the client. It's always a matter of perspective. Some people are more comfortable answering questions that exclude rather than include. It's probably that left-brain vs. right-brain thing.

Ask the Inclusion or Exclusion Questions (for Reports).

This is one of my personal favorites.

Here we are, well into the 21ˢᵗ century, but so many people still want to see reports being the primary output of systems. A report, of course, if a solution to some question – it's a *how* are we going to provide certain information, in some context.

Rather than trying to tell your clients or SMEs that true business analysis doesn't address "how" something is done (such as issuing a report) but focuses on what is required to meet a need – which really means the essential data, not how it is delivered – it's best to find out the reason the client needs the report.

DEPOSIT

Data Attributes

- date of deposit
- name of depositor

If the client says, *"We need a sales report for widgets in the northeast region"* we can ask either or both of the Inclusion and Exclusion Questions, as follows:

"If we <u>do not</u> know about {the sales results for the northeast region} what will it <u>prevent</u> us from doing that we must be able to do?"

Or ….

"If we know about {the sales results for the northeast region} what will it <u>enable</u> us to do that we could not do if we didn't know about it?"

The client's answer to either question can then be translated into a *business event* – a situation or circumstance that the system has to deal with.

5. The Business Rules Table – How to Find the Questions to Ask

Contents

The single most difficult issue in business analysis has always been finding the right questions to ask clients and subject-matter experts (SMEs). The analyst's quandry has always been, *How do I know what I should ask these people? What should my first question be? And what should I ask next?*

Every business and system analysis methodology has always lacked this fundamental foundation – a method to find the exact, in-context questions to ask clients and SMEs. The only way we can be assured of the completeness of any business requirements specification is to somehow know that we have asked all the right questions, and none have been missed. Anything less makes not a business system specification, but a business *speculation*. Business requirements analysis isn't horseshoes. *"Close is good enough"* just isn't acceptable for the sophisticated, integrated, expensive business systems we need to have today.

The Kinds of Questions

Agile business analysis means nothing if we can't find all the correct questions to ask our stakeholders. It's not "agile" to leave unasked, and unanswered, questions on the floor. Therefore, to be able to start and finish business requirements analysis for any project, all of the following questions must be answered or resolved.

1. **How do I find all the right questions to ask?** How do I quickly find all the questions to ask our clients and SMEs? How do I know what the questions should be? (The operative words here are *find*, *all* and *quickly*.)

2. **How do I know all the right questions have been asked?** How do I find unanswered questions? How do I find the ones no one ever seems to find, or the ones we promised to come back to later and need to keep track of? How do I know we're done? How do I know we have found all the questions that need to be asked? (In other words, how can I know what I don't know?)

3. **How do I find the real limits of the project?** How do I find the questions that determine the real scope of the project? How do I prevent 'scope creep' during the project? How do I avoid surprises? (Or, how can I turn the scope issue into something real rather than trying to pin Jell-O to a wall?)

4. **How do I create a small, understandable and business-focused requirements document that everyone can understand?** How can I put all the related documentation in the same place, without redundancy, so I can find it again? How do I make the documentation brief, event-based, and not like a Victorian novel, so we can easily maintain it and find elements? How can I write it in business language, and not base it on the technology we're implementing? How can I make sure it focuses on the business and not on the technology solution? (And, how can we release and distribute in an "agile" fashion using modern media?)

5. **How do I describe data access requirements based on the business needs?** If we need a database design, how can I quickly determine the data accesses required by the business needs, so database designers don't have to go out and reinvent the business wheel? (And how can I, as an analyst and not a database designer, do this magic?)

5.1 How to Find the Questions to Ask Clients

All of the questions listed above can be answered and resolved by using the questions outlined in Chapter 3 of this book, the *Inclusion / Exclusion Questions* and the BUSINESS RULES TABLE.

- The BUSINESS RULES TABLE (BRT) is a question generator. It requires a specific syntax – a *language of structure* – so we can ask questions of clients and SMEs. This syntax eliminates personal and subjective evaluations of whether a question (or answer) is a 'good' one. All BRT-generated questions, and all answers from clients, have an equal value. This means we never have to be concerned with someone else's intuitive understanding.

- The BUSINESS RULES TABLE enables the analyst to easily identify and structure all questions to be asked about the business domain, in the context of specific business processes.

- The BUSINESS RULES TABLE enables the analyst to write a clear statement for the desired business policy, in plain language, in the context of a specific business process.

- The BUSINESS RULES TABLE enables the analyst to know where to document the client's answer, and to know where to find the answer in the future.

- The BUSINESS RULES TABLE enables the business analyst to find *business events* (conditions, situations and circumstances) the client did not recognize to be part of the project's scope, and therefore the supporting business processes that would otherwise be missed.

- The BUSINESS RULES TABLE enables the analyst to know when there are no more questions to ask the client about the project's business requirements.

The resulting documentation, written in plain and simple business language, can be easily read and evaluated by the client or subject-matter experts. The succinctness of the documentation enables SMEs to evaluate individual business processes and to determine if any new processes and data effectively contribute to the organization's mission, goals and direction.

Governing business rules, which come from the questions generated by the BUSINESS RULES TABLE, are the rules or policies that govern the existence or behavior of {the Object we are questioning}, in the context of a specific business process. Everything we learn about an Object is documented as a set of rules that govern the client's business, in a specific circumstance. These rules become the key part of the business requirements specification. They represent functionality and required (or denied) behavior in a specific situation.

Each Object that is part of a process supporting a *business event* (Fig. 5-1) becomes part of a matrix called the BUSINESS RULES TABLE. The symbols used in the BRT (see Fig. 5-2) are shorthand notation for specific answers to the questions that are asked. Although the BRT contains the shorthand notation, the actual context-specific rules are documented in plain language, using declarative statements.

Symbols used in the BUSINESS RULES TABLE to symbolize this shorthand, also known as *ratio of occurrences* (or cardinality), are shown in Fig. 5-2.

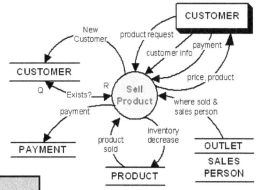

Fig. 5-1: Business Process diagram:
Sell Product

1	=	One only
N	=	Numerous (more than one)
0	=	None (means "never")
NA	=	Does not apply (= 0 [zero] occurrences)

Fig. 5-2: Notation for Business Rules Table (BRT)

Using a *language of structure* to ask questions of clients results in business rules specific to a process. These business rules are documented, as declarative statements, also specific to a business process.

From a data perspective, a process can also be seen as a relationship among Objects, behaving in a specific context.

A BUSINESS RULES TABLE is produced for each **Business Process Diagram**. An example of the completed BUSINESS RULES TABLE for the process **"Sell Product"** is shown in Fig. 5-3. The business process **"Sell Product"** supports the *business event* "**The Customer Buys a Product**".

BRT		Salesperson	Customer	Outlet	Product	Payment
1	**Salesperson**		N,0	1,N	N,0	N,0
1	**Customer**	1,N,0		1,N	1,N,0	1,N,0
1	**Outlet**	N	N		N	N
1	**Product**	1,N,0	1,N,0	1,N		1,N,0
1	**Payment**	1,N	1	1	1,N	

These are the 'Anchor' Objects.

**Fig. 5-3: Business Rules Table –
Sell Product**

SALESPERSON

Someone who sells the company's products.

Business Rules

- May have served several **CUSTOMERs**, but not at the same time.
- May never serve a **CUSTOMER** (e.g., may leave the company before serving a customer)
- Must have worked in one or more **OUTLETs** (e.g., may be transferred; or may work part-time in several outlets)
- May have sold several **PRODUCTs** to a customer
- May never have sold a product to a **CUSTOMER** (e.g., left the company before serving a customer)
- May have been credited with several **PAYMENTs** for products sold, from which commissions are calculated
- May never have been credited with a **PAYMENT** (e.g., left the company before serving a customer)

These are the business rules that come from the BRT for "Salesperson".

**Fig. 5-4: Business Rules for
Salesperson Object – in context
of "Sell Product" process**

BUSINESS RULES TABLE questions have a *language of structure* to get good answers. "Good" means nothing less than complete and accurate. Each Object must be queried with three (3) specific questions to uncover all the business rules relevant to the specific process in which it participates, and to be able to find other *business events* required to support the target business area. Above is an example of the type of rules that would result from the table entries above, for the Object SALESPERSON. The rule notation in Fig. 5-3 is read from left to right, and translates into the text in Fig. 5-4.

Each Object is placed in the BUSINESS RULES TABLE twice – once as an entry in the row on the left and once in a column at the top. We add Objects to the table only as they are discovered when we determine the Objects necessary to support a business process. An Object can intersect or *join* with several other Objects in the table. It is not possible that an Object never joins with any other Object. While it is possible that a single Object can be alone in a process, it must join with at least one other Object when all the BUSINESS RULES TABLEs are combined for the purpose of database design.

We start at the first row on the left with the first Object.

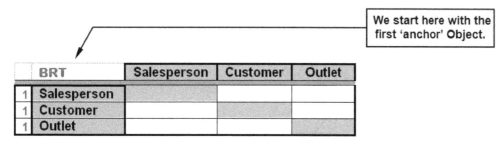

Fig. 5-5: Business Rules Table – Where to Start

We then ask questions about Objects that appear in a specific **Business Process Diagram**. (We'll visit what the specific questions are in a moment.) We ask our questions of only two Objects at one time... in binary pairs, if you like. This enables us to ask a series of stable question and get specific, stable answers.

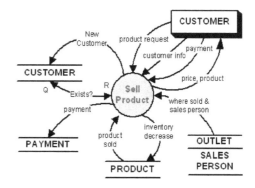

Fig. 5-6: Business Process Diagram – Sell Product

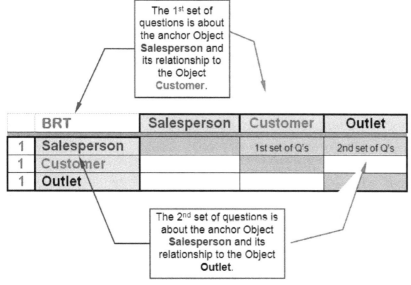

Fig. 5-7: Business Rules Table – Relationship between Objects

So, how does this work? Let's work through an example using just three of the Objects identified in the **Business Process Diagram** for **"Sell Product"**.

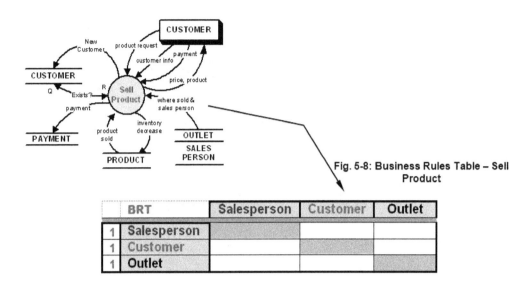

Fig. 5-8: Business Rules Table – Sell Product

	BRT	Salesperson	Customer	Outlet
1	Salesperson			
1	Customer			
1	Outlet			

From the process **"Sell Product"**, place the Objects in the BUSINESS RULES TABLE – once in a row on the left, and once in a column across the top. Place the number "1" in front of each anchor Object. This will help us focus on a single instance of the anchor Object when we ask the questions that arise from this table. (I did not place all of the Objects from the **"Sell Product"** process into the BRT, just to conserve some space.)

We start with the first anchor Object, and we structure the questions as follows:

Structure: "For a single, specific {anchor OBJECT} how many {intersecting OBJECTs} might {verb construct}?"

Let's put that into an English-language structure we can all understand.

"For a single, specific SALESPERSON how many CUSTOMERs might he or she serve?"

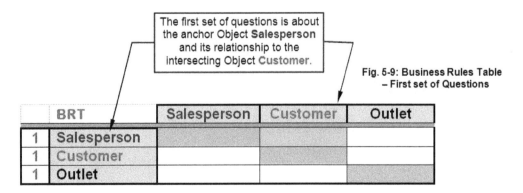

The first set of questions is about the anchor Object **Salesperson** and its relationship to the intersecting Object Customer.

Fig. 5-9: Business Rules Table – First set of Questions

	BRT	Salesperson	Customer	Outlet
1	Salesperson			
1	Customer			
1	Outlet			

The questions that come from this table must always be put into a context. The context is the verb you chose. For example, what do salespersons do in the **"Sell Product"** process? They **sell to** or **serve** customers. In this example, then, the context must be something like the verb *to serve* or *to sell*. I have chosen *to serve* since it seems easier to work with. Words like "associated" or "related" should never be used since they are far too abstract and only have meaning to the person using them.

Never attempt to answer this first, general question.

This initial question is only intended to help us focus our thinking. It's just a mental placeholder, so we can get on with the more specific questions. We immediately follow this initial question with three very specific questions, each soliciting a clear and unambiguous answer.

QUESTION # 1:

Structure: "Could the {anchor OBJECT} {relationship context verb} just one {intersecting OBJECT}?"

Or, in plain English:
"Could the SALESPERSON serve just one CUSTOMER?"

QUESTION # 2:

Structure: "Could the {anchor OBJECT} {relationship context verb} several {intersecting OBJECTs}?"

Or, in plain English:
"Could the SALESPERSON serve several CUSTOMERs?"

QUESTION # 3:

Structure: "Might the {anchor OBJECT} never {relationship context verb} any {intersecting OBJECTs} at all?"

Or, in plain English:
"Might the SALESPERSON never serve any CUSTOMERs at all?"

So far, we have a total of four questions, except the initial "placeholder" question doesn't require an answer.

PLACEHOLDER QUESTION:

"For a single, specific SALESPERSON how many CUSTOMERs might he or she serve?" (Do not wait for answer.)

This is followed immediately by three specific questions, each requiring a response from the client or subject matter expert.

BRT	Salesperson	Customer	Outlet
1 Salesperson		?	
1 Customer			
1 Outlet			

QUESTION # 1: "Could the **SALESPERSON** serve just one **CUSTOMER**?"

Fig. 5-10: Business Rules Table – Questions in the Intersection Cell

QUESTION # 2: "Could the SALESPERSON serve several CUSTOMERs?"

QUESTION # 3: "Might the SALESPERSON never serve any CUSTOMERs at all?"

Each of these questions is asked in what we call a client-interactive "requirements *discovery* session". Discovery sessions with subject-matter experts are very similar to technical JAD sessions, but *discovery* sessions focus entirely on the business requirements and not on system solutions or design. **J**oint **A**pplication **D**esign (or Development) is a session in which subject-matter experts and system developers interact to determine system functionality and output. In business discovery sessions, answers to questions are captured by an expert scribe, based on the BUSINESS RULES TABLEs for each **Business Process Diagram**.

Let's play through the answers to our questions – we'll make up some answers along the way, pretending subject-matter experts are present – and populate the BUSINESS RULES TABLE with the values representing our made-up answers. From these answers we'll also generate plain-language text that documents the rules in Objects.

BRT	Salesperson	Customer	Outlet
1 **Salesperson**		?	
1 Customer			
1 Outlet			

Fig. 5-11: Business Rules Table – Questions in the Intersection Cell

Start with the **PLACEHOLDER QUESTION: "For a single, specific SALESPERSON how many CUSTOMERs might he or she serve?"** But don't wait for answer. Immediately go on with the three follow-on questions.

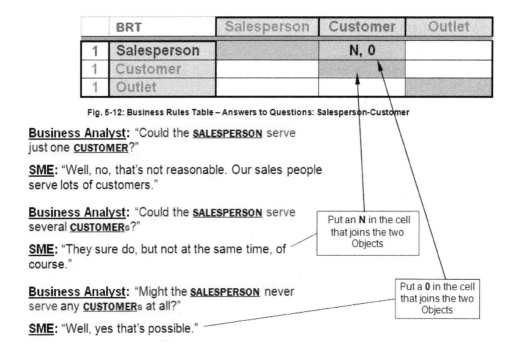

BRT	Salesperson	Customer	Outlet
1 **Salesperson**		N, 0	
1 Customer			
1 Outlet			

Fig. 5-12: Business Rules Table – Answers to Questions: Salesperson-Customer

Business Analyst: "Could the SALESPERSON serve just one CUSTOMER?"

SME: "Well, no, that's not reasonable. Our sales people serve lots of customers."

Business Analyst: "Could the SALESPERSON serve several CUSTOMERs?"

SME: "They sure do, but not at the same time, of course."

Business Analyst: "Might the SALESPERSON never serve any CUSTOMERs at all?"

SME: "Well, yes that's possible."

Put an **N** in the cell that joins the two Objects

Put a **0** in the cell that joins the two Objects

You will recall that earlier we reviewed the notation we use to record the ratio of occurrences between Objects. Ratio of occurrences, or cardinality, specifies how many instances (or occurrences) of an intersecting Object there are for a single anchor Object. Now, by itself, that's not very interesting information, and it doesn't seem to have much to do with business requirements analysis. But the moment we put that into the context of a business process, then we've defined the nature of the relationship between the intersecting Objects, and we can define the rules of that relationship, as specified by our subject-matter experts. Analysts don't have to agree with the rules the SMEs specify; but we do have to accept that they know more about their business than we do. I've repeated the notation so we can all work from the same page.

1	=	One only
N	=	Numerous (more than one)
0	=	None (means "never")
NA	=	Does not apply (= 0 [zero] occurrences)

Fig. 5-13: Notation for Business Rules Table (BRT)

By revisiting the 3rd Question we find that the SME gave us a technically correct but not very enlightening answer:

Business Analyst: "Might the **SALESPERSON** never serve any **CUSTOMER**s at all?"

SME: "Well, yes that's possible."

With this answer, we enter a "**0**" in the **BUSINESS RULES TABLE** cell (at the intersection of **SALESPERSON** and **CUSTOMER**) but we must go on to a follow-on question.

Business Analyst's Follow-on Question: "Under what circumstances might that be true – that they might never serve a customer?"

SME: "Well, they could leave the company before serving their first customer."

Whenever there is a "never" response from a client, you must always ask one additional question – "**Under what circumstances might that be true?**" This is the final Question and is only asked when the client responds to the 3rd Question with "never".

Each of the rules you have now discovered must also be documented in plain language. This isn't difficult, especially since you have already selected the context (verb construct) that you will use. Let's review the questions (and answers) in our example.

Business Analyst's 1st Question: "Could the **SALESPERSON** serve just one **CUSTOMER**?"

SME: "Well, no, that's not reasonable. Our sales people serve lots of customers."

Since the answer was "no" then there is nothing to add to the **BUSINESS RULES TABLE** and nothing to write up as the business rule.

Business Analyst's 2nd Question: "Could the **SALESPERSON** serve several **CUSTOMER**s?"

SME: "They sure do, but not at the same time, of course."

With this answer we now know that a salesperson may serve many customers, since serving none is not a reasonable scenario. With this answer we enter **"N"** in the cell that joins **SALESPERSON** with **CUSTOMER**.

BRT	Salesperson	Customer	Outlet
1 Salesperson		N	
1 Customer			
1 Outlet			

Fig. 5-14:
Notation for
Business Rules
Table (BRT)

We then write the rule in plain language under the 'anchor' Object (**SALESPERSON**). The rule can be written as *"may have served several customers, but not at the same time"*.

When we use 'may' as in "may have served several customers" we are also implying the salesperson "may not have served several customers". Therefore, before we chose 'may' instead of 'must' it's important to know the answer to the next question, since the words we chose to write our rules do have precise meanings.

SALESPERSON

Someone who sells the company's products.

Business Rules
- May have served several **CUSTOMER**s, but not at the same time
- May never serve a **CUSTOMER**

Data Attributes
- salesperson name
- salesperson address
- salesperson phone # (mv)
- salesperson fax #
- salesperson email address (mv)

Unique Identifier
Salesperson-ID

Fig. 5-15: Object Business Rules

Business Analyst's 3rd Question: Might the **SALESPERSON** never serve any **CUSTOMER**s at all?"

SME: "Well, yes they could."

With this answer we also place a **"0"** (zero) in the in the cell that joins **SALESPERSON** with **CUSTOMER**. The rule can be written as *"may never serve a customer"*.

BRT	Salesperson	Customer	Outlet
1 Salesperson		N, 0	
1 Customer			
1 Outlet			

Fig. 5-16: Notation for Business Rules
Table (BRT)

Whenever we get a "never" response to this 3rd question we must ask a fourth follow-on question to determine the condition that makes it true.

Business Analyst's 4th Question: "Under what circumstances might that be true?"

SME: "Well, they could leave the company before serving their first customer."

In this case, because we got a "never" response to the 4th question, we must qualify the business rule we previously recorded. In this case we take the original rule (*"may never serve a customer"*) and add (*e.g., may leave the company before serving a customer*). As with the original statement, this rule is allocated to the anchor Object **SALESPERSON**.

Whenever a "never" response is given by a client, they must support the "never" condition with an example (or several). In turn, you must determine if the circumstances identified in the example is <u>a *business event* that has not yet been included</u> in the project's scope… and if so, is it in-scope or out-of-scope?

In the example we are using…

- May never serve a **CUSTOMER** (e.g., may leave the company before serving a customer)

…the example states that the salesperson may leave the company. The question you must therefore ask the client is, "*Is this something – the salesperson may leave the company before serving a customer – that we want to keep track of?*" If so, should we include the new *business event* "**The Employee Terminates**" (quits, dies, retires) in the project's scope?

SALESPERSON
Someone who sells the company's products.
Business Rules
• May have served several **CUSTOMERs**, but not at the same time
• May never serve a **CUSTOMER** (e.g., may leave the company before serving a customer)
Data Attributes
• salesperson name
• salesperson address
• salesperson phone # (mv)
• salesperson fax #
• salesperson email address (mv)
Unique Identifier
Salesperson-ID

Fig. 5-17: Object Business Rule with example of "never" response to 4th BRT Question

The simple fact that a SME mentioned the example – stimulated by our question – forces us to consider its inclusion. If the SME's answer is "*yes, it's something we want to keep track of*" we must add it to our parking lot of *business events* that make up the project's scope. If the client's answer is "*no, it's not part of the scope*" then we won't include it – although we do keep track of *business events* found to be out-of-scope as well. However, it's not usual for a SME to use an example of a situation that could arise, and then say it's not something they want to know about. That's OK. But, in the end, it's either in or it's out.

I have found it is easier to get a response when asking if "we want to keep track of" something, rather than "Is this within the project's scope?" Earlier, we discussed how all systems just keep track of things. (If you don't keep track of something, you can't know about it.) Therefore, if the client wants to "keep track of" something, it means it's inside scope. This is also why so many projects are called "XYZ Tracking Project".

Also, two Business Event Lists are maintained – one for **In-Scope Business Events** and another for **Out-of-Scope Business Events**. This enables us to keep track of those *business events* that were discussed but determined to be out-of-scope. The out-of-scope *business events* could become in-scope on a future project. By keeping track we're also able to answer questions such as, "did you discuss ….?"

The 4th BRT Question is a primary method used to discover *business events* that are within a project's scope. That's why it is so important to listen carefully to what clients and subject-matter experts have to say, especially to their "never" answers, and to get the circumstances that make the "never" responses true.

This procedure of asking 3 or 4 specific questions (which we simply call the 'BRT Questions') is repeated for all the Objects that intersect with the anchor Object **SALESPERSON**. After we have finished asking questions of all the Objects that have a relationship with **SALESPERSON** – specific to a process – then we go on to the next anchor Object, which is **CUSTOMER** in our example. Because there are three very specific questions (and sometimes a fourth) you will never fumble trying to figure out what the questions should be or what comes next. You will find the 'BRT Questions' procedure to be very fast and effective. And you will find that your clients relate to these questions very well. They sometimes struggle to answer, but that's because the questions are so specific and call for a precise answer. Many interesting discussions and policies come out of these questions.

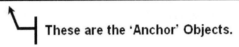

BRT		Salesperson	Customer	Outlet
1	**Salesperson**		N, 0	1, N
1	**Customer**			
1	**Outlet**			

Fig. 5-18: Business Rules Table (BRT) – Relationships between Objects

These are the 'Anchor' Objects.

Where do we put the rules? All rules are allocated to and documented under the Object that is the 'anchor' Object in the question.

And when we're all done we have all kinds of business rules attributed to all the Objects that we need to support a specific process. Our limited example, **SALESPERSON**, would look something like the entry in Fig. 5-19. I didn't go through the entire table with all the Objects since that would simply take too long. We will play through a more complete example later.

And how do we go about asking the 'BRT Questions' of all the Objects that are part of a business process, so we can find all the rules?

Immediately upon completing a **Business Process Diagram** we start asking the 'BRT Questions' of our clients. As a result, we gain an understanding of the business rules in a specific context (a process) right away, which enables us to progressively understand better each answer we get from our clients. This approach also enables us to learn incrementally, which means that we don't have to start the project with a whole lot of knowledge.

SALESPERSON

Someone who sells the company's products.

Business Rules
- May have served several **CUSTOMER**s, but not at the same time
- May never serve a **CUSTOMER** (e.g., may leave the company before serving a customer)
- Must have worked in one or more **OUTLET**s (may be transferred or may work part-time in several outlets)

Data Attributes
- salesperson name
- salesperson address
- salesperson phone # (mv)
- salesperson fax #
- salesperson email address (mv)

Unique Identifier
Salesperson-ID

Fig. 5-19: Object with Business Rules

5.2 The Value of Asking the Questions

It's important to recognize that analysis is all about asking questions ... and thus finding the answers. The ability to do this quickly, without spinning wheels, is a function of asking the right questions, in context, the very first time. It's not about getting the answers from ourselves (and out of our own head) based on our hypothetical understanding of the client's business system, without ever talking to the client and subject-matter experts. It's about getting down with the clients and SMEs, and asking them all the relevant questions that have to be asked. And, it's about doing it quickly and effectively.

Sadly, many business system analysts – experienced ones and brand new ones – think it takes too much time to ask all the required questions of clients and SMEs. So they don't. The interesting thing about all the precise questions that come out of the individual BUSINESS RULES TABLES is that ... they actually help us get the work done faster than by not asking the questions. The questions identified by the individual BUSINESS RULES TABLES focus on nothing but the rules of behavior between one group of data and another (i.e., Objects), in a context where these data comes together. It doesn't get any tighter or more concise than that.

How many times have clients gone off on tangents that appear to have little to do with the objectives of the project? How many times have teams experienced loss of focus in meetings or client-interactive sessions? How often have we heard the refrain, *"my client doesn't know what they want"*? All of these challenges can be attributed to meetings without a way of keeping everyone in focus and on target. And all of these challenges take time, time, time. It is simply faster and much more effective to go directly to the questions to be asked, ask them, and get immediate answers in variations of "yes", "no", "maybe" or "sometimes" – all of which can be decoded. Even though there may be scores of questions to ask our clients, it's a whole lot faster and better to know exactly what the questions are than to have to meander through the business analysis without focus. The other benefit is that you know when the entire job is done. It's not a guess. You know.

So, how fast can it get? Well, let's remember that any charlatan can finish faster than you simply by not doing some of the work required. But to know the work is absolutely complete *and* it was finished fast, that's another matter. And that truly is "agile". I will give you a metric later in the book, so we can have a measurable definition of "fast".

I mentioned earlier that at the center of their being most systems do just one thing: They keep track of stuff, so we can find the "stuff" later – or use it to make new "stuff". Therefore, based on the principle of finding the answer first and then discovering the question, it is the business analyst's job to discover what the client needs *to find*, and under what circumstances. By finding the circumstances (the *business events*) we can identify what it is we need to know, and therefore identify what we need to record or remember.

So what does all of this accomplish? By asking questions generated by Object relationships in the BRT, it enables the following:

- It enables us to quickly find the specific business rules that determine required and disallowed behavior in a specific context.

- It enables us to find *business events* that had not yet been mentioned by the clients, and have not yet been discovered.

- It enables us to find Objects and data attributes that we need which have not yet been discovered.

- Based on discovering new *business events* (via the 4ᵗʰ 'BRT Question'), we may discover new Objects not previously defined; therefore we will discover new data attributes and new business rules too.)

- It enables us to eliminate scope creep due to errors of omission – things we didn't know to ask about, or our clients didn't think to tell us about.

The rules that come from the 'BRT Questions'– always in the singular context of a specific *business event* (a circumstance, condition or situation) – are a different way of prescribing the behavior of the system, from an exclusive business context. Therefore, the **Business Process Diagrams** (and accompanying text), along with Object definitions and the rules derived from the 'BRT Questions' eliminate the need for other behavior models at the business specification level. That reduces the amount of work needed considerably, but no facts or business requirements are missed. This is, at least in my definition of the universe, truly agile. (Yes, I will discuss how long this takes later.)

Also, all of the business rules that come from the 'BRT Questions' lead directly to test cases.

Each business rule is a clear (and brief) contextual specification of required (or denied) behavior. A test case of functionality can be easily built around each of these business rule statement. Since this is done up-front as part of the business discovery, it eliminates the need to spend an lot of time figuring out business functionality later; thus, more time is saved, and "agile" business analysis takes on more meaning.

5.3 How to Write Clear Business Rules

By asking the 'BRT Questions' we can easily generate all the business rules needed for the project and the affected business areas, with each rule stated in a specific context. Each of the business rules is constructed from the responses we get after asking the 'BRT Questions', and all rules are written in plain language. Each rule is attributed and documented under the anchor Object that forms part of the 'BRT Question'. An example of how rules are attributed to an Object (**SALESPERSON**) is illustrated in Fig. 5-21, based on the limited **BUSINESS RULES TABLE** (Fig. 5-20).

	BRT	Salesperson	Customer	Outlet
1	Salesperson		N, 0	1, N
1	Customer			
1	Outlet			

Fig. 5-20: Business Rules Table – Salesperson Relationships

Business rules should be written as simple, single-subject declarative statements. This helps the reader understand exactly what we mean when we document the rules, and we never have to rely on someone else's comprehension of the language or their intuitive understanding.

The 'BRT Questions' we ask our clients solicit clear, unambiguous answers, which can only be *"yes," "no"* or *"sometimes"* and *"maybe"* (which we'll get to soon). We use shorthand (e.g., 0, 1, or N) to note our clients' answers, and we call this shorthand *cardinality* or, better stated, *the ratio of occurrences between the anchor Object and its intersecting Objects*. The ratio of occurrences that's entered in the cell that joins two Objects indicates how we should write the business rules.

For example:

SALESPERSON
Someone who sells the company's products.
Business Rules
• May have served several **CUSTOMER**s, but not at the same time
• May never serve a **CUSTOMER** (e.g., may leave the company before serving a customer)
• Must have worked in one or more **OUTLET**s (may be transferred or may work part-time in several outlets)
Data Attributes
• salesperson name
• salesperson address
• salesperson phone # (mv)
• salesperson fax #
• salesperson email address (mv)
Unique Identifier
Salesperson-ID

Fig. 5-21: Object with Business Rules

- If there is a **1** only we write, "**must** be **only one {OBJECT}**" as the rule statement.

- If there is a value of **1, N** only we write, "**must** be **one or more {OBJECTs}**" as the rule statement.

- If there is a value of **N** only we write, "**must** be **several {OBJECTs}**" as the rule statement.

- If there is a value of **1, N, 0** we write, "**must** be **one or more {OBJECTs} ... unless there are none**"; or we can write "**may** be **several {OBJECTs} ... unless there are none**" as the rule statement. We can also write two rules for the **1, N, 0** relationship, such as "**may** be **one or more {OBJECTs}** ..." followed by "**may never** be **an {OBJECT}...**".

- If there is a value of **N, 0** we write "**must** be **more than one {OBJECT} ... unless there are none**"; or we can write "**must** be **several {OBJECTs} ... unless there are none**" as the rule statement.

- If there is a **0** value we write "**will never** have an **{OBJECT}...**" as a separate rule statement.

In all of the above I have used the relationship verb "to be" or "to have" to join the anchor and intersecting Objects. Below, there are examples of these rules, written in plain language, with verb constructs other than the generic "to be".

- If there is a **1** only we can write, under the **CUSTOMER** Object, "**must** receive **only one PAYMENT**" as the rule statement.

BRT		Customer	Payment
1	Customer		1
1	Payment		

Fig. 5-22: BRT Object with "1" entry

- If there is a value of **1, N** we can write, under the CUSTOMER Object, "**must** receive **one or more** PAYMENTs" as the rule statement.

BRT	Customer	Payment
1 Customer		1, N
1 Payment		

Fig. 5-23: BRT Object with "1,N" entry

- If there is a value of **N** only we can write, under the CUSTOMER Object, "**must** receive **several** PAYMENTs" as the rule statement.

BRT	Customer	Payment
1 Customer		N
1 Payment		

Fig. 5-24: BRT Object with "N" entry

- If there is a value of **1, N, 0** we can write, "**must** receive **one or more** PAYMENTs ... **unless there are none**"; or we can write "**may** receive **several** PAYMENTs ... **unless there are none**" as the rule statement. We can also write two rules for the **1, N, 0** relationship, such as "**may** receive **one or more** PAYMENTs" ..." followed by "**may never** receive **a** PAYMENT...".

BRT	Customer	Payment
1 Customer		1, N, 0
1 Payment		

Fig. 5-25: BRT Object with "1,N,0" entry

- If there is a value of **N, 0** we can write "**must** receive **more than one** PAYMENT ... **unless there are none**"; or we can write "**must** receive **several** PAYMENTs ... **unless there are none**" as the rule statement.

BRT	Customer	Payment
1 Customer		N, 0
1 Payment		

Fig. 5-26: BRT Object with "N,0" entry

- If there is a **0** value only, we write "**will never** receive **a** PAYMENT..." as a separate rule statement.

BRT	Customer	Payment
1 Customer		0
1 Payment		

Fig. 5-27: BRT Object with "0" entry

As you can imagine, it's very important to be precise (i.e., *exact, as in measurement or amount*) and concise (i.e., *expressing much in few words*) when writing the business rules. The shorthand notation of 1, N and 0 tells us just about everything, but it doesn't put the relationship in the context of a chosen verb construct. Therefore, we also write out the rule in plain language, joining the two related Objects in a relationship described by the chosen verb. While the simple 1, N and 0 may be enough for database designers, the business folks need to see the rule expressed clearly.

5.4 How to Find Complementary Business Events

The *business event* is the foundation for all business processes. In other words, if there is no situation or circumstance to deal with (which is how we define a *business event*) then there is no need for a process. Finding *business event*, then, is the most important job of all.

Most *business events* have complementary *business events* – counterparts. Some *business events* must have opposite ends and predecessor and subsequent *business events*, or the project would not be complete in its logical coverage. Finding these is not a strange journey to a mysterious land. All we have to do is to identify the complementary, opposite, predecessor or subsequent *business event* and then ask the client if it is a *situation* or *circumstance* that they want to keep track of. A couple of examples of questions you might want to ask to determine *business events* that fall into these categories follow.

- You have identified the *business event* **"The Customer Buys a Product"** as being within the scope of your project. Does the complementary *business event* **"The Customer Returns a Product"** also fall inside the scope of the project? Are these returns something you want to keep track of?

- **"It is Time to Order a Product from a Supplier"** has been identified as a *business event* inside your project's scope. Does the subsequent *business event* **"The Product Arrives from the Supplier"** also belong to the project? Do you want to keep track of products that arrive from suppliers?

- **"A Vendor Applies for Approval to be a Recognized Vendor"** has been identified as a *business event* inside your project's scope. Do the related *business events* **"The Vendor is Suspended"** and **"The Vendor Ceases Operation"** also belong to the project? Do you want to keep track of suspended vendors or vendors that cease operations?

As we discussed earlier, the "keep track of" question is far better to use than asking if something is inside a project's scope. Asking about scope is a bit abstract for most people (notice how they scrunch their eyebrows as they think about this), whereas asking "do you want to keep track of xyz" becomes a whole lot easier to deal with.

Finding these complementary or related *business events* is making sure we ask the client all the follow-on questions that come as a result of discovering other *business events*. Finding the opposite end of a *business event* is making sure nothing is left unasked. Finding these complementary *business events* is establishing the limits to the project by stepping out to its perimeter and beyond and then determining where the scope line comes to rest. Scope creep will always be a challenge unless there is some way to determine the limits to the project. You can use the **BUSINESS RULES TABLE** and the 'BRT Questions' to determine what's in and what's out, but you also need to look for the complementary *business events* that make up the whole.

5.5 Good Questions are Closed-Ended

Open-ended questions are good for stimulating discussion but not so good for getting clear and specific answers. Therefore we rarely ask open-ended questions like, *"what do we need to know about customers?"* Not only will an answer take a long time, but we have no reasonable hope of achieving specific answers with such a question. This kind of question, while it might create interesting discussion, really just transfers the responsibility for analysis from the business analyst to the client or subject-matter expert. Most (but not all) open-ended questions do not lend anything of value to "agile" business analysis. Instead, we have to ask simple and closed-ended questions about the data (Objects) that's needed to support a process. We do this with closed-ended questions through the **BUSINESS RULES TABLE** and the 'BRT Questions', which tends to encourage direct and unusually concise answers. They cause answers such as *"yes,"* *"no"* and *"no, that's not what I mean."*

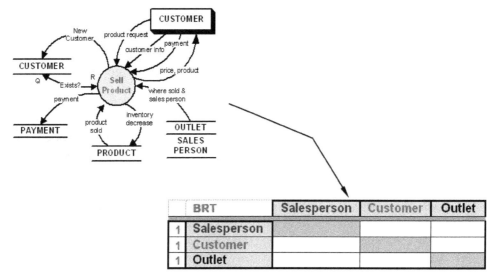

Fig. 5-28: Business Rules Table – Questions about Objects specific to a Process

While I strongly support the idea of open-ended questions to stimulate discussion and brainstorming – which is sometimes very necessary – I equally strongly oppose this approach if the objective is to get concise answers to specific questions quickly. The idea of "agile" business analysis also means getting clear and concise answers to questions quickly. Since the 'BRT Questions' have a specific syntax, they are designed to elicit exact answers rapidly.

The idea of using closed-ended questions based on a specific predefined syntax also removes business system analysis from the realm of 'art', as so many have called it (an elitist idea, even though it's in the title of this book). The 'art', as I understand it, has always been finding the questions to ask. And whoever was good at finding better questions – and therefore got better and faster answers – was considered to be the best and most experienced analyst. The **BUSINESS RULES TABLE** and the 'BRT Questions' enable all of us to become artists.

5.6 What to do when the Answer is "It depends ..."?

Sometimes, when we ask questions of clients or SMEs we get answers like *"well, it depends..."* or *"maybe"* or *"sometimes"*. While these answers are often seen as frustratingly vague or evasive, and may even appear defensive, it's really quite the opposite.

Sometimes, in real life, the answer is ... *"it depends"*. This is simply a conditional response; that is, under one circumstance the answer is *"no"*, while under another circumstance the answer is *"yes"*. You will recall that a *business event* is a "condition or circumstance ...." One of the two circumstances suggested by an 'it depends' type of answer is most likely a *business event* that you have already found, while the other one has not yet been discovered and added to your **Project Business Event List**. This kind of answer, then, is an opportunity to find a new *business event* that's not so obvious. To find it, we ask the client, *"Can you give me a couple of the situations or circumstances you're thinking about?"* Undoubtedly, they will, and you will then discover one or more new *business events* that weren't considered before. Add the new *business events* to your **Project Business Event List (Parking Lot)**, and then –working with your project subject-matter experts – develop the new **Business Process Diagrams** that support those *business events*.

5.7 How to Use Verb Context in the 'BRT Questions'

So far, I have said very little about how to select the verb construct to bind the two Objects in the 'BRT Question' together so you can have a context for the question. Let me remind you of how the 'BRT Questions' are structured:

QUESTION # 1:

Structure: "Could the {anchor OBJECT} {relationship context verb} just <u>one</u> {intersecting OBJECT}?"

Or, in plain English:
"Could the <u>SALESPERSON</u> serve just <u>one</u> <u>CUSTOMER</u>?" (Answer: *"Yes."*)

QUESTION # 2:

Structure: "Could the {anchor OBJECT} {relationship context verb} <u>several</u> {intersecting OBJECTs}?"

Or, in plain English:
"Could the <u>SALESPERSON</u> serve <u>several</u> <u>CUSTOMER</u>s?" (Answer: *"Yes."*)

QUESTION # 3:

Structure: "Might the {anchor OBJECT} never {relationship context verb} <u>any</u> {intersecting OBJECTs} at all?"

Or, in plain English:
"Might the <u>SALESPERSON</u> never serve <u>any</u> <u>CUSTOMER</u>s at all?" (Answer: *"Yes."*)

QUESTION # 4: *"Under what circumstances might that be true?"* (Answer: *"They leave the company before they serve their first customer."*)

All of these questons are based on the **Business Rules Table** in Fig.5-29, with the answers written as 1, N, 0 under **CUSTOMER** and across from **SALESPERSON**.

BRT		Customer
1	Salesperson	1, N, 0
1	Customer	

Fig. 5-29: Partial Business Rules Table –
Salesperson : Customer

So, how did we know to use the verb *'to serve'*? Lucky guess? How do we know what the verb construct should be for any 'BRT Question'?

The verb you choose to use is determined by the business process you are dealing with. For example, if the process you're working on has to do with the sale of products to customers, the **Business Process Diagram** (Fig. 5-30) will have a verb assigned to it that defines the process under which the data is related.

One way to find an appropriate verb to define the relationship between two Objects is to ask the clients or subject-matter experts who are present in your requirements *discovery* sessions. After all, they know their business.

However, if you do this I guarantee that you will get lots and lots of debate about what the right verb could be. If there are seven people in the room with you, you'll get eleven opinions on what's right and what's wrong. The reason for this is because you're asking them an open-ended question *("So, what verb might we use here?")*, which is designed for discussion rather than a direct answer. So, don't go there. You'll spin wheels 'til the cows come home.

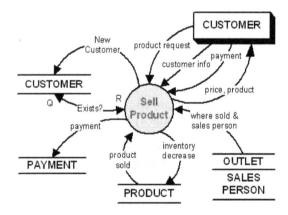

Fig. 5-30: Business Process diagram –
"Sell Product"

It is far better that you select what you think is an appropriate verb (right or wrong) and go with that. The important point is that the verb you chose must be contextual – that is, in the context of the business process – and must make sense in your 'BRT Questions'. The chosen verb will not necessarily be the one you used in the **Business Process Diagram**, like **"Sell Product"** in the process above (Fig. 5-30). But your chosen verb will reflect the context of that process. In the example we used earlier, based on this process, we used the verb "to serve" since this worked better in constructing the 'BRT Questions'.

But what about those situations when you have no idea what the right verb might be? What then? Out of all your verb choices in the language, you clearly can't just make one up without it making some kind of sense. So, what to do?

The answer, as with all good things, is with Shakespeare. The Bard had many good things to say, and arguably his most famous of all was The Question; which is precisely what we are discussing now – the 'BRT Question'. My friend Shakespeare wrote, *"To be or not to be ... that is the question."*

To be.

But to use this effectively we have to start with the very first placeholder question. An example is below.

PLACEHOLDER QUESTION: **"For a single, specific SALESPERSON how many CUSTOMERs might there be?"** (Do not wait for an answer.)

We follow this immediately with the next three (and possibly four) 'BRT Questions'. However, to use the verb *'to be'* we have to slightly restructure the questions, as follows:

- 1st Question: **"Could there be just one CUSTOMER?"** (Answer: *"Yes."*)

- 2nd Question: **"Could there be several CUSTOMERs?"** (Answer: *"Yes."*)

- 3rd Question: **"Might there never be any CUSTOMERs at all?"** (Answer: *"Yes."*)

- 4th Question: **"Under what circumstances might that be true?"** (Answer: *"The salesperson leaves the company before they serve their first customer."*)

BRT		Customer
1	**Salesperson**	1, N, 0
1	Customer	

Fig. 5-31: Partial Business Rules Table – Salesperson : Customer

To make the questions work, the subject (**SALESPERSON**) is now mentioned in the placeholder question only, and it is implied in the subsequent questions. But it works, even though it can sometimes be awkward. I certainly wouldn't want to see a **BUSINESS REQUIREMENTS DOCUMENT** with the verb *'to be'* documented throughout all the Objects in the project. However, the purpose of this Shakespearean tactic is not to find the final verb, but to find a way of starting so your business partners and subject-matter experts can move ahead quickly. If necessary, you can change the verb construct later. This approach works extremely well; and has kept many discovery sessions rolling along without those awkward discussions when everyone in the room is arguing about what the right verb might be.

5.8 Opposite Cardinality in the Business Rules Table?

There is a commonly held misperception that opposite ends of a relationship between intersecting Objects must be the same. This is incorrect. Let me explain.

In the **BUSINESS RULES TABLE** in Fig. 5-32, the relationship cell **SALESPERSON-CUSTOMER** contains **"NA"**, which means the client has decided that this relationship is 'not applicable' to their business requirements. There could

BRT		Salesperson	Customer
1	Salesperson		NA
1	Customer	1, N, 0	

Fig. 5-32: Partial Business Rules Table – Salesperson : Customer

be any number of reasons why they have no interest in this relationship. One possibility is that it's outside the scope of the project. In such a case, this relationship cell would produce no business rules that can contribute to the project.

The opposite end of this relationship, **CUSTOMER-SALESPERSON**, contains **1, N, 0** which would produce a full set of rules, and may even identify a new *business event* in the reason for the "0" relationship.

It is definitely not true that the relationship between two Objects must be the same from both directions. Neither is it true that a relationship between two Objects will be different in the opposite direction.

BRT	Salesperson	Customer
1 Salesperson		NA
1 Customer	1, N, 0	

Fig. 5-33: Partial Business Rules Table –
Salesperson : Customer

6. The Business Processes – How to Define Functionality

Contents

6.1 The Business Requirements Document

6.2 Finding the Business Requirements – 6 Steps

6.3 The Anatomy of a Business Requirement

6.4 The Non-Serial Incremental Approach

6.5 The Object-Task Table

The business processes are arguably the most important part of the system requirements to your business partners and subject-matter experts. They think in terms of *what the system should do*, while the analyst must think in terms of what information the system <u>must know about</u> and <u>have access to</u> so it can support the business. That means we really have to focus on the Objects and the business rules. The Objects define the data we have to keep track of, and the business rules define the circumstances under which required data must exist. Your clients and subject-matter experts, however, will naturally want to focus on the processes required by the system, and what those processes should do.

Before exploring business processes we need to better understand the components that make up those processes, and we need to understand that a 'process model' can't stand on its own. The BUSINESS REQUIREMENTS DOCUMENT must consist of **all** required documentation, not just diagrams that describe the processes.

6.1 The Business Requirements Document

The BUSINESS REQUIREMENTS DOCUMENT is organized first by *business event* and secondly by Object, with each Object being defined only once.

You will recall that a *business event* is an essential <u>condition</u>, a <u>circumstance</u>, a <u>situation</u>, a <u>state</u> or an <u>external requirement</u> that the target business area must respond to or deal with in order to successfully support the organization's key business objectives, goals, or mission.

A *business event* also does not reflect **_how_** something is done; it represents **_what_** must be done without regard to a particular technology or a particular way of doing things.

You will recall that *business events* come in four flavors:

Situation Event – non-controlled
  "The Customer Buys a Product"
  "The Product Shipment Arrives from a Supplier"
  "The Customer has Exceeded Their Credit Limit"

External Event – based on third party need
> **"The Government Requires Notification of Employee Earnings"**
> **"The Customer Requests a Higher Credit Limit"**

Temporal Event – based on time
> **"The Customer's Credit Card Expires"**
> **"It Is Time to Pay the Supplier"**
> **"It Is Time to Increase the Customer's Credit Limit"**

Internal Event – based on a decision
> **"The Company Decides to Cancel the Customer's Credit Card"**
> **"The Company Decides to Issue a Loan to the Customer"**

Also, *business events* never start with a verb. That's because a *business event* is not a process. A *business event* is a condition, circumstance, state or external requirement that must be supported by a process. The process that supports a *business event* is illustrated by, preferably, a **Business Process Diagram**, which is similar to (looks like) but not the same as a data flow diagram.

Data flow diagrams are discussed extensively in Tom DeMarco's delightful original work, *Structured Analysis and System Specification*. Scores of other books have been published since then, with almost all of them based on his earlier work. DeMarco's is still the easiest to read and understand. However, while the **Business Process Diagram** looks very much like a data flow diagram, it is limited to one process only, rather than several. This, too, goes to the idea that we should "partition the effort to minimize complexity" and therefore be more "agile" in approaching business requirements.

What we do to deal with a *business event* is documented in the BUSINESS REQUIREMENTS DOCUMENT with the content described on the next page. The documentation in the BUSINESS REQUIREMENTS DOCUMENT is organized by *business event* first and by Object second.

Some of my colleagues insist that both data models and process models are necessary for a complete requirements specification. I respectfully disagree with that approach. That's very old-school, and takes a lot of unnecessary time. Data models – for which I use the Chen-type of **Object-Relationship Diagram** in this book – represent essentially a database view. Our business partners and clients really have no interest in the database view. Their primary interest is in business functionality, and appropriate deployment of technology to support their business needs. However, in addition to business behavioral rules, the accesses to data that are required by the target business area are illustrated in the BUSINESS RULES TABLEs that support each process. While this is mostly transparent to your business partners, database analysts and designers should recognize BUSINESS RULES TABLEs as prescriptions for database access based on the requirements of the business.

The Business Requirements Document

Project Business Event List

(from the *Project Scope Blitz*)

- List of project *business events* from the *Project Scope Blitz*, including business area ownership and involvement, and requirement priority.

SALES AND PROCUREMENT PROJECT
AIR Telecom Inc.

List of Potential Events	SALES	MARKETING	PURCHASING	ACCOUNTING	Priority (1, 2, 3)
1 A Customer Buys a Product	*	*		*	1
2 A Customer Requests an Unavailable Product	*	*			1
3 A Product is Returned by a Customer	*	*		*	1
4 It is Time to Determine a Salesperson's Commissions	*			*	2
5 It is Time to Order a Product from a Supplier	*	*	*	*	1
6 It is Time to Pay a Supplier for Product Delivered	*	*	*	*	1

Total Number of Events = 6
Pilot & Copilot: Days to BRD = 2.7
Pilot Only: Days to BRD = 4.4

Fig. 6-1: A Short Project Business Event List

For each Event (*n* occurrences)

- A **Business Process Diagram** that support the *business event*.
- A task-based narrative for the Business process.
- References or links to Object definitions.
- A list of Business Areas affected by the Business process
- A Business Rules Table for Objects supporting the business process.
- Any Implementation (design solution) considerations.

AIR Telecom Inc.

Sales and Procurement
Business Requirements Document

August 23

For each Object (*n* occurrences)

- Definition of the Object.
- Business Rules for the Object.
- Data attributes for the Object.
- Primary (unique) identifier.

The Business Rules Table (BRT)

- Matrix of intersecting Objects.
- Cardinality (0,1,N) for each Object.

BRT	customer	product	payment
1 customer		1,N,0	1,N,0
1 product	1,N,0		1,N,0
1 payment	1	1,N	

Fig. 6-2: Example of a Business Rules Table

Business Process Diagram symbols

Business Process Diagram. The **Business Process Diagram** illustrates the required tasks and planned responses of the target business area to a specific *business event*. Each **Business Process Diagram** must have a written narrative to describe the process. This narrative supports the diagram so readers of the documentation can understand the business requirements. The diagram must have definitions of all the participating Objects, their data attributes, and business rules. A single **Business Process Diagram** can support more than one *business event*.

Fig. 6-3 is an illustration of the elements of a **Business Process Diagram**, and Fig. 6-4 is a diagram specific to the *business event* **"The Customer Buys a Product".**

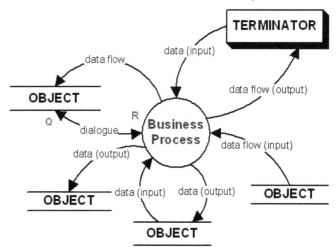

Fig. 6-3: Elements of a Business Process Diagram

While a picture is worth a thousand words, this diagram is not sufficient to describe business requirements: It needs a brief narrative, Object definitions, data attributes and business rules before it is complete.

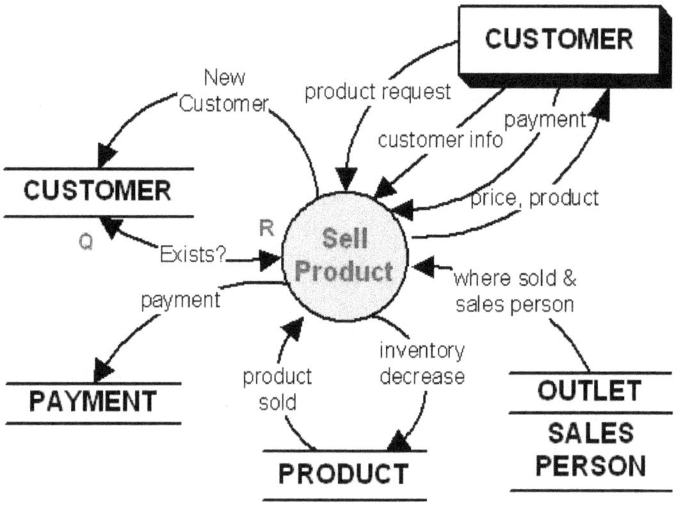

Fig. 6-4: Business Process Diagram – Sell Product

Terminator. A Terminator is a source of information or destination for information from a process. A Terminator, which may be inside or outside your organization, is not directly under the control of the business process which receives or sends information to it. A Terminator has its own set of processes and data, but these are outside the domain of the process that interfaces with it. *Use Case* practitioners might call a Terminator an "Actor", but that's only part of the story. It is definitely not a **Primary Actor** (one who does something in the system, since that implies a "how" or a technology. There are three kinds of technologies: Software, hardware and peopleware). However, a Terminator can be either or both a **Secondary Actor** (provides a service or data) and an **Offstage Actor** (has an interest in

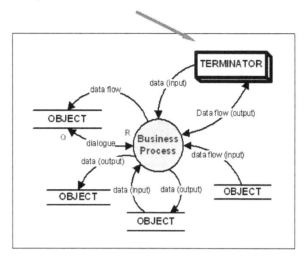

Fig. 6-5: Business Process diagram – The Terminator

the system, and receives data). A Terminator is simply a source or a destination of information. Some, but not all Terminators are also Objects in our business processes; but only if we need to remember something about the Terminator, or need to look it up (among several) so information can be sent to it.

Object. An Object is a repository of data shown in **Business Process Diagrams**.

- An Object is a repository of logically grouped non-redundant data.

- An Object in a **Business Process Diagram** is exactly the same as an Object in an **Object-Relationship Diagram** (an Object by any other name is still an Object; the shape of it doesn't matter), but is a different shape because the IT industry established these standards many years ago, when the two sides (data and process) weren't really seeing eye-to-eye.

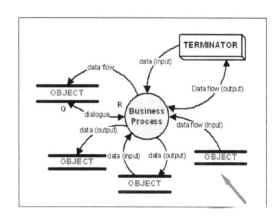

Fig. 6-6: Business Process Diagram
– The Object

- An Object in a **Business Process Diagram** contains all the data items attributed to the Object, in accordance with **The 5 Rules of Business Data** (see Chapter 4.4).

- An Object in a **Business Process Diagram** contains all the business rules attributed to it from the BUSINESS RULES TABLE specific to that **Business Process Diagram** (see Chapter 5: The Business Rules Table).

Process Narrative. A task-based process narrative must be written for each **Business Process Diagram** in plain language. It must specify clearly what is to be done with each data flow and describes the planned response to support the business process. It can be written in either of two styles: point form or structured narrative.

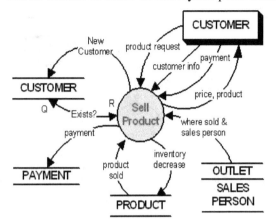

Fig. 6-7: Business-Process diagram
– with 2 narrative styles

Point Form Style

For each request for a product from the customer:

- Find out if the **CUSTOMER** exists in our system.
- Find the **PRODUCT** sold.
- If it is available, give it to the **CUSTOMER** with the price.
- Accept the **PAYMENT** from the **CUSTOMER**.
- Remember the **PAYMENT**.
- Remember the **SALESPERSON** who served the **CUSTOMER**, and in which **OUTLET**.
- Reduce inventory by the quantity of **PRODUCT** sold.
- If it is a new **CUSTOMER**, get the **CUSTOMER** information from the customer.
- Remember the new **CUSTOMER** information.

Fig. 6-8: Task-based Narrative –
Point Form Style

Structured Narrative Style

For each request for a product from the customer, find the **PRODUCT**. If it is available give it to the **CUSTOMER** with the cost. Accept the **PAYMENT** from the **CUSTOMER**. Remember the **PAYMENT** and the sales transaction, including the **SALESPERSON** who served the **CUSTOMER**, and in which **OUTLET**. Reduce inventory by the quantity of the **PRODUCT** sold. If it is a new customer, remember the **CUSTOMER**.

Fig. 6-9: Task-based Narrative
– Structured Narrative Style

Data flow. A *data flow* represents the directional movement of information between a process and an Object or Terminator. A data flow must always be labeled for its contents when the data flow is between a process and a Terminator. However, it does not have to be labeled if it is between a process and an Object. This is because an Object is about one thing, and one thing only. While a data flow may only contain some of the data in an Object, the Object itself is not mystery data. An Object is *something* specific. It is helpful, however, to always label a data flow since this makes it clear what is "riding" the data flow. You don't have to use data item names. Label it any way you like, as long as the label communicates effectively what the data flow is all about. This means the reader has to understand it, not just the writer.

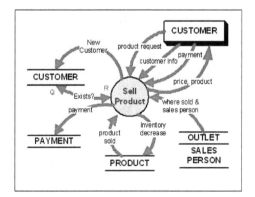

Fig. 6-10: Business-Process diagram
– illustrating data flows (bold lines)

Dialogue Data flow. A dialogue data flow is a data flow with arrows at each end showing the "dialogue" between a process and (a) an Object that contains data, or (b) a Terminator. For example, to query the **CUSTOMER** Object we can put the query "*exists*?" on the data flow, and a "Q" (for query) and "R" (for response) on each end of the data flow to illustrate that there is a dialogue.

Strict use of data item names on a data flow is not required, although this was the convention in the past. You can put anything you like on the data flow if it helps you to communicate better. If an Object is well named and properly attributed with data, without redundancy, then it will not be a mystery to know what data the Object consists of. One thing for

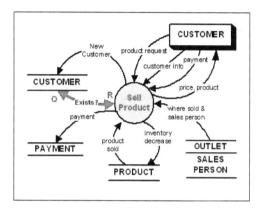

Fig. 6-11: Business-Process diagram
– illustrating dialogue data flow
(bold lines)

sure: An Object will not be a variety-show data store containing all kinds of information about all kinds of things. Because Objects are limited it enables you to use data flows better, even putting verbs on them.

Stacked Objects. Diagrams can sometimes get pretty busy, especially if there are a lot of participating Objects. So, we sometimes stack Objects to conserve space, as you see in Fig. 6-12. But we can't stack all the Objects, making one big stack, which would not be helpful in understanding the diagram. Objects should only be stacked if they are related to the subject of the data flows – such as the example in Fig. 6-12.

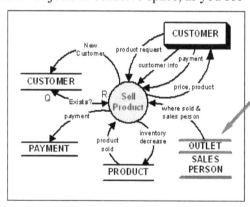

Fig. 6-12: Business-Process diagram
– illustrating related stacked Objects

6.2 Finding the Business Requirements – 6 Steps

Each *business event* or circumstance encountered by the business must be handled by the business in a prescribed manner; i.e., with a planned response. This means the circumstance or condition the business encounters must first be recognized as <u>part of a process</u>; i.e., there must be a stimulus that identifies the existence of the *business event*.

> A "***business event***" is an *essential* business condition, situation, circumstance, state or external requirement which the affected business area must respond to or deal with in order to carry on operations to successfully support its key business objectives.

The stimulus that tells us what circumstance the business has encountered – what the *business event* is – can be either temporal (like a date or a specific day), or it can be a specific value of data, such as a **CUSTOMER** exceeding their *credit limit*. Time can also be represented by data, such as a *due date*.

- **The customer buys a product**
- **It is time to order a product from a supplier**
- **The product arrives from a supplier**
- **It is time to pay a supplier**

The stimulus, regardless of the form it takes, identifies the *business event*. For example, "**It Is Time to Pay a Supplier**" is a condition that exists *at a specific time*. Usually it's the *due date*, which would be the stimulus that identifies the existence of the *business event*. This is part of a process that supports the *business event* "**It Is Time to Pay a Supplier**".

Once the stimulus has been identified we have to determine what should be done with the information. For example, if we know that the *due date* tells us that "**It Is Time to Pay a Supplier**", the question becomes "<u>what do we want to do about it?</u>" After shaping the process with the client – i.e., finding out *what we want to do about it* – then we ask the question, "and <u>what do we want to record or remember about this?</u>"

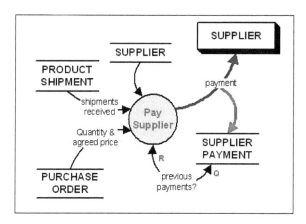

Fig. 6-13: Business-Process diagram – Pay Supplier, showing planned response, with narrative

- Periodically, find those shipments received from suppliers that have not been completely paid.
- Determine the amount owed based on the amount of product received and the agreed price.
- Deduct any previous payments against the same purchase order.
- Pay the supplier, and remember the payment.

In the example in Fig. 6-13, we <u>pay the supplier</u> (this is *what we do about it*), and we <u>record the payment</u> (this is *what we remember about it*).

In essence, we asked just three basic questions, which enabled us to build the **Business Process Diagram** in Fig. 6-13.

1. "How do I know that "It Is Time to Pay a Supplier"? (The answer identifies the stimulus.)

2. "What do I want to do about it?" (The answer tells us about the process itself.)

3. "What do I want to remember or record about what I've done?" (The answer tells us what we will record, and therefore look up at some other time.)

The 6 Steps to a Business Requirements Document

There are six basic steps to follow to complete the BUSINESS REQUIREMENTS DOCUMENT.

1. **Conduct Project Scope Blitz.**
2. **Plan the Project's Discovery Sessions.**
3. **Develop a Business Process.**
4. **Identify Business Objects.**
5. **Query a Business Rules Table**
6. **Issue the Business Requirements Document**

S T E P 1. Conduct Project Scope Blitz: This is the starting point for all projects. Convene a ½-day or 1-day Project Scope Blitz, as an interactive discovery session with the project's sponsors, clients, subject-matter experts, other key people and interested senior persons.

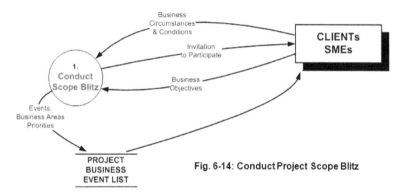

Fig. 6-14: Conduct Project Scope Blitz

The Process:

- Determine the best time to conduct a *Project Scope Blitz*.

- Issue a <u>Scope Blitz Discovery Invitation</u> to all clients and prospective subject-matter experts.

- At the scheduled time, conduct the *Project Scope Blitz* with clients and subject-matter experts.

- During the *Project Scope Blitz* with clients and SMEs, determine *business event* that are in-scope (as many as possible, but apply the 80/20 Rule, since other *business events* will be found during the detailed discovery sessions).

- Record *business events* that are mentioned but are out-of-scope.

- Issue the PROJECT BUSINESS EVENT LIST to all participants as soon as practical after the *Project Scope Blitz*.

> - **The customer buys a product**
> - **It is time to order a product from a supplier**
> - **The product arrives from a supplier**
> - **It is time to pay a supplier**

Fig. 6-15: Partial Project Business Event List

S T E P 2. Plan Discovery Sessions: After finishing the ½-day or 1-day Project Scope Blitz, and a short (or long) list of *business events* has been produced, it's time to plan the detailed client-interactive discovery sessions for the project.

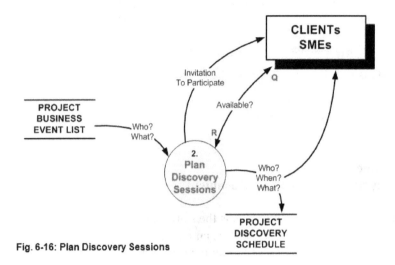

Fig. 6-16: Plan Discovery Sessions

The Process:

- Based on the **PROJECT BUSINESS EVENT LIST** produced from the *Project Scope Blitz*, determine the availability of clients and subject-matter experts to participate in detailed client-interactive discovery sessions for the project.

- Create a **PROJECT DISCOVERY SCHEDULE**, with participants and dates, for each *business event* on the **PROJECT BUSINESS EVENT LIST**.

- When the schedule is complete, issue the **PROJECT DISCOVERY SCHEDULE** and a formal "Invitation to Participate" in the discovery sessions to affected clients and SMEs.

S T E P 3. Develop a Business Process and

S T E P 4. Identify Business Objects.

Developing a business process and identifying the Objects that support that business process must be done together, at the same time. These are not, and cannot be, separate activities. Data and process are completely integrated – they have a symbiotic relationship – just like verbs and nouns are used together to make a sentence. Also, data attribution at the high level (i.e., finding a home for those data items that are needed) is done while defining the business process. Other, detailed data items can be attributed to Objects outside these discovery sessions.

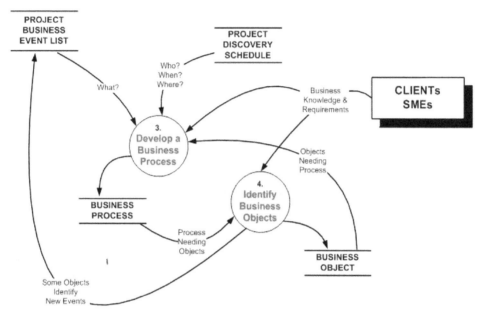

Fig. 6-17: Develop a Business Process and
Identify Business Objects

The Process:

- Periodically, based on the **PROJECT DISCOVERY SCHEDULE**, meet with subject-matter experts to develop business requirements for the business.

- For each *business event* on the **PROJECT BUSINESS EVENT LIST**, develop the supporting **BUSINESS PROCESS**, based on discovery dialogue with project subject-matter experts.

- By dialogue with business subject-matter experts, determine the **BUSINESS OBJECT**s that are required to support the **BUSINESS PROCESS**.

- At a high level (apply the 80/20 Rule), attribute data to **BUSINESS OBJECT**s according to **The 5 Rules of Business Data**.

- For those Objects and data items that identify the need for additional *business events*, add those *business events* to the **PROJECT BUSINESS EVENT LIST**.

- For those Objects that identify the need for additional **BUSINESS PROCESS**es, develop those additional **BUSINESS PROCESS**es.

S TE P 5. Query a Business Rules Table: After completing a **Business Process Diagram**, create a **BUSINESS RULES TABLE** for the diagram, populated with the Objects that are part of the **Business Process Diagram**.

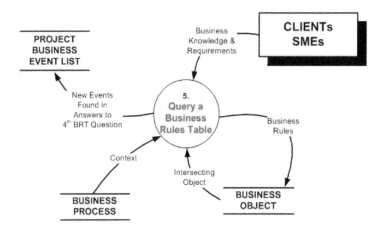

Fig. 6-18: Query a Business Rules Table (BRT)

The Process:

NOTE: This is not a discrete process. Querying the **BUSINESS RULES TABLE** is done immediately after each **Business Process Diagram** is finished.

- For two intersecting **BUSINESS OBJECTS** specific to a **BUSINESS PROCESS**, determine the Business Rules in the context of the **BUSINESS PROCESS**, by asking the BRT Questions.

- For each Business Rule determined, attribute the Rule to the **BUSINESS OBJECT** that forms the anchor (subject) of the BRT Question.

- In the **BUSINESS RULES TABLE**, annotate the Rules (1,N and/or 0) in the intersection cell of the two queried **BUSINESS OBJECTS**.

- Write each Business Rule in plain language under the **BUSINESS OBJECT** to which the Rule has been attributed.

S T E P 6. Issue the Business Requirements Document: After completing **Business Process Diagrams** for all the *business events* on the PROJECT BUSINESS EVENT LIST, including the ones found during the detailed discovery sessions with clients and subject-matter experts, all the documentation is organized as part of the BUSINESS REQUIREMENTS DOCUMENT. This document is then issued to those who need it.

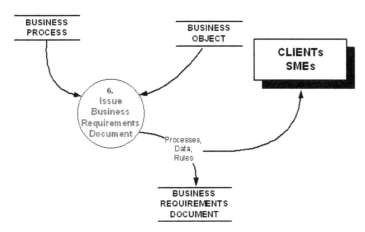

Fig. 6-19: Issue Business Requirements Document

The Process:

- For each BUSINESS PROCESS that has been completely defined, record it as part of the BUSINESS REQUIREMENTS DOCUMENT.

- When done, issue the BUSINESS REQUIREMENTS DOCUMENT to clients and subject-matter experts, as required.

We will discuss different and more agile ways of organizing the documentation and distributing it later in the text. The traditional way of documenting, distributing and getting sign-offs is quite contrary to how an agile organization can operate.

6.3 The Anatomy of a Business Requirement

The example we have selected to go through in considerable detail is a (partial) personal *accounts payable* system. We all have one of these, whether we use software to manage paying our bills or we manage it directly out of our checkbook. Since it is intended as an example of how to go through the 6 Steps to create a business requirements specification, we are not going to go down every possible road in terms of variable answers to questions or other such considerations. It's an example, and much in real life can be different.

Parsing the Business Processes

The first step is to conduct a *Project Scope Blitz* to produce a short (or long) list of *business events* – conditions, circumstances, situations and other external requirements – that the target business area must include in its scope. One of the objectives of the initial *Project Scope Blitz* is to get together with all the senior project people – the sponsors, the key stakeholders, the business and subject-matter experts – and outline how the work will progress, what it will look like and how long it will take. In other words, to manage expectations. Part of managing expectations is to get a real handle on the project's scope, and to have the agreement of the key people involved. The way to accomplish this, we have found, is to create a list of in-scope *business events*. (There's more involved in a *Project Scope Blitz*, but we'll get to that later.)

We can get initial *business events* from the business and subject-matter experts by leading an interactive session that searches out the desired *business events* for the project. This presumes that your business experts know their business and they have a pretty good idea of what they need to support their business needs – not the technology application, but the business functionality.[10]

You certainly don't have to find all the *business events* that might make up your project. That would be difficult, at best. All you need is a few entries on a short list to get you started. If you have just a few *business events*, then you will be able to find all the others through answers to your 'BRT Questions', and specifically the fourth question – "under what circumstances would that be true?"[11]

In this example we'll limit ourselves to starting with just two *business events*. However, we expect to find other *business events* through the 'BRT Questions', and if we do (and they are in scope) we'll add them to our **Project Business Event List (Parking Lot)**[12] so we can work on them later.

---

[10] Your clients do know their business. With well-structured and focused questions we will get very precise answers from them.

[11] See Part 5, The Business Rules Table – How to Find the Questions to Ask.

[12] The **Project Business Event List** is the list of *business events* first produced from the interactive *Project Scope Blitz*. During the detailed discovery sessions with subject-matter experts, several new *business events* are usually discovered (*business events* that were not on the original list, and some that were not even thought to be part of the project). These are usually found in answers to the fourth 'BRT Question', although some are also found when the Object and Data Inclusion and Exclusion Questions are asked. As new in-scope *business events* are discovered, they are added to the **Project Business Event List (Parking Lot)**, and we can return to them when it's time to do so. In this way, progress is also very visible to clients, and there is no "*trust me, we'll deal with it later*".

In our example we won't actually work through the newly discovered *events*, but we will add them to our list, so you can see how quite a few new *events* can be found through the '<u>BRT Questions</u>'.

The two *business events* we will work through are

➔

Project Business Event List

▪   A Bill Arrives from a Supplier

▪   It is Time to Pay a Supplier

Fig. 6-20: Initial Project Event List

The first *business event* is, "**A Bill Arrives from a Supplier**".

Business Process Diagrams

The first question we ask is, *"How do I know that ... (insert event statement here).* For example, for our *business event* "**A Bill Arrives from a Supplier**" the question would be *"How do I know that <u>a bill arrives from a supplier?</u>"*

In this case the answer could be, *"We know the bill arrived from the supplier because we received it in the mail."*

The "mail" can, of course, mean many things. It could mean the bill arrived in the mailbox attached to your house or apartment, or it could be the mailbox in your computer. If we specify either of these "physical" options at this stage in the project, then we are biasing the solution design, or at the very least we are limiting ourselves to our current way of thinking. This would make it all the more difficult to discover re-engineering opportunities when we look at the potential design solutions later.

Instead, we look for the basic concept behind "mail" and the *net flow of data*. What this means is ... we look for the source of the data, rather than the physical handler, such as an email system or postal delivery. In our earlier definition of a Terminator we said, *"It is a source of input..."* from outside the system. In this example we get the bill from a supplier. We illustrate this by using **Business Process**

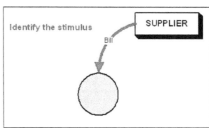

Fig. 6-21: Business process "stimulus"

Diagram symbols, showing the process as a bubble, and the data we received from the supplier as a data flow with an arrow from the supplier as input to the process in our system.[13]

The second question is, *"What are we going to do about it?"* In our accounts payable example it means we have to determine what we're going to do with the bill after we receive it. While the immediate response might simply be, *"pay it,"* that's covered by our second *business event*, "**It is Time to Pay a Supplier**".[14]

(At all times, we must stay focused on the current *business event* to the exclusion of all others. In other words, **Business Process Diagrams** are joined by data, through Objects,

---

[13] Note that a stimulus that identifies a *business event* and initiates a process does not always come from a Terminator. A stimulus can also be time, or data that's part of an Object.

[14] Remember the First Principle of Analysis – Simplicity: "Partition the effort to minimize complexity." This means breaking it down into small pieces so we can focus on one manageable piece at a time.

and never through the flow of data. By trying to join various processes by way of data flows, rather than data items that make up Objects, we would end up with meta-*business events* that include everything, such as **"A Bill Arrives from a Supplier"** <u>and</u> **"It Is Time to Pay a Supplier"**. If you end up doing a whole lot of things that are lumped together this way, you're probably violating our First Principle, "partition the effort to minimize complexity".)

Returning to what we're going to do with the bill we receive from the supplier (such as a phone bill), the question was *"What are we going to do about it?"* Our project subject-matter expert has informed us, *"We only accept bills from recognized and*

approved suppliers." With that information we can add two data flows to our **Business Process Diagram**, as shown on the right. Each data flow represents a task.

In a real business system we would, of course, check the bill against a purchase order to determine its legitimacy. However, our example (minimized to reduce complexity) is a personal accounts payable system.

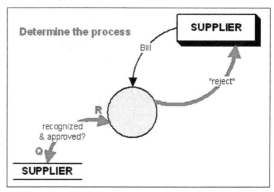

Fig. 6-22: Business process "tasks"

The last question to our subject-matter expert (SME) is, *"What do we need to record or remember about this process?"* In our example this means – now that we have received a bill and checked that it's from a recognized supplier – that we want to record the bill received from the supplier. We can draw this as illustrated in our model below.

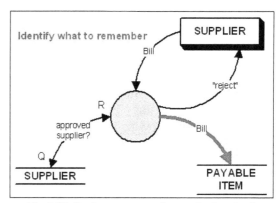

Fig. 6-23: Business process "remembering data"

Before we go on to the next part, let's review how to determine the direction of the arrow on a diagram. Data flows (and their arrowheads) can only go in two directions – in or out of the process (the bubble). The data flow either goes out of the process or it comes into the process.

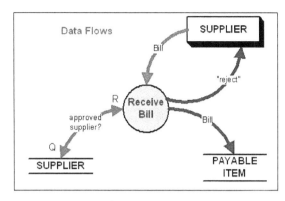

Fig. 6-24: Direction of data flows

When a data flow comes into the process (the bubble) it means we are retrieving data from an Object or we have received data from a Terminator.

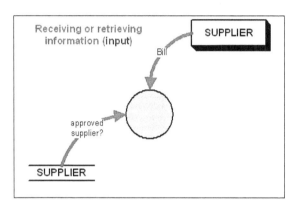

Fig. 6-25: Data flows coming into a process

When a data flow goes out of a process, it means we are recording data in an Object or we are sending some form of data to a Terminator (i.e., to a destination outside the system or business unit's immediate processes).

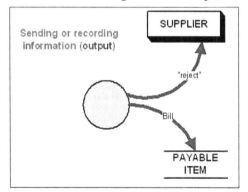

Fig. 6-26: Data flows going out of a process

When there is a dialogue data flow there are arrowheads on each end of the data flow. This represents two separate data flows – one to find the right record or data, and another to return the data – for the same subject data. By drawing a single data flow in this manner, we're just conserving space, and we're illustrating that something specific is directly related; i.e., two ends of the same thing. The 'Q' represents "query", and the 'R' represents "response". In the example in Fig. 6-27 we could read it as, *"Find the record of an approved supplier that matches the query.*

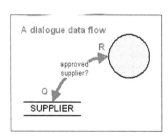

Fig. 6-27: Dialogue Data flow

If the query finds that the supplier is on record and approved, tell me. If not, tell me that too."

This now leaves us with a complete diagram for the *business event* **"A Bill Arrives from a Supplier"** (as shown on the right, Fig. 6-28). But lots of things haven't been done yet:

We haven't given a name to the process and labeled it; nor have we written a narrative to describe it. We also haven't done any data discovery and attribution; and we haven't completed the **BUSINESS RULES TABLE** to find and document the business rules for Objects that support this particular circumstance (**"A Bill Arrives from a Supplier"**).

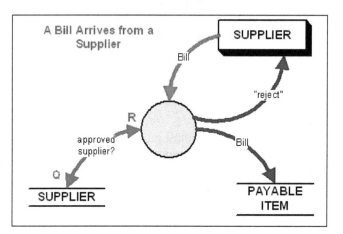

Fig. 6-28: Business process to support the Business event 'A Bill Arrives from a Supplier'

Some of these things are done in parallel with the drawing of the **Business Process Diagram** to support a *business event*. This is particularly true for how we go about discovering Objects and how we go about attributing data items that we find. Creating the **BUSINESS RULES TABLE**, asking the 'BRT Questions', and generating the business rules is the very last thing that's done after the diagram has been completed, including writing the descriptive narrative and attributing data to the Objects.

You will recall that the very first question we asked our subject-matter experts was, *"How do I know that a bill arrives from a supplier?"* This resulted in finding the stimulus (bill arrives from supplier), which led to the partial diagram on the right.

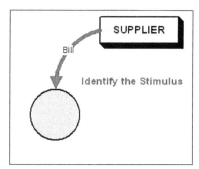

Fig. 6-29: Business process with "stimulus" identified

As the subject-matter experts answer the next question *("What are we going to do about it?")*, your SMEs could respond with an answer that might be at the highest level of abstraction or at the lowest level of detail. As an analyst, it is your responsibility to decipher what they have said and to determine what's a data item and what's an Object.

Because we now have to find the data that supports the process, we usually supplement the original question with another: *"What do we need to know about or remember about this process?"* For each noun, you must determine if it consists of *two or more component parts*. If it does, it's a noun "with substance" and it complies with Business Data Rule # 3 (see Part 4: The Business Object). That's an Object. If the noun does not consist of more than one data item, then it's just another data item for which you have to find a home.

Another way of initially identifying Objects that are needed to support a *business event* situation – and perhaps the best way to start – is to use the nouns you find in the *business event* statement itself. For example, in the *business event* **"A Bill Arrives from a Supplier"** there are two nouns – **bill** and **supplier**.

Are these nouns "of substance"? Can we imagine each of them consisting of two or more data items? Sure … we can imagine the Object **BILL** consisting of data such as *due date* and *amount due*. The other Object, **SUPPLIER**, could include data items such as *supplier name*, *supplier address*, *contact name* and *phone number*.

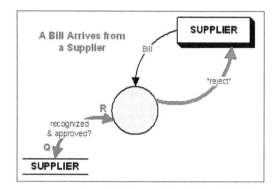

Fig. 6-30: Business process with
SUPPLIER Object

Since **SUPPLIER** is clearly an Object (see below), then we must ask our subject-matter experts if they want a record of authorized suppliers. If the answer is *"yes,"* then we have an Object that we must document – and we can immediately attribute some of the data we uncovered.

SUPPLIER
- supplier name
- supplier address
- contact name
- phone #

Fig. 6-31: SUPPLIER data attributes

For **BILL** we must ask our subject-matter experts if we want to remember (or record) the *due date* and *amount due*. If the answer is *"yes,"* then this is also an Object that we must include, and we can immediately attribute the data we uncovered.

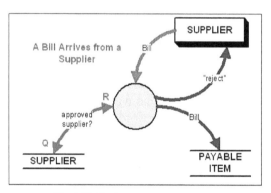

Fig. 6-32: Business process with
PAYABLE ITEM Object

PAYABLE ITEM
- Due date
- Amount due

Fig. 6-33: PAYABLE
ITEM data attributes

These questions should all stimulate other questions. We might even find the subject-matter experts want to call the bill a **PAYABLE ITEM**, and want to include some other data attributes (which we won't include here, so we can keep the example small).

Discussions with clients and subject-matter experts will tend to bring out the remaining Objects and the data that make up the Objects. In this particular example, there are no more Objects needed to support the *business event* **"A Bill Arrives from a Supplier"**.

How do we know that we have put the data attributes with the right Objects? Business Data Rule # 1 (see Part 4: The Business Object) states, *"Attribute the data item to the Object it describes best, and to no other Object."* It appears that _due date_ and _amount due_ describe **PAYABLE ITEM** best, while _supplier name_, _supplier address_, _contact name_ and _phone #_ best describe **SUPPLIER**.

The next step is to write a plain yet descriptive narrative. The narrative has to be clear, concise, unambiguous, in plain business language – and brief.

You will notice that at this time we have left the bubble that denotes the process unlabeled – blank and unnamed. That's intentional, and we're going to leave it unnamed until we have written the descriptive narrative necessary to support the diagram.

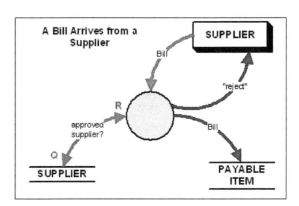

Fig. 6-34: Business process supports the Business event 'A Bill Arrives from a Supplier'

Our objective is to write a narrative that clearly explains the **Business Process Diagram** in as much detail as necessary, but no more. Our narrative must be in plain language – easily understood by our business partners – without any technobabble. We must stay away from writing great prose or even a novel. All of these are unnatural to our business partners. The end result must be a narrative that's easily understood by the business partners and the technical team[15].

So, where do you start? To help with the structure of the sentences, we have identified a few key words that will help you develop a usable narrative that's understandable to all. These five key words can be used to build just about any narrative:

1. **"For each ..."**
2. **"Periodically ..."**
3. **"Determine ..."**
4. **"Remember (or record) ..."**
5. **"Find (or identify) ..."**

But how do we know exactly how many narrative statements are needed for any given business process? Is it simply stream-of-consciousness? Is it roaming around the china shop of words until we figure out what the text should be, based on brute thinking force? Does it require a major in English? Does it involve smoke and mirrors? Or will just plain magic do the trick?

---

[15] The system specification narrative has been debated for many years now. As incredible as it may seem, there are many who still teach how to write "Structured English" or (sigh) "Tight English", vintage when wheels were square. We're now well into the 21st century and there are many who are still teaching the methods and tools of the 1960s and 1970s. There is a new "Structured Narrative" today that is much better suited to today's world. There is also a clear difference between a technical system specification and a business requirements specification. The descriptive narratives in this book are intended for use with business requirements and not for technical system specifications.

Well, there is a way.

We determine the narrative needed by identifying an implicit task[16] for each data flow that comes into or goes out of the process. Visually, it looks like the illustration on the right; although we don't draw those little nodes on our real diagrams, we just write the descriptive narratives.

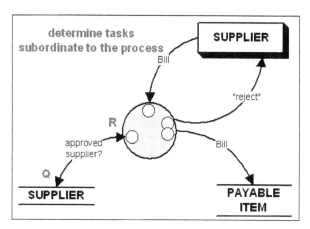

Fig. 6-35: Business process with "task nodes" illustrated

Each of these nodes must have an explanatory narrative; or, better put, each node must be referenced in some way in the descriptive narrative that you write. You can use at least two different styles when producing your narrative, the Structured Narrative Style, or the Point Form Style. You can also develop your own style, as long as your narrative text refers to each of the data flows entering or leaving the process. You may have to add additional text to describe the transformation of data, such as calculations or other formulas.

For the **Business Process Diagram** below (which supports the *business event* **"A Bill Arrives from a Supplier"**), you could produce a narrative similar to either of the styles below the diagram.

 Fig. 6-36: Business process with two types of descriptive narratives based on task nodes

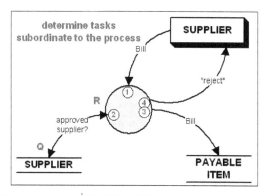

Structured Narrative Style

For each **bill** received, determine if it is from a recognized and approved **supplier**. If it is, remember it. If the **supplier** is not recognized, reject the **bill**.

Point Form Style

1. Receive the **bill**.
2. Determine if it is from a recognized and approved **supplier**.
3. If it is, record it.
4. If the **supplier** is not recognized, reject the **bill**.

---

[16] A 'task' is an activity that is subordinate to a 'process'. A process consists of several tasks.

This form of *functional decomposition*[17], which is really process decomposition, is relatively straightforward. It enables you to quickly determine the tasks that make up a process.

Before we go on with our next *business event* in our accounts payable example, let's look at another example of process decomposition that enables us to easily write the narrative for the process.

For the diagram below, our objective is to pay the supplier for products received. Previous payments may already have been made (or not). After process decomposition to identify the subordinate tasks, we could have a task list, and narrative, as follows:

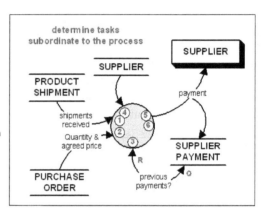

Fig. 6-37: Another business process with two types of descriptive narratives based on task nodes

Point Form Style

1. Find **product shipment**s not completely paid.
2. Determine the amount owed, based on the amount of **product** received and the agreed price.
3. Deduct any previous **payment**s made against the same **purchase order**.
4. Find the **supplier**'s location and preferred method of payment.
5. Pay the **supplier**.
6. Record the **payment**.

Structured Narrative Style

Periodically, find those **shipment**s received from **supplier**s that have not been completely paid. Determine the amount owed based on the amount of **product** received and the agreed price. Deduct any previous **payment**s against the same **purchase order**. Pay the **supplier**, and remember the **payment**.

Once again, you can write itemized tasks (Point Form Style), or you can write simple sentences (Structured Narrative Style), as shown above.

The *business event* in this case is **"It Is Time to Pay a Supplier"**. If a *business event* starts with **"It Is Time to ..."** we can often start the narrative with *"Periodically ..."* The writing style you chose to use is the one you are most comfortable with.

---

[17] Originally, *functional decomposition* was used to divide engineering systems into segments such that each block on a block diagram could be described without an "and" or "or" in the description. Similarly, if you use the Point Form Style of narrative, each task that supports a process should stand alone and not link with other tasks using "and" or "or" in the descriptive text. However, pragmatism will suggest that you could often use one simple "and" statement, rather than two (e.g., "Receive the video request and payment from the customer," rather than two separate statements, "Receive the video request from the customer" and "Receive the payment from the customer". But, since we're all wired a little different, you can choose any style you like, as long as it helps you communicate.

The new element we introduced into this diagram is what is called a *split* or *divergent data* flow. In the example diagram on the right, it means you are sending the payment to two places: the physical payment goes to the supplier (which could be a check or an electronic funds transfer); and the payment data is recorded so we can keep track of the supplier payment. While these two data flows that diverge represent the same thing (payment information), they will certainly be physically different in the implemented system.

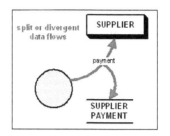

Fig. 6-38: Business process with "split" or "divergent" data flow

In this example, relationships between Objects are absolutely necessary[18]. If the Objects are not somehow joined, we would not be able to find what we need. For example, we need to find the **SUPPLIER** record for a specific **PURCHASE ORDER**. We also need to find all the **SUPPLIER PAYMENT** records for a specific **PURCHASE ORDER**. These relationships necessitate *foreign keys* to join the Objects that need to be joined. (For a review of *Pointers to Related Objects*, see Part 4: The Business Object.) For us to create a business requirements specification that also consists of a prescription for the database design – but transparent to the client and the SMEs – we need to define which Objects must be joined to which other Objects under different circumstances (*business events*). We will do this through the **BUSINESS RULES TABLE**.[19]

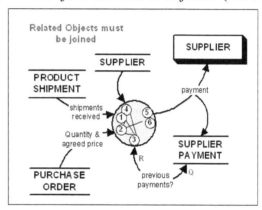

Fig. 6-39: Business process – Objects must be joined so they can be relational

We now have a complete diagram and narrative for the *business event* **"A Bill Arrives from a Supplier"**. We have also identified the Objects and data items we need to support the process.

SUPPLIER
- supplier name
- supplier address
- contact name
- phone #

PAYABLE ITEM
- Due date
- Amount due

Point Form Style
1. Receive the **bill**.
2. Determine if it is from a recognized and approved **supplier**.
3. If it is, record it.
4. If the **supplier** is not recognized, reject the **bill**.

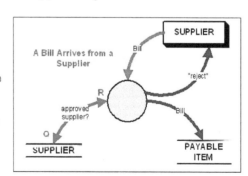

Fig. 6-40: Complete but unnamed Business process

---

[18] This is because Objects such as **SUPPLIER** only contain information about that specific Object, and not about any other Objects (such as payments from the supplier). It's all based on the 5 Rules of Business Data, particularly Rule # 1, "Attribute the data item to the Object it describes best, and to no other Object."

[19] See Part 5, The Business Rules Table.

But we haven't named the process yet, which is the last thing we do before we build out the BUSINESS RULES TABLE.

We didn't name the process earlier (as you wanted to do) because that would have created an unconscious bias to make the narrative fit the name of the process. We have found that one of the best ways of freeing our mind from any predetermined path, or bias, is to name the process last, after the narrative is written.

Naming a process is a lot easier than it appears. The first word in the process label is <u>always a verb</u>. The next word or two is always the subject of the process. The subject usually includes a noun. For our example *business event* **"A Bill Arrives from a Supplier"** we have to ask ourselves, *What are we really doing here?* Since we are receiving a bill from a supplier we can name the process **"Receive Bill"**. That gives us a strong verb and a subject.

Labels for processes must be strong and to the point, not abstractions. Abstractions that you want to stay away from include weak verbs such as "process" and "handle". For example, "Process Employee Pay" sounds like something we do to sausages. It's far better to say "Pay Employee". Another example of a weak label is, "Handle Payables", which sounds more like a juggling act than the more specific "Pay Supplier".

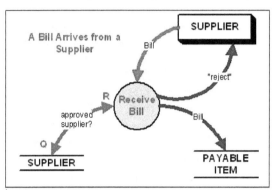

Point Form Style
1. Receive the **bill**.
2. Determine if it is from a recognized and approved **supplier**.
3. If it is, record it.
4. If the **supplier** is not recognized, reject the **bill**.

SUPPLIER	PAYABLE ITEM
• supplier name	• Due date
• supplier address	• Amount due
• contact name	
• phone #	

Fig. 6-41: Complete Business process with Object descriptions, descriptive narrative and process name.

Examples of strong and pointy process labels include:

Pay Supplier
Open Account
Ship Product
Reserve Seat
Receive Loan Application
Receive Payment

Although we haven't completed the BUSINESS RULES TABLE, we have done the **Business Process Diagram**, so we can now check off this *business event* from our PROJECT BUSINESS EVENT LIST.

Fig. 6-42: Project Business Event List

Now that we have created a **Business Process Diagram** that describes part of the business requirement (i.e., the *essential* requirement, without defining how it will be implemented), we can proceed with the Business Rules Table, where we will define the remaining business requirements for this specific process.

Take the Objects that are in the **"Receive Bill" Business Process Diagram** and build up a Business Rules Table for those Objects, so we can ask a series of specific questions.

Build the table, as follows, by placing the Objects **SUPPLIER** and **PAYABLE ITEM** in the diagram in the rows and columns indicated. Put a '1' in front of each of the Objects in the anchor position to the left. This will help you focus on a single occurrence of the anchor Object when you ask the questions that arise from this table.

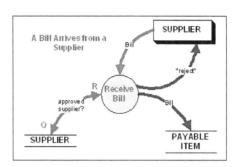

Fig. 6-43: "Receive Bill" business process

BRT	Supplier	Payable Item
1 Supplier	---	
1 Payable Item		---

Fig. 6-44: Basic BRT structure

For the time being, blank out the intersection of like Objects, such as **SUPPLIER+SUPPLIER** and **PAYABLE ITEM+-PAYABLE ITEM**. We'll discuss those later.

After placing each of the Objects into the Business Rules Table that we found in the **Business Process Diagram**, we start with the first 'anchor' Object and ask the 'BRT Questions' of it. You can usually use the verb you assigned to the process ('RECEIVE') to structure the 'BRT Questions'.

PLACEHOLDER QUESTION: **"For a single, specific SUPPLIER how many PAYABLE ITEMs might we receive?"** We don't wait for an answer to this first question. It is just a mental placeholder. We immediately go on with the three follow-on questions, soliciting a response from our subject-matter experts for each of them.

QUESTION # 1: **"Could we receive just one PAYABLE ITEM from the SUPPLIER?"** This question isn't intended to exclude the two following questions, but your SMEs may be tempted to respond with an expanded answer such as, *"Yes, and we might get several bills from them…"* which already answers the next question. If the answer is **NO** we enter nothing in the cell joining the two Objects that make up the question. But if the answer is **YES**, we put a '1' in the **SUPPLIER+PAYABLE ITEM** intersection cell.

BRT	Supplier	Payable Item
1 Supplier	---	1
1 Payable Item		---

Fig. 6-45: SUPPLIER+PAYABLE ITEM relationship in "Receive Bill" context

QUESTION # 2: **"Could we receive many PAYABLE ITEMs from the SUPPLIER?"** This kind of closed-ended question tends to draw out specific responses. Again, if the answer is **NO** we enter nothing in the cell joining the two Objects that make up the question. But if the answer is **YES**, we put an 'N' in the **SUPPLIER+PAYABLE ITEM** intersection cell.

BRT		Supplier	Payable Item
1	Supplier	---	1, N
1	Payable Item		---

Fig. 6-46: SUPPLIER+PAYABLE ITEM relationship in "Receive Bill" context

QUESTION # 3: **"Might we never receive any PAYABLE ITEMS from the SUPPLIER at all?"** Notice that this question does not ask, *"Could there be none…"* which is a completely different kind of question. What we're looking for here is, firstly, an <u>exclusion</u> from the possibility of any other answers than those given to the first two 'BRT Questions'. Secondly, we're looking for the <u>inclusion</u> of a possible exception as being part of normal business policy. In other words, this question serves the dual purpose of verifying answers already given, and a search for legitimate exceptions to those answers.

When there is a **YES** to this kind of question (i.e., *"We might **never** receive a **payable item** from a **supplier**…"*) we find that SMEs often like to discuss the exceptional situation at length, as if it was a newly discovered business policy.

On the other hand, if the answer is **NO** (i.e., *"We might **not ever** receive any **payable items** – therefore we will always receive one or more **payable items** from a **supplier**…"*) then we enter nothing in the cell joining the two Objects that make up the question. But if the answer is **YES**, we put a '0' in the **SUPPLIER+PAYABLE ITEM** intersection cell.

Notice that we ask this third question from the perspective of all time; that is, the word "never" is intentionally chosen to mean just that – **never** – spanning all time up to now, the current time. Time is an interesting element – it just keeps right on moving, no matter what we do. So this

BRT		Supplier	Payable Item
1	Supplier	---	1, N, 0
1	Payable Item		---

Fig. 6-47: SUPPLIER+PAYABLE ITEM relationship in "Receive Bill" context

question really covers the period from the time a supplier is entered into our system until the current time, which keeps moving. You certainly can substitute the words "not ever" if you wish.

When a client or subject matter expert answers "yes" to this third question, we must always follow up with a fourth question:

QUESTION # 4: **"Under what circumstances might that be true?"**

Let's partition this a bit more so we can understand it better.

All the suppliers that make up our **SUPPLIER** Object are "approved" suppliers. These are the only ones that are part of our list of suppliers. (It sort of makes sense that our list would not include the entire world of suppliers.)

In this example we have just asked the subject-matter expert, **"Might we never receive any PAYABLE ITEMs from the SUPPLIER at all?"** And the SME, quite reasonably replied, *"That's right, we might never receive a payable item from a supplier."*

The question, of course, is … how does a someone get to become an approved supplier, and yet we don't do any business with that supplier? To find out we have to ask the follow-up question **"Under what circumstances might that be true … *that we might never get a payable item from a supplier?"*** In this example, our client's answers could be several:

"They could have gone out of business before we ordered anything from them."

"We did order from the supplier, but they were never able to ship the product to us, so eventually we just stopped doing business with them."

Both of the above, and more, are possible answers in this circumstance. It is the analyst's responsibility, and challenge, to ferret out as much information as possible from the client or subject-matter experts.

So what does it accomplish for us to uncover these "never" situations? Plain and simple, it goes directly to the issue of completeness of the business requirements. It enables us to find *business events* – situations or circumstances – that we may not have found previously. Remember that our definition of a *business event* is "… an essential business condition, a state, an external requirement, or a circumstance …" and our fourth follow-on question is **"Under what circumstances might that be true?"** In other words, with this question, we're really looking for *business events*. And a complete business requirement means finding all the *business events* the target business area must deal with.

Let's look at each of the scenarios we have painted.

1. "They could have gone out of business before we ordered anything from them."

Based on this answer we must follow up with the subject-matter experts and ask if the *business event* **"The Supplier Goes Out of Business"** is something that could be within the scope of the project. For an Accounts Payable project, it seems reasonable that we would want to know if one of our suppliers went out of business. If our subject-matter expert says, *"Yes, we would like to know"* then add this new *business event* to the PROJECT BUSINESS EVENT LIST (PARKING LOT)[20].

> **Project Business Event List
> (Parking Lot)**
> - A Bill Arrives from a Supplier
> - **It is Time to Pay a Supplier**
> - **The Supplier Goes Out of Business**

Fig. 6-48: Business Event List
Parking Lot with discovered events

---

[20] The Project Business Event List, originally generated during the *Project Scope Blitz*, is now expanded into a Parking Lot of *business events* discovered during the detailed discovery sessions.

2. "We did order from the supplier, but they were never able to ship the product to us, so eventually we just stopped doing business with them."

From that answer we must follow up with the subject-matter expert and ask if the *business events* **"The Supplier is Unable to Fill the Product Order"** or **"Product Does Not Arrive from Supplier"** are circumstances we need to know about in our system. If so, are they within the scope of the project? If our subject-matter experts says, *"Yes, we need to know this"* then we add both new *business events* to our PROJECT BUSINESS EVENT LIST (PARKING LOT). (We'll add both *business events* because they seem to be a little different.)

Project Business Event List (Parking Lot)

- A Bill Arrives from a Supplier
- It is Time to Pay a Supplier
- The Supplier Goes Out of Business
- The Supplier is Unable to Fill the Product Order
- Product Does Not Arrive from Supplier

Fig. 6-49: Business Event List Parking Lot with discovered events

There are other ways to find new *business events*, too. One of the best ways is simply *listening* carefully to the client or SME. But listening for what? You will recall that we specified that suppliers must be "approved" before they can be on our list of suppliers. In this case we have to ask, *"How did the supplier get to be approved?"* Since it hasn't been covered yet, is there a *business event* such as **"Supplier Applies to Become an Approved Supplier"**? To find out we ask our SMEs. If their answer is, *"Yes, we receive applications from suppliers who want to become approved suppliers,"* then we add this to our list of new *business events* too.

Project Business Event List (Parking Lot)

- A Bill Arrives from a Supplier
- It is Time to Pay a Supplier
- The Supplier Goes Out of Business
- The Supplier is Unable to Fill the Product Order
- Product Does Not Arrive from Supplier
- Supplier Applies to Become an Approved Supplier

Fig. 6-50: Business Event List Parking Lot with discovered events

As you can see, the process of going through the 'BRT Questions' produces a lot of information that goes directly to the heart of the project. The 'BRT Questions' not only help us find business rules (we'll get to the details of that in a moment), but they help us find hidden *business events* too, like the ones above.

Let's review.

We started with two original *business events* (**"A Bill Arrives from a Supplier"** and **"It is Time to Pay a Supplier"**), supported by two Objects (**SUPPLIER** and **PAYABLE ITEM**). We also attributed some data to the two Objects; and we found several new *business events* to add to our list. We also determined the ratio of occurrences (0, 1, N) between two Objects. For the first *business event* that we worked on (**"A Bill Arrives from a Supplier"**), there now only remains the task of writing the business rules that come from the BUSINESS RULES TABLE, and to assign those rules to the right Objects.

BRT		Supplier	Payable Item
1	Supplier	---	1, N, 0
1	Payable Item		---

Fig. 6-51: SUPPLIER+PAYABLE ITEM relationship

For the first anchor Object – **SUPPLIER** – we know that we could receive one or several **PAYABLE ITEM**s, or we may never receive any at all, for which we have several examples. These rules (noted with the symbols **1,N,0**) must be documented as declarative statements in the correct context (i.e., with the proper verb) under the anchor Object **SUPPLIER**. In this example, the **PAYABLE ITEM**s rules for **SUPPLIER** might read something like this:

SUPPLIER

Business Rules

- We can receive one or more **PAYABLE ITEM**s from a **SUPPLIER**.

- We may never receive a **PAYABLE ITEM** from a **SUPPLIER** (e.g., may go out of business before we order a product; may not have been able to fill the only order from us).

Data Attributes

- supplier name
- supplier address
- contact name
- phone #

Fig. 6-52: SUPPLIER Business Rules

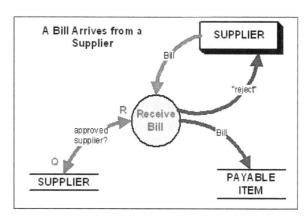

Fig. 6-53: Business Rules are in the context of the process for which the BRT was built.

The next step is to ask the 'BRT Questions' of the second anchor Object, **PAYABLE ITEM**. Let's play it out.

PLACEHOLDER QUESTION: **"For a single, specific PAYABLE ITEM that we have received, how many SUPPLIERS might it come from?"** Don't wait for an answer for this first question – it's your mental placeholder – just immediately go on with the three follow-on questions.

QUESTION # 1: **"Could the PAYABLE ITEM be from only one SUPPLIER?"** In this example the answer from our subject matter experts is, *"Yes, of course, what did you think? So,* with a **YES** answer, we put a **'1'** in the **PAYABLE ITEM+SUPPLIER** intersection cell.

	BRT	Supplier	Payable Item
1	Supplier	---	1, N, 0
1	Payable Item	1	---

Fig. 6-54: PAYABLE ITEM+SUPPLIER relationship

QUESTION # 2: **"Could the PAYABLE ITEM be from several SUPPLIERs?"** Our SME tells us the answer is **NO**, so we enter nothing in the cell joining the two Objects that make up the question.

BRT	Supplier	Payable Item
1 Supplier	---	1, N, 0
1 Payable Item	1	---

Fig. 6-55: PAYABLE ITEM+SUPPLIER relationship

QUESTION # 3: **"Might the PAYABLE ITEM not be received from any SUPPLIER at all?"** Once in a while this question addresses the intuitively obvious – such as this one. Of course a payable item must come from an approved supplier, otherwise it can't be recognized as a payable item ... someone else's perhaps, but not ours. Even through the answer to the question seems self-evident, we still have to confirm with our subject-matter experts. The answer, of course, is *"No"* – a payable item must come from a supplier, therefore we enter nothing new in the **PAYABLE ITEM+SUPPLIER** intersection cell.

BRT	Supplier	Payable Item
1 Supplier	---	1, N, 0
1 Payable Item	1	---

Fig. 6-56: PAYABLE ITEM+SUPPLIER relationship

Sometimes, when there is a painfully obvious answer to a question you need to ask (such as verifying that a single, specific bill can only come from one supplier), it is easier to ask the client the 'BRT Question' differently than to try to solicit a double negative to mean *"yes"*. The question **"Might the PAYABLE ITEM not be received from any SUPPLIER at all?"** can cause, at the very least, a pained quizzical look on the face of the client or subject-matter expert. As they try to process this question, they are also wondering how you could ask such a question. What is probably going through their mind is the question, *"Say what?"* A far better way of approaching this is to make a declarative statement with the answer, thus soliciting disagreement (which you probably won't get). For example, in this case, I would make the statement, **"And a PAYABLE ITEM can only come from one SUPPLIER, right?"** If they disagree, they will tell you. Otherwise, you'll get a fast nod of their collective heads and you can go on to the next questions or issues.

After you have asked the questions and got the answers, and entered them into the **BUSINESS RULES TABLE**, the new rules have to be written as declarative statements under the Object **PAYABLE ITEM**, which might read as follows:

BRT	Supplier	Payable Item
1 Supplier	---	1, N, 0
1 Payable Item	1	---

PAYABLE ITEM

Business Rules
• A **PAYABLE ITEM** can be received from one **SUPPLIER** only.

Fig. 6-57: Business Rules for Payable Item

Data Attributes
• Due date
• Amount due

The BUSINESS REQUIREMENTS DOCUMENT – the complete set of requirements documentation – is built incrementally. We record the requirements as we go through the analysis process and discover the business requirements with our clients and subject-matter experts. This incremental approach is possible because the requirements documentation doesn't have to be written serially or like a novel. In addition to being Object-based, it is focused on the individual **Business Process Diagrams**, and each component stands on its own. Therefore, the document is not produced serially, it is created in components: *Business event*, business process, Objects, data attributes, descriptive narrative, Business Rules Table, and context-specific business rules. This, in itself, speeds up the process significantly compared to old-school approaches.

> **Project Business Event List**
> **(Parking Lot)**
> - ~~A Bill Arrives from a Supplier~~
> - It is Time to Pay a Supplier
> - The Supplier Goes Out of Business
> - The Supplier is Unable to Fill our Product Order
> - Product Does Not Arrive from Supplier
> - The Product Received from the Supplier is Defective
> - Supplier Applies to Become an Approved Supplier

Fig. 6-58: Business Event List Parking Lot with discovered event

To demonstrate this progression, let's look at the second *business event* on our list is, **"It Is Time to Pay a Supplier"**.

Once again, the first question we ask is, *"How do I know that it is time to pay a supplier?"* The answer, of course, is *"We know because we have a due date."* You will recall earlier we attributed *due date* and *amount due* to the Object **PAYABLE ITEM**. The diagram and the accompanying data would, therefore, look like this.

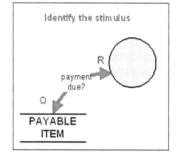

Fig. 6-59: Business process queries 'due date' to identify if it time to pay a supplier

PAYABLE ITEM

Business Rules
- A **PAYABLE ITEM** can be received from one **SUPPLIER** only.

Data Attributes
- Due date
- Amount due

Fig. 6-60: PAYABLE ITEM data attributes

This is also an example of where a stimulus that identifies a *business event* and initiates a process does not come from a Terminator, but instead comes from data that's part of an Object. This is the most common way of identifying if **"It Is Time ..."** for something.

The second question is, *"What are we going to do about it?"* In this example our client told us that we pay the balance of the account after calculating any previous payments that were made to the supplier. Therefore, we must first determine if any previous payments to the supplier have been made.

To know if there were any previous payments we must have an Object called **PAYMENT**. Its data attributes would include *amount paid* (which includes previous payments), *date paid* and *method of payment*. There could be several previous payments.

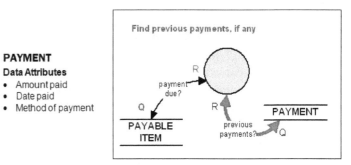

Fig. 6-61: Business Process Diagram and Object data – finding previous payments

After we determined if there were any previous payments, we can calculate the remaining balance that's due.

We also need to identify the **SUPPLIER** we're going to send the payment to; and we can find that supplier by locating which one is linked[21] to the **PAYABLE ITEM**.

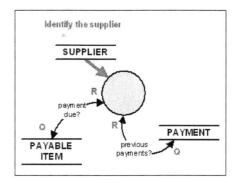

Fig. 6-62: Business process identifies supplier

And then we can send the payment to the supplier.

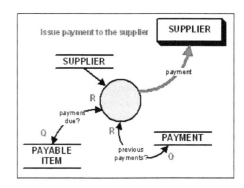

Fig. 6-63: Business process issue payment to supplier

---

[21] Using the **PAYABLE ITEM**'s *foreign key* to find it.

The last question to our subject matter expert is, *"What do we need to record or remember about this process?"* In this example we want to remember the payment sent to the supplier, including the method of payment and when it was made. We can draw this as illustrated in our diagram on the right, below. The data attributes for the **PAYMENT** Object are also listed below.

PAYMENT
Data Attributes
* Amount paid
* Date paid
* Method of payment

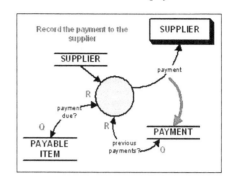

Fig. 6-64: Business process remembers payment issued

This now leaves us with a complete **Business Process Diagram** for the *business event* **"It Is Time to Pay a Supplier"** (as shown on the right). But, once again, lots of things haven't been done yet: We still haven't named the process; nor have we written a descriptive narrative. We have only done a little bit of data attribution; and we haven't completed the BUSINESS RULES TABLE to define our business rules for the new Object, **PAYMENT**.

The very first question about this *business event* to our subject-matter experts was, *"How do I know that it is time to pay a supplier?"* This resulted in finding the stimulus (there was a *due date* for the **PAYABLE ITEM**), which eventually led to the full diagram.

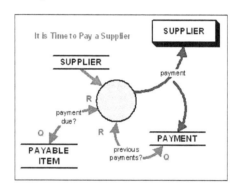

Fig. 6-65: Business process almost done

As you draw the diagram for the process, your discussions with the subject-matter experts tend to bring out the remaining Objects and the data that make up the Objects. In this particular example, there are no more Objects or data needed to support the *business event* **"It Is Time to Pay a Supplier"**.

The next step is to write a descriptive narrative of the **Business Process Diagram**. The narrative has to be clear, concise, unambiguous, in plain business language – and brief.

So far, we have left the bubble that represents the process unlabeled. The process name is only assigned after we have written the narrative necessary to support the diagram.

Our objective is to write a narrative that explains the **Business Process Diagram** in as much detail as necessary, but no more. Our narrative must be in plain language, without

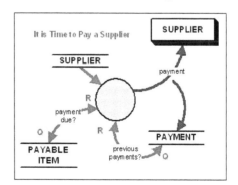

Fig. 6-66: Business process needs a descriptive narrative

any technobabble. The end result must be a narrative that's easily understood by the client, subject-matter experts, and a technical team.

We determine the narrative needed by identifying the tasks associated with each data flow that comes into or goes out of the process. For our **"It is Time to Pay a Supplier"** *business event* example, it looks like the illustration in Fig. 6-67; although we don't draw those little nodes on our real documentation, we just write the narratives.

Each of these nodes must be referenced in some way in the narrative that you write. You can use at least two different styles when producing your narrative, the <u>Structured Narrative Style</u>, or the <u>Point Form Style</u>. You can also develop your own style, as long as your narrative text refers to each of the data flows entering or leaving the process. You may have to add additional text to describe the transformation of data, such as calculations or other formulas.

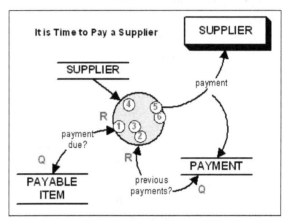

Fig. 6-67: Nodes identify tasks to be part of descriptive narrative

To write a narrative in this way is relatively easy and without pain. It enables you to quickly determine the tasks that make up a process without getting writer's block. Both types of narratives have been done for this example.

Point Form Style

1. Find bills (**PAYABLE ITEM**s) that are due to be paid.
2. Find previous **PAYMENT**s that have been made against individual bills (**PAYABLE ITEM**s), if any.
3. Determine the amount to be paid to a **SUPPLIER** (*amount due* minus previous *amount paid*).
4. Locate the **SUPPLIER** for the **PAYABLE ITEM**.
5. Pay the **SUPPLIER**.
6. Record the **PAYMENT**.

Structured Narrative Style

For each bill (**PAYABLE ITEM**) that is due for payment, determine the balance to be paid based on previous partial **PAYMENT**s against the bill. Pay the **SUPPLIER** and remember the **PAYMENT**.

We now have a complete diagram and narrative for the *business event* **"It is Time to Pay a Supplier"**. We have also identified the Objects and data attributes we need to support the process.

But we haven't named the process yet, which is the last thing we do before we build out the Business Rules Table for this process.

You will recall that a *business event* name (such as **"It is Time to Pay a Supplier"**) <u>never</u> starts with a verb. The name of the process that supports a *business event*, however, <u>always</u> starts with a verb.

So what are we really doing in this process? We're sending a payment to a supplier; therefore, we can name the process **"Pay Supplier"**. That gives us a strong verb and a subject.

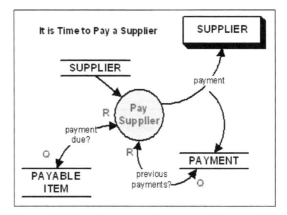

Fig. 6-68: A named Business Process diagram

Although we haven't completed the <u>Business Rules Table</u> for the new <u>**PAYMENT**</u> Object yet, we can now check off this *business event* from our <u>Project Business Event List (Parking Lot)</u>,

The <u>Business Rules Table</u> has to include all Objects that support a process. Although we did work through a BRT for the earlier process **"Receive Bill"** the context has now changed, so there will be different rules produced from the table. Therefore, all Objects that support the process **"Pay Supplier"** must be queried.

<u>**Project Business Event List (Parking Lot)**</u>

- ~~A Bill Arrives from a Supplier~~
- ~~It is Time to Pay a Supplier~~
- **The Supplier Goes Out of Business**
- **The Supplier is Unable to Fill our Product Order**
- **Product Does Not Arrive from Supplier**
- **Supplier Applies to Become an Approved Supplier**

Fig. 6-69: Making progress against the Business Event List Parking Lot

Take the Objects that are in the diagram for the **"Pay Supplier"** process and build up a <u>Business Rules Table</u> for those Objects.

Build a table, just like the previous example, by placing the Objects (<u>**SUPPLIER**</u>, <u>**PAYABLE ITEM**</u> and <u>**PAYMENT**</u>) in the rows and columns indicated. Put a **'1'** in front of each of the Objects in the anchor position to the left. This will help you focus on a single occurrence of the anchor Object when you ask the questions that arise from this table.

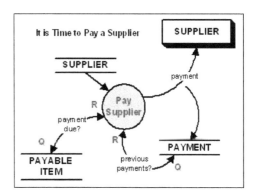

Fig. 6-70: Business process **"Pay Supplier"**

For the time being, blank out the intersection of like Objects.

	BRT	Supplier	Payable Item	Payment
1	Supplier	---		
1	Payable Item		---	
1	Payment			---

Fig. 6-71: Business Rules Table for process "Pay Supplier"

We can now start with the first 'anchor' Object and ask the 'BRT Questions'. You can usually use the verb you assigned to the business process (Fig. 6-70) to structure your 'BRT Questions'. If that verb doesn't work, then select another verb construct based on the concept behind the process. The idea is to ask the 'BRT Questions' based on the context of the process.

PLACEHOLDER QUESTION: **"For a single, specific SUPPLIER how many PAYABLE ITEMs might be due to be paid to them?"** We don't wait for an answer to this first question. It is just a mental placeholder. We immediately go on with the three follow-on questions, soliciting a response from our subject-matter experts for each of them.

QUESTION # 1: **"Could there be just one PAYABLE ITEM due to be paid to a SUPPLIER?"** Our SME answers, *"Yes, and there might be several bills to be paid to a supplier too..."* which already answers the next question. Since the answer is **YES**, we put a **'1'** in the **SUPPLIER+PAYABLE ITEM** intersection cell.

	BRT	Supplier	Payable Item	Payment
1	Supplier	---	1	
1	Payable Item		---	
1	Payment			---

Fig. 6-72: SUPPLIER-PAYABLE ITEM relationship in "Pay Supplier" context

QUESTION # 2: **"Could there be many PAYABLE ITEMs due to be paid to a SUPPLIER?"** The answer is **YES**, so we put an **'N'** in the **SUPPLIER-PAYABLE ITEM** intersection cell.

	BRT	Supplier	Payable Item	Payment
1	Supplier	---	1, N	
1	Payable Item		---	
1	Payment			---

Fig. 6-73: SUPPLIER+PAYABLE ITEM relationship in "Pay Supplier" context

QUESTION # 3: **"Might we never have any PAYABLE ITEMs that are due to be paid to a SUPPLIER at all?"** The answer is **YES**, so we put a **'0'** in the **SUPPLIER-PAYABLE ITEM** intersection cell.

	BRT	Supplier	Payable Item	Payment
1	Supplier	---	1, N, 0	
1	Payable Item		---	
1	Payment			---

Fig. 6-74: SUPPLIER-PAYABLE ITEM relationship in "Pay Supplier" context

When the answer is "yes" to this third question, we must always follow up with a fourth question:

QUESTION # 4: **"Under what circumstances might that be true?"**

"They could have gone out of business before we ordered anything from them."

"We did order from the supplier, but they were never able to ship the product to us, so eventually we just stopped doing business with them."

These are the same responses we got when we asked the SMEs about the **SUPPLIER+PAYABLE ITEM** relationship in the context of the **"Receive Bill"** process earlier.

That being the case, we don't have to add any new *business events* to our list since they have all been added before.

Now we need to write the business rules for the new relationship (based on context of the **"Pay Supplier"** process, Fig. 6-76) between **SUPPLIER** and **PAYABLE ITEM**.

	BRT	Supplier	Payable Item	Payment
1	Supplier	---	1, N, 0	
1	Payable Item		---	
1	Payment			---

Fig. 6-75: SUPPLIER+PAYABLE ITEM relationship in "Pay Supplier" context

For the first anchor Object – **SUPPLIER** – we now know that we could issue a payment for one or several **PAYABLE ITEMS**, or we may never pay any at all. These rules are documented as declarative statements under the anchor Object **SUPPLIER** (in the context of the **"Pay Supplier"** business process it supports). In this example, the **PAYABLE ITEMS** rules attributed to **SUPPLIER** might read something like those below (Fig. 6-77).

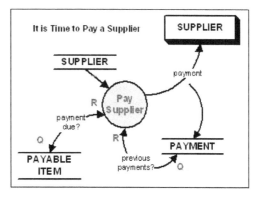

Fig. 6-76: Business process "Pay Supplier"

SUPPLIER

Business Rules

- We can receive one or more **PAYABLE ITEM**s from a **SUPPLIER**.

- We may never receive a **PAYABLE ITEM** from a **SUPPLIER** (e.g., may go out of business before we order a product; may have sent us a defective product on their only order from us; may not have been able to fill the only order from us).

★ We can pay one or more **PAYABLE ITEM**s for a **SUPPLIER**.

★ We may never have a **PAYABLE ITEM** to pay for a **SUPPLIER** (e.g., may go out of business before we order a product; may not have been able to fill the only order from us).

Data Attributes

- supplier name
- supplier address
- contact name
- phone #

Fig. 6-77: SUPPLIER Business Rules

The next step is to ask the 'BRT Questions' of the next Object (**PAYMENT**) that intersect with the anchor Object, **SUPPLIER**. Let's play this one out.

PLACEHOLDER QUESTION: **"For a single, specific SUPPLIER how many PAYMENTs might we issue (pay) to them?"** We don't wait for an answer to this first question.

QUESTION # 1: **"Could we issue just one PAYMENT to a SUPPLIER?"** Our SME answers, *"Yes, we might only ever make one payment to a supplier…"*. Put a **'1'** in the **SUPPLIER+PAYMENT** intersection cell.

	BRT	Supplier	Payable Item	Payment
1	Supplier	---	1, N, 0	1
1	Payable Item		---	
1	Payment			---

Fig. 6-78: SUPPLIER+PAYMENT relationship in "Pay Supplier" context

QUESTION # 2: **"Could we issue <u>many</u> PAYMENTs to a SUPPLIER?"** The answer is **YES**, so we put an **'N'** in the **SUPPLIER+PAYMENT** intersection cell.

	BRT	Supplier	Payable Item	Payment
1	Supplier	---	1, N, 0	**1, N**
1	Payable Item		---	
1	Payment			---

Fig. 6-79: SUPPLIER+PAYMENT relationship in "Pay Supplier" context

QUESTION # 3: **"Might we never issue <u>any</u> PAYMENTs to a SUPPLIER at all?"** The answer is **YES**, so we put a **'0'** in the **SUPPLIER+PAYMENT** intersection cell.

	BRT	Supplier	Payable Item	Payment
1	Supplier	---	1, N, 0	**1, N, 0**
1	Payable Item		---	
1	Payment			---

Fig. 6-80: SUPPLIER+PAYMENT relationship in "Pay Supplier" context

When the answer is "yes" to this question, we always follow up with a fourth question:

QUESTION # 4: **"Under what circumstances might that be true?"**

"While they were on our list of approved suppliers, we just never ordered anything from them."

There may be other reason, too, but we won't list them here.

This circumstance begs the question, *"Do we need to know about those suppliers who don't do business with us after a certain period of time?"* The answer from our subject-matter expert was *"No, we don't care,"* so we don't have to add any new *business events* to our list on the right.

Now we need to write the business rules for the new relationship between **SUPPLIER** and **PAYMENT**. The **PAYMENT** rules attributed to **SUPPLIER** might read something like this:

Project Business Event List (Parking Lot)
- A Bill Arrives from a Supplier
- It is Time to Pay a Supplier
- The Supplier Goes Out of Business
- The Supplier is Unable to Fill our Product Order
- Product Does Not Arrive from Supplier
- Supplier Applies to Become an Approved Supplier

Fig. 6-81: The Project Business Event List

SUPPLIER

Business Rules

★ We can issue one or more **PAYMENT**s to a **SUPPLIER**.

★ We may never issue a **PAYMENT** to a **SUPPLIER** (e.g., we just didn't order anything from them).

Fig. 6-82: More SUPPLIER Business Rules

You go through exactly the same process for the other Objects that support the process **"Pay Supplier"**, those Objects being **PAYABLE ITEM** and **PAYMENT**. When you're done, and you have all the answers to the questions, you will end up with the following entries in the BUSINESS RULES TABLE.

BRT		Supplier	Payable Item	Payment
1	Supplier	---	1, N, 0	1, N, 0
1	Payable Item	1	---	1, N
1	Payment	1	1	---

Fig. 6-83: Business Rules Table (BRT) for "Pay Supplier" process

The answers in the BRT spell out policy quite nicely:

★ A specific **PAYABLE ITEM** can be from one **SUPPLIER** only. (Makes sense.)
★ A specific **PAYABLE ITEM** can have one or several **PAYMENT**s made against it. (In effect, this says there can be partial payments.)
★ A specific **PAYMENT** can only be issued to one **SUPPLIER**. (This, too, makes sense.)
★ A specific **PAYMENT** can only be for one **PAYABLE ITEM**. (This is because, in our example, accounting is done on an open item basis rather than balance forward.)

All of these rules are attributed to their respective anchor Objects.

Earlier I asked you to blank out the intersection of like objects, such as the cells for **SUPPLIER+SUPPLIER**, **PAYABLE ITEM+PAYABLE ITEM** and **PAYMENT+PAYMENT**. That's because if we ask the same questions of these recursive relationships[22] as we would of all the other Objects, we would find it very challenging. For example, for the **"Pay Supplier"** process, the series of 'BRT Questions' for **PAYABLE ITEM** would read as follows:

---

[22] A recursive relationship occurs when there is a relationship between an Object and itself. For example, a one-to-many recursive relationship occurs when an **EMPLOYEE** is the manager of other **EMPLOYEE**s. In that scenario, the **EMPLOYEE** Object is related to itself, and there is a one-to-many relationship between one **EMPLOYEE** (the manager) and many other **EMPLOYEE**s (the people who report to the manager).

PLACEHOLDER QUESTION: **"For a single, specific PAYABLE ITEM how many other PAYABLE ITEMS might we <u>pay</u> for?"** Say what? This doesn't seem to make a lot of sense.

QUESTION # 1: **"Could we pay for just <u>one</u> PAYABLE ITEM … PAYABLE ITEM?"** How do we even structure this question? There's clearly a problem here.

QUESTION # 2: **"Could we pay for <u>many</u> PAYABLE ITEMS …. PAYABLE ITEM?"** Again, how do we even structure this question? This isn't working.

QUESTION # 3: **"Might we <u>never</u> pay <u>any</u> PAYABLE ITEMS … PAYABLE ITEM at all?"** What kind of sentence structure could we use to make this into a sensible question?

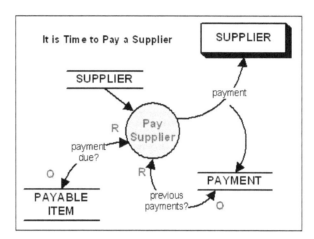

**Fig. 6-84: Business process
"Pay Supplier"**

Of course, none of those questions work in this context – and they usually don't work when trying to ask questions about the relationship between like Objects. So how do we ask these important questions?

By changing how we ask.

BRT	Supplier	Payable Item	Payment
1 Supplier	---	1, N, 0	1, N, 0
1 Payable Item	1	---	1, N
1 Payment	1	1	---

Fig. 6-85: The remaining questions to ask in a Business Rules Table (BRT) for the "Pay Supplier" process

If you are querying the intersection of like Objects – or even if the standard 'BRT Questions' just don't seem to work or don't make too much sense – then change how you ask the placeholder question to the following (in a **"Pay Supplier"** context):

SUPPLIER Substitute Placeholder Question: **"If I know about one SUPPLIER that we pay, under what circumstances would I ever want to find another, related SUPPLIER that we pay?"**

<u>PAYABLE ITEM</u> Substitute Placeholder
Question: **"If I know about one PAYABLE ITEM that we pay for, under what circumstances would I ever want to find another, related PAYABLE ITEM that we pay for?**

<u>PAYMENT</u> Substitute Placeholder Question: **"If I know about one PAYMENT that is issued to a supplier, under what circumstances would I ever want to find another, related PAYMENT to that supplier?**

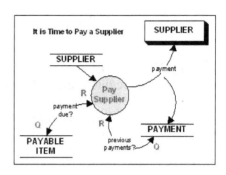

Fig. 6-86: Business process "Pay Supplier"

The difference between this substitute placeholder Question and the regular one is that we <u>do</u> expect an answer from our subject-matter experts.

With this question, we are looking for a *circumstance* – which, as we know, is really a *business event*. The answers that our SMEs give us identify *business events* (circumstances) that may or may not already be on our **PROJECT BUSINESS EVENT LIST (PARKING LOT)**. Answers such as, *"We want to know about multiple payments to a supplier so we can determine how much business we're giving them"* will lead to a new *business event*, **"Company Wants to Know Historical Payments to a Supplier (for a Period)"**. If this *business event* – regardless of how it is stated – is already on the **PROJECT BUSINESS EVENT LIST (PARKING LOT)**, there's nothing to add to the list. If it's not, however, a new *business event* has been discovered and it has to be added to the list if it is determined to be in scope.

Once you have the answer to the <u>substitute placeholder question</u>, the regular three (or four) '<u>BRT Questions</u>' still have to be asked of the subject Object.

Can the discovery of a *business event* lead to additional questions that, in turn, can find other *business events*? You bet. A good example is the answer we just looked at.

The new *business event*, **"Company Wants to Know Historical Payments to a Supplier (for a Period)"** is essentially a report, regardless of the form it will finally take. Any time a report or a list is required, the question an analyst must ask is, *"If I know about the historical payments we made to a supplier, what does that tell us?"*

Earlier we looked at <u>Inclusion Questions</u> for Objects and data items (Part 4). This same kind of question can be applied to potentially discover new *business events* from already identified *business events*.

Project Business Event List (Parking Lot)

- ~~A Bill Arrives from a Supplier~~
- ~~It is Time to Pay a Supplier~~
- The Supplier Goes Out of Business
- The Supplier is Unable to Fill our Product Order
- Product Does Not Arrive from Supplier
- Supplier Applies to Become an Approved Supplier
- Company Wants to Know Historical Payments to a Supplier (for a Period)

Fig. 6-87: The Project Business Event List with another event added

<u>The Inclusion Question</u> **(for Events)**

"If we know about {the EVENT} what will it <u>enable</u> us to do that we could not do if we didn't know about it?**"**

<u>The Exclusion Question</u> **(for Events)**

"If we <u>do not know</u> about {the EVENT} what will it *prevent* us from doing that we must be able to do?**"**

What kind of answers might you get?

INCLUSION: **"If we know about {<u>the historical payments to a supplier (for a period)</u>} what will it <u>enable</u> us to do that we could not do if we didn't know about it?"** Answer: *"It enables us to do comparative research of how much business we're doing with certain suppliers so we can negotiate better financial terms with some of them."*

EXCLUSION: **"If we do not know about {<u>the historical payments to a supplier (for a period)</u>} what will it <u>prevent</u> us from doing that we must be able to do?"** Same answer, different perspective: *"It would prevent us from knowing how much business we're doing with certain suppliers, which would in turn prevent us from negotiating better financial terms with some of them."*

Both answers suggest another *business event* not previously discovered, **"It Is Time to Negotiate Better Financial Terms with a Supplier"**, which must be added to our list.

When an identified *business event* is essentially a report or a list of some kind – regardless of how it will actually be designed and implemented – you must take it one more step and ask *"What does that tell us?"* or *"What does it prevent us from doing if we don't have it?"*

<u>Project Business Event List</u>
<u>(Parking Lot)</u>
- ~~A Bill Arrives from a Supplier~~
- ~~It is Time to Pay a Supplier~~
- **The Supplier Goes Out of Business**
- **The Supplier is Unable to Fill our Product Order**
- **Product Does Not Arrive from Supplier**
- **Supplier Applies to Become an Approved Supplier**
- **Company Wants to Know Historical Payments to a Supplier (for a Period)**
- **It is Time to Negotiate Better Financial Terms with a Supplier**

Fig. 6-88: The Project Business Event List with another event added

Finding reports or lists to be produced is one of the easier things to do. Clients and SMEs will always have a long list of lists and reports they want. For an analyst to simply accept a requirement for a list or report is not analysis, it's just regurgitation of what the subject matter-expert thinks should be done. But please note that the SME is not a 'business systems analyst'. You are. And you are the one that has to do the analysis to find out what the real requirements are, rather than the surface requirements. And a report or list is a surface requirement because people *do something* with reports, usually to uncover other information that's not directly on the report. While this isn't always the case, it often is.

Finally, from our two starting *business events* (**"A Bill Arrives from a Supplier"** and **"It Is Time to Pay a Supplier"**) we managed to get all of this:

1. Two **Business Process Diagrams** (**Receive Bill** and **Pay Supplier**).
2. A descriptive narrative for each of the two business processes.
3. Discovery of three Objects (**PAYABLE ITEM**, **SUPPLIER** and **PAYMENT**).
4. The necessary data attributes for each of the three Objects.
5. Business rules for each of the three Objects.
6. A list of six (6) additional *business events* that had not been found originally.

As an added benefit, we also got a prescription for database design (the required data accesses) based on the business requirements[23].

Object-Relationship Diagrams

The examples we worked through were all **Business Process Diagrams**. Could we have developed **Object-Relationship Diagrams**[24] instead? Yes, we could have. However, it's more difficult to determine the process required for an object model than for a process model, mostly because we don't see the flow of data, we only see the relationship of Objects. It's also more difficult to get SMEs on board, since they are accustomed to working with the process activity, not a simplified static view of data. In the end, however, everything would be the same except the diagrams.

A Bill Arrives from a Supplier

Fig. 6-89: Object-Relationship diagram for event "Bill Arrives from Supplier"

It Is Time to Pay a Supplier

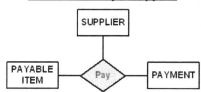

Fig. 6-90: Object-Relationship diagram for event "It Is Time to Pay a Supplier"

6.4 The Non-Serial Incremental Approach

Business requirements for any project are developed incrementally, but it certainly should not be done serially. Using the approach in this book, you can uncover the processes, data and business rules for any *business event* at any time, in any sequence. Each can stand on its own during discovery sessions. Although many Objects are shared by different business processes, there isn't any dependency by one process on another; therefore, the sequence with which you analyze the different *business events* is unimportant. The only thing that matters is your comfort level with the sequence in which you work.

Most organizations with business systems are mature, integrated and complex; therefore, there isn't just one 'beginning' for the analyst on a project. There could be

---

[23] The notation (0,1,N) in the **BUSINESS RULES TABLE** translates easily into the accesses required in a Conceptual Data Model, while the Objects with data attributes provides the composition of the data model.

[24] See Part 3.3: The Different Diagramming Conventions.

many 'beginnings', depending on the number of business areas involved and on their perspectives. Most projects in mature organizations involve several business areas; therefore, there are often as many perspectives on where things begin and end, as there are business areas represented.

This non-serial approach to analysis is also possible because the BUSINESS REQUIREMENTS DOCUMENT doesn't have to be written sequentially either. The document that's produced to define the business requirements, just like the business, should not be a serial description of business processes, like the old manufacturing or paper flow systems from the past. In today's world, that would be difficult to produce, although I see that many people still try. The document you produce will be organized by *business event* (business condition), which is then a whole lot easier to read and understand.

Below is a diagram to illustrate what needs to be done to develop a business process and identify required Objects.

Develop a Business Process and Identify Business Objects

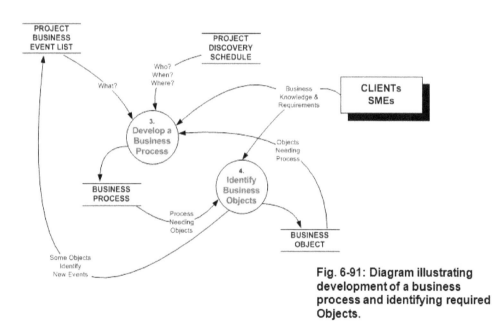

Fig. 6-91: Diagram illustrating development of a business process and identifying required Objects.

After a **Business Process Diagram** has been developed to represent requirements, including the Objects that are need, the BUSINESS RULES TABLE must be queried in the context of the business process.

Query a Business Rules Table

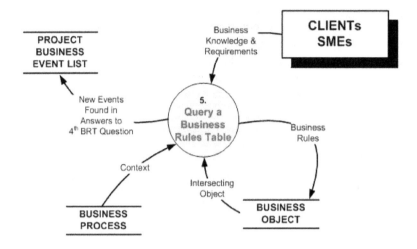

Fig. 6-92: Query a Business Rules Table

The details of these processes can be found in Part 2.7: The 6 Steps of Business System Analysis.

6.5 The Object-Task Table

The **Object-Task Table** helps you find *business events* that may have been missed.

This table lists all the Objects used in a project, and indicates whether the Objects have been created, viewed, modified (sometimes) and/or removed (deleted or archived). These four tasks represent the full life-cycle of an Object. Since an Object must appear more than once in any business scenario, this table helps to determine if we have identified all the scenarios in which each Object participates. An Object such as CUSTOMER, for example, that is viewed only (e.g., by looking up a *customer name* and *email address*) and not referenced in any other way, clearly begs at least three questions: (1) *Under what circumstances was it created*? (2) *Is it ever modified (updated)*? (3) *Under what circumstances is it removed*?

The **Object-Task Table** is a working tool only. It does not make up part of the business requirements documentation. In other words, this table does not become part of the BUSINESS REQUIREMENTS DOCUMENT.

The **Object-Task Table** is only used after all discovery sessions with clients and SMEs have been done for your project, including diagrams, narratives and all the BUSINESS RULES TABLES. Its purpose is only to find *business events* that were missed.

The **Object-Task Table** looks like the one below (Fig. 6-93). The Objects that populate the table are found in the **Business Process Diagrams** that were worked up for the project.

	OBJECT-TASK TABLE			
primary functions →	Create	View	Change	Retire
Product	✓	✓	✓	✓
Supplier		✓		
Payable item	✓			
Payment	✓	✓		

Fig. 6-93: An Object-Task Table

By listing all the Objects that are part of your project and then reviewing each process diagram that support the individual *business events*, you can then determine if the Objects have been <u>created</u>, <u>viewed</u>, <u>changed</u> (sometimes) and/or <u>retired</u> (deleted or archived)[25].

If an Object has not had a full life-cycle in your project, then it must be 'completed' in another. An example of this is an Object such as **SUPPLIER**. To be part of your project, **SUPPLIER** must be <u>created</u> somewhere, <u>viewed</u> (so we can see what it contains, such as a *supplier address*), perhaps <u>changed</u> or updated, and finally <u>retired</u> or archived. If all of this has not been done with a specific Object, such as **SUPPLIER**, then we have missed a *business event*. The only question is whether the missed *business*

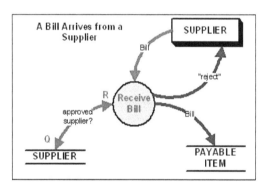

Fig. 6-94: A Business Process Diagram for the event 'A Bill Arrives from a Supplier'

event is inside the scope of your project, or if it belongs to another project or system. In either case, it must be documented accordingly, so project people will know that it has been addressed.

In the context of *your* project, the **Object-Task Table** shows clearly what is missing for any Object. If one of your project's Objects has not been <u>created</u>, then how can you possibly <u>view</u> or <u>update</u> it?[26]

---

[25] The data that make up some Objects, such as long-term statistical or research data, may never be removed if the data is part of a metric database. However, this is the exception to the rule. Most Objects are eventually archived, such as expired **CONTRACTs** or removed **SUPPLIERs**.

[26] This is very similar to the poorly named 'CRUD matrix' (create, retrieve, update, delete), which results in the *Business Transaction Model*. This was developed by Haim Kilov, and presented at the First International Conference on Systems Integration, 1990, in a paper entitled *"From semantic to object-oriented data modeling"*. Just like the Object-Task Table, the Business Transaction Model correlates the major business processes with the general entities (Objects) defined in what they call the Enterprise Data Model. So, we're not so far apart here. The term CRUD, however, is unacceptable to me since it incorrectly implies the analysis is of little value.

7. The Business Requirements Document – How to Package the Requirements

Contents

Up to this point we have focused on the information required to create a business requirements specification at the *business event* level. We have approached the target business areas and partitioned the analysis effort into small and manageable pieces. Now that we know what processes and data are needed to support the *business events* within the project's scope, we can package this information for distribution and future use.

7.1 The Business Interfaces Diagram

The <u>Business Interfaces Diagram</u> (also sometimes known as the "Context Diagram") identifies the interface communications needed between the target project and its outside world, without dictating the specifics of the technology to be employed.

The <u>Business Interfaces Diagram</u> is a powerful tool to graphically illustrate communication needs between the business areas in your project and its outside world. The whole diagram fits nicely on a single page, although a diagram for a project in real life can sometimes get quite busy. But, because it fits on a page, you can present and describe the whole business system in just a few minutes. Senior management generally really likes presentations you can make against this diagram.

To build this diagram, first just draw a big circle representing the target system. Put the project's name inside the circle.

Then go back and look at the individual **Business Process Diagrams** for the project. On each diagram, find the Terminator (if there is one)[27] and the data flow that either comes from or goes to that Terminator. Add the data flows to the <u>Business Interfaces Diagram</u>.

Fig. 7-1: TORDIS Context bubble – The starting point

---

[27] Not all Business Process Diagrams will have a Terminator.

For example, the diagram on the right has only one Terminator (**Hospital**) and two data flows connected to it: one coming from the **Hospital** as a source of information (the *organ request*); and the other providing information to the **Hospital** (*"non-member reject"*). Add these two data flows to the Business Interfaces Diagram (Fig. 7-3, below).

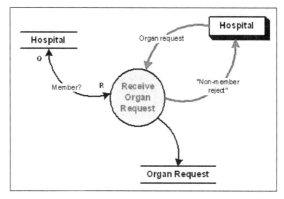

Fig. 7-2: Business process with data flows to Terminator identified

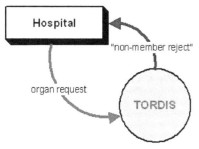

Fig. 7-3: Building up the Business Interfaces Diagram

After adding the data flows coming from and going to the **Hospital** Terminator, the TORDIS Business Interfaces Diagram will look like the picture on the immediate left.

Using another diagram – *Receive Organ* – we have one new data flow to add to the Business Interfaces Diagram, which now would look like the diagram below (Fig. 7.5).

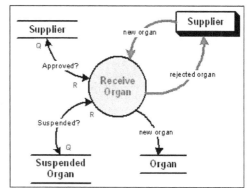

Fig. 7-4: Business process with data flows to Terminator identified

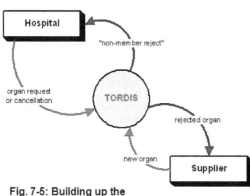

Fig. 7-5: Building up the Business Interfaces Diagram

By going through each of the **Business Process Diagrams** for a project, and identifying each data flow from or to a Terminator, we end up with a <u>Business Interfaces Diagram</u> that could look like this example for the TORDIS project below (Fig. 7-6).

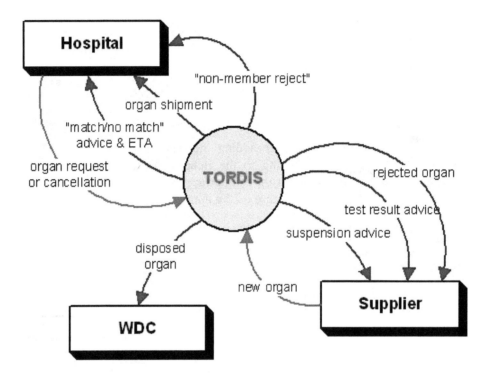

Fig. 7-6: TORDIS Business Interfaces Diagram

This diagram is now easily explained and presented to your clients or senior management. You can "talk through" each of the data flows that come into and leave TORDIS; and you can explain what happens inside it. The diagram clearly shows the interfaces with the outside world that need technology applied, and who is involved.

7.2 How to Package the Business Requirements

The finished BUSINESS REQUIREMENTS DOCUMENT will include the following:

★ **Business Interfaces Diagram** – a single picture to identity outside interfaces.

★ **Business Process Diagrams** – the individual business processes, with accompanying documentation.

You may be surprised at how little this seems to be. First, that's because it's a business requirements specification, not a software engineering specification. Business requirements can be lean, brief and succinct without missing a thing. Second, when you take a close look at the components of the business requirements, you find it is very dense with all kinds of information: The process model with clear narratives, participating Objects, data items, and business rules that succinctly specify system behavior. The absence of technology and an implementation bias enable the document to be quite small, and to be completed very quickly.

Being the highest-level view, the Business Interfaces Diagram illustrates the communications interfaces needed between the outside world[28] and the project's business area(s). It can be used as the foundation for a communication and/or transportation network with suppliers, vendors, partners, banks, and even customers.

The individual **Business Process Diagrams** and their accompanying documentation describe the required processes and the data that supports those processes, without referring to any specific technology architecture or solution design.

The BUSINESS REQUIREMENTS DOCUMENT can be produced as a complete document or as a partial document – specific to a business area – and issued to those who should have it.

How to Bring an Agile Approach to the Development and Distribution of Project Documentation

Traditionally, software acquisition or system design doesn't start until all the business requirements analysis has been completed. And that's a bit of a problem. In most cases, that's a very long time and is very frustrating for management who really want to get on with "the real work": Implementing the software.

To create an even bigger challenge, once all the business requirements analysis has been completed, there's the approval process. In some organizations, this can be a painful process, fraught with the politics of budgets and turf. In other organizations, the people signing off on business requirements simply look at the (conventional) size of the document (*War and Peace* comes to mind) before grumbling their consent without actually reading the document. I can't blame them.

To send out a document that details all the business requirements to everyone who was involved in the project – to all the stakeholders – and to do this after all the work has been done does not seem to be in keeping with the principles of a modern business nor that of a lean, agile organization.

---

[28] The project's "outside world" can be internal or external to the organization.

This is, quite frankly, exactly how it was done in 1970. It's difficult to get better results with methods that are from a previous century. I would suggest it's time to change.

Let's face it – this old-school approach is contrary to quality management principles, too. The approval process is, after all, a way of managing the quality of the product; and, as such, should be an integral part of the business requirements process itself. To go through a major "approval" at the end of the process, for the first time, seems like a recipe for failure to me.

In a mature organization, it's quite common that stakeholders for a project could number 30 or more – perhaps many more – people.

Imagine for a moment a project that has 30 stakeholders and subject-matter experts involved in a project. Imagine also that the Financial Management group on the project is directly involved with only 12 *business events*. The Reservation area team is involved in only 7 of the project's *business events*. Product Testing is involved with 3 *events* … and a few other groups are involved in various other *events*. No one, not one business unit, is involved in or concerned with all the *business events*.

That kind of distribution of stakeholders is pretty well normal for any project.

That being the case, why should we distribute the entire document to everyone? The Financial Management area has nothing to do with a *business event* like **"It is Time to Test an Organ for Disease"**; nor is it their responsibility to review and approve the business processes required by another business area.

A BUSINESS REQUIREMENTS DOCUMENT can potentially consist of scores of pages.[29] But, if a business area is involved in only a part of the project (which is almost always the case), their willingness to wade through all the pages of a document could be very low. On the other hand, there are those who want to see everything that's documented for the project, but they really have little to do with it all. These folks sometimes get in the way and delay progress.

On scores of projects, we have found that it can be very productive to issue a subset of the BUSINESS REQUIREMENTS DOCUMENT to the different stakeholders and subject-matter experts involved, rather than the whole thing to everyone. For example, for the Product Testing area of the TORDIS project, we could create a BUSINESS REQUIREMENTS DOCUMENT that consists of the components on the next page.

A Business Interfaces Diagram ('Context Diagram') showing the required interfaces with the system's outside world.

---

[29] Traditionally, the size of the finished document is a function of the complexity of the project and the number of people involved. This is not the case for event-based projects, as described in this book. The size of the finished BUSINESS REQUIREMENTS DOCUMENT is entirely a function of the number of *business events* and the number of Objects that support the business processes. This makes event-based project documentation much smaller than conventional documentation; thus much more "agile" in context.

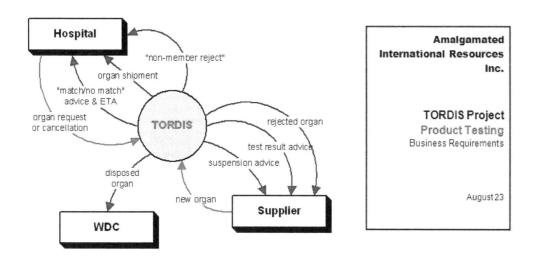

Fig. 7-7: TORDIS Business Interfaces Diagram

Individual Business Process Diagrams showing the processes that belong to the business area for which the document has been prepared. (In this example, there would be only three <u>Product Testing</u> processes.) Business process documentation must include – as well as the diagrams – descriptive narratives, Object definitions, data attributes and business rules for the Objects that support the business area the document is focused on.

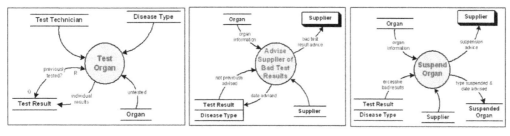

Fig. 7-8: The 3 Product Testing business processes

By partitioning the BUSINESS REQUIREMENTS DOCUMENT in this manner we not only increase the focus, but we significantly reduce the volume of reading required by the clients and subject-matter experts in any business area. This can lead to faster and better turnaround. It certainly minimizes any potential distractions.

There's another important factor: The BUSINESS REQUIREMENTS DOCUMENT could only be produced with the knowledge contributed by the subject-matter experts. They participate in and contributed actively in detailed discovery sessions, and they are probably very aware of what they contributed. Their contribution is reflected in the pages of this document; and the document – when it issued by separate business areas – is clearly focused on the knowledge about that business area, without the distractions of all the other contributions by other SMEs from other areas. And since the document is theirs – and most people don't disagree with themselves – they will probably pay far better attention to the document than if it is a variety show of all the different business areas.

However, to take this idea to an even higher level of responsiveness and "agile", I suggest the following strategy.

Discovery sessions with subject-matter experts are conducted on the basis of one or more specific *business events*.[30] For each *business event*, you will create a **Business Process Diagram**. You'll do the process diagram, identify supporting Objects, attribute data items to the Objects, and determine business rules specific to the business process. All of this will be done with the direct interactive participation and contribution of your subject-matter experts.

As soon as possible after you've wrapped up a discovery session with subject-matter experts, and you have cleaned up all the resulting specifications and documentation – issue the business requirements dealing with the *business event* to all the stakeholders and SMEs who participated in your discovery session.

"As soon as possible" could be the same day, but is certainly within a day or two. The sooner it's done, the more responsive you'll be seen to be, and the more enthusiastic the response from your SMEs will be too.

Three things are important in this very agile and lean process.

First – your documentation for a single *business event* will be very small. Typically, you will be asking them to review just 3 or 4 pages. It will consist of two pages describing the process that supports the *business event*. The diagram will be on one page and the process narrative will be on the other page, if it doesn't fit under the diagram. For each of the Objects identified in the process diagram you will have a definition, data attributes and business rules. Since most diagrams only have 3 or 4 Objects, usually not more than six, this makes the documentation pretty lean. Send this to the subject-matter experts who participated in the discovery session. Ask them to read and review the document, particularly the business rules for the Objects, since these define the behavior of the new system. Give them a deadline for feedback or their approval that it represents what you discussed in the discovery session.

Second – what your SMEs receive will look exactly like the diagrams you drew in the actual discovery session, just a little prettier ... so they will recognize what they are reviewing. Most of them will be very comfortable with this, since you have already spent some time on the business process and the business rules in the discovery session. Also, all the information contained in the very slim document is their knowledge, not yours. They will recognize it as such.

Third – your fast and timely distribution of the documentation means it's still fresh in their minds. As they read, they will recall what was discussed. This provides the

---

[30] Discovery sessions – how they are conducted and with whom – will be discussed in detail in the next chapter.

continuity you need to get good feedback. It will also stimulate them to get the feedback back to you as quickly as possible.

I have found this to be an exceptionally fast, agile and lean way of getting good feedback quickly, and a good way of keeping subject-matter experts involved past the very interactive discovery sessions. It's a way of overcoming the "out of sight, out of mind" syndrome, which can have so much effect of project progress.

What tools can you use for documentation?

Let's get one issue out of the way. I am opposed to the use of technical software (you know the kind) because every one of them is designed to help software engineers, not your business partners. What they see and what they get is totally alien to their business world.

In terms of what works well, the most commonly used is still simple documents, emailed internally. But Wikis are starting to become more popular; and I would recommend the use of an expert-moderated Wiki for any project.

A Wiki is particularly good for teams that are dispersed across the country, around the world, or even in different offices across the city. Feedback can be almost instant, and knowledge will be contributed by the people who have the knowledge.

A Wiki has two lives. The first is when it is the knowledge repository consisting of the business requirements specification preceding software installation. The second is its life after the software is implemented. The transition from a business requirement Wiki to a Business Area Wiki takes place when stakeholders and subject-matter experts start to maintain the knowledge contained in the business requirements as a knowledge set of the business areas. Since this includes all areas and interfaces, not just those features developed as software support. The Wiki becomes a teaching and learning tool for the affected business areas.

The intent of any Wiki is to make changes easy to do, not difficult. Traditional documentation is always difficult to maintain, and is never maintained very well, if at all.

When a Business Area Wiki is developed this way, maintenance of the business documentation now becomes the responsibility of the client and the SMEs in the different business areas.

The documentation you need, whether for a single business event, or all of them, is summarized on the following page.

The Business Requirements Documentation

Project Business Event List
(from the *Project Scope Blitz*)

- List of project **business events** from the *Project Scope Blitz*, including business area ownership and involvement, and requirement priority.

SALES AND PROCUREMENT PROJECT
AIR Telecom Inc.

	List of Potential Events	SALES	MARKETING	PURCHASING	ACCOUNTING	Priority (1, 2, 3)
1	A Customer Buys a Product	★	★		★	1
2	A Customer Requests an Unavailable Product	★	★			1
3	A Product is Returned by a Customer	★	★		★	1
4	It is Time to Determine a Salesperson's Commissions	★			★	2
5	It is Time to Order a Product from a Supplier	★	★	★	★	1
6	It is Time to Pay a Supplier for Product Delivered	★	★	★	★	1

Total Number of Events = 6
Pilot & Copilot: Days to BRD = 2.7
Pilot Only: Days to BRD = 4.4

Fig. 7.9: Example of a Project Business Event List

For each Event (*n* occurrences)

- A **Business Process Diagram** that support the **business event**.
- A task-based narrative for the business process.
- References or links to Object definitions.
- A list of Business Areas affected by the business process
- A Business Rules Table for Objects supporting the business process.
- Any Implementation (design solution) considerations.

For each Object (*n* occurrences)

- Definition of the Object.
- Business Rules for the Object.
- Data attributes for the Object.

AIR Telecom Inc.

Sales and Procurement
Business Requirements
Document (BRD)

August 23

The Business Rules Table (BRT)

- Matrix of intersecting Objects.
- Cardinality (0,1,N) for each Object.

BRT		customer	product	payment
1	customer		1,N,0	1,N,0
1	product	1,N,0		1,N,0
1	payment	1	1,N	

Fig. 7-10: Example of a Business Rules Table

7.3 Are Composite Diagrams Still OK?

In one of my seminars, someone once said, *"I was taught to do several process diagrams together on a page – more or less seven – to integrate related processes for an area? Should I join some of the event-based diagrams together to make composite diagrams?"*

No – normally, we don't. When using an event-based approach to analysis, we have not found any particular reason to do this, except that it was a necessity with the original 'structured analysis' methods. It was done that way because the data flow diagrams of 'structured analysis' resulted from how you approached progressive decomposition of higher level diagrams.

Let me suggest that you ask the Inclusion Question to deal with this issue: *"If we join the process diagrams together, what will this enable us to do that we couldn't do if they were not joined together?"* … or, as an Exclusion Question, *"If we don't join the process diagrams together, what will this prevent us from doing that we must be able to do?"*

The usual answer is, *"We need a composite diagram so we can get the bigger picture."* Well, that's interesting, but what do we mean by "the bigger picture"?

What are we really looking for here? And how will we recognize it when we see it? My understanding is that "the bigger picture" is an issue left over from another way of doing things in earlier years. Almost all older systems were serial and procedural in nature; therefore, it was very important to see how things were connected and how data moved from one process to another. The systems of yesterday were generally monoliths, with almost everything happening as serial progression. Most communication was by way of data flows rather than through Objects and their data.

Today, we know that it's not necessary to take this same serial approach. Instead, we can take an approach based on *business events*. A set of *business events* is really just a set of circumstances that a system has to deal with, not serial in nature, and all the supporting data is Object based.

So, how do we see "the bigger picture"? Well, it depends on what someone needs to know about the so-called "bigger picture".

If we want to see how we can access information, we can extract a prescription for database design[31] by generating a conceptual data model from the BUSINESS RULES TABLE.

The Conceptual Data Model, created by database designers, is one view of the "bigger picture" – as a composite diagram – and tells the software engineers how Objects of related information are logically joined, and how to get from one Object to another to find related information.

---

[31] A "prescription" for database design is not a solution design. It is simply a specification that states, "these are the data relationships and accesses you need to be able to build a database solution" to meet the data access requirements specified by the business.

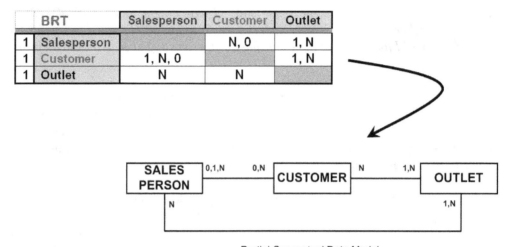

Partial Conceptual Data Model

Fig. 7-11: Business Rules Table with corresponding Chen ER diagram

In the example above, the notation in the **BUSINESS RULES TABLE** converts easily into a partial conceptual data model diagram. The only things that remain to be done are to resolve the many-to-many relationships between Objects (an easy process), and complete the data attribution to Objects.

Do individual diagrams need to be joined together into a series of composite diagrams? I don't think so.[32] In all the projects I have ever worked on, using this event-based approach to business requirements analysis, I have never found the need. But if it makes you feel better to do it, there's no real harm in it. Be forewarned, however, that it takes longer (because there's extra work to do), and I would suggest there is no benefit in the exercise. If you can't identify the reason for the need, don't do it.

---

[32] Although joining some of these business processes together when developing a solution design is another matter.

8. The Discovery Sessions – How to Involve Your Subject-Matter Experts

Contents

8.1 The Risks and Reward of Discovery Sessions

8.2 What is a Requirements Discovery Session?

8.3 Key Success Factors

8.4 Tips and Techniques for Discovery Sessions

A 'requirements discovery session' is an interactive approach to conducting meetings with clients and subject-matter experts to probe and establish a project's business or organizational requirements. These highly interactive sessions include clients, business partners, subject-matter experts, business analysts, executives and some system professionals. These discovery sessions are based on the sound principles of JAD[33], but with greater flexibility and more suited to the 21st century. Discovery sessions are even faster than conventional RAD[34] sessions.

Requirements discovery sessions produce great savings by shortening the elapsed time required to gather business system requirements and by improving the completeness and quality of the requirements gathered. This reduces significantly the number of costly downstream requirements changes. Requirements discovery sessions have been extremely successful with many organizations worldwide, private and government alike. However, the success of a requirements discovery session is not just a function of the business analysis methodology you use, it requires a well-practiced professional to lead the sessions (a senior practitioner) and the unreserved participation of clients, business partners, subject-matter experts and executives. In other words, there must be a real commitment by the organization's client base, not just words of support. "Real commitment" means putting in the time necessary to participate in discovery sessions – which is a lot less than the time required by conventional analysis methods.

There are two kinds of requirements discovery sessions: the *Project Scope Blitz* and the detailed discovery session.

---

[33] Joint Application Development or Joint Application Design (JAD) was developed by Chuck Morris of IBM Raleigh (North Carolina) and Tony Crawford of IBM Toronto (Canada) in the late 1970's. In 1980 Crawford and Morris taught JAD in Toronto and Crawford led several workshops to prove the concept. The results were encouraging and JAD became a well accepted approach in many companies. In time, JAD developed and gained general industry approval as a best practice. Crawford defines JAD as an interactive systems design concept involving discussion groups in a workshop setting. Originally, JAD was designed to bring system developers and users of varying backgrounds and opinions together in a productive and creative environment. The meetings were a way of obtaining system requirements and specifications.

[34] Rapid Application Development (RAD) is based on JAD, but moves along faster by applying the 80/20 Rule in development and scope selectivity.

8.1 The Risks and Rewards of Discovery Sessions

There are two major risks when planning requirements discovery sessions. Whether the discovery session is intended to be a front-end *Project Scope Blitz* or a series of <u>regular detailed discovery sessions</u>, there are often unrealistic productivity expectations (a) before the discovery session, and (b) after discovery sessions.

Also, when an organization embarks on a series of discovery sessions without being fully committed to the highly interactive nature of these sessions, it can fail or fall short of the mark. But if an organization devotes the right amount of time and the right people, the results will be substantial. Some of the benefits of a requirements discovery session include:

- It accelerates the business revitalization and process re-engineering process.

- It accelerates the business requirements learning process.

- It massively increases productivity by shortening the iteration cycle.

- It ensures the highest quality possible, because of direct participation by clients and subject-matter experts.

- It ensures the most complete business requirements analysis in the shortest period of time.

- It helps to develop mutual respect between business system analysts and clients.

- It provides a forum for exploring focused, in-context business revitalization ideas.

- It helps to deliver what the client needs and wants, quickly.

- It opens the door to success.

How the requirements discovery session is conducted is what sets it apart from other approaches to gathering business requirements. Critical ingredients for a successful discovery session include leadership from a trained and experienced practitioner and an expert scribe (also a business specialist); as well as participation by executive sponsors, key decision makers and *real* subject-matter experts[35]; and the ability to work without the usual daily interruptions[36].

---

[35] A real subject-matter expert has in-depth practical knowledge of the business areas affected by the project, and their work processes. This person also understands why work processes are organized the way they are, and what these processes are to achieve. This is not a surrogate user; nor is it a recent business school graduate who can fill the gap.

[36] Discovery sessions can last anywhere from an hour to several days, depending on the critical nature of the project. Discovery sessions should be uninterrupted, as much as possible, since the absence of key people delays progress.

8.2 What is a Requirements Discovery Session?

The Project Scope Blitz. The objectives of a *Project Scope Blitz* are as follows:

- To quickly identify many of the *business events* that will be part of the target system.

- To determine the business areas or departments that have responsibility for responding to and dealing with the identified *business events*.

- To accurately predict the amount of time required to complete the detailed discovery sessions with clients and SMEs, and to prepare the BUSINESS REQUIREMENTS DOCUMENT.

- To establish work priorities – what *business events* will be done first, and which ones will be done later.

- To enable planning the schedule for detailed discovery sessions with clients and subject-matter experts.

- To determine the effort and cost of the project's business system requirements analysis.

Detailed Discovery Sessions. The objectives of a detailed discovery session are as follows:

- To quickly get all subject-matter experts on the same page, at the same time.

- To quickly uncover and discover the project's business requirements for one or more *business events* in a single session with one or more subject-matter experts.

- To enable the business system analyst to focus on a small component (a *business event*) and to quickly learn about the business requirements in support of that *business event*.

- To discover complete and accurate business requirements, focused and in context – not just "goodness and light".

- To achieve "buy-in" and ownership from clients and subject-matter experts.

- To develop mutual respect by all participants – subject-matter experts and business system analysts.

How long does a Discovery session take?

The Project Scope Blitz. *Project Scope Blitz* sessions take about a half-day, sometimes a little more. For an average project, if the client has a good handle on what they need, a half-day session is often enough.

It's important before planning the regular detailed discovery sessions for a project to estimate how many *business events* there will be and how much time is needed for each one. You also need to know who should participate – clients and subject-matter experts.

SALES AND PROCUREMENT PROJECT
AIR Telecom Inc.

List of Potential Events	SALES	MARKETING	PURCHASING	ACCOUNTING	Priority (1, 2, 3)
1 A Customer Buys a Product	★	★		★	1
2 A Customer Requests an Unavailable Product	★	★			1
3 A Product is Returned by a Customer	★	★		★	1
4 It is Time to Determine a Salesperson's Commissions	★			★	2
5 It is Time to Order a Product from a Supplier	★	★	★	★	1
6 It is Time to Pay a Supplier for Product Delivered	★	★	★	★	1

Total Number of Events =	6
Pilot & Copilot: Days to BRD =	2.7
Pilot Only: Days to BRD =	4.4

Fig. 8-1: A short Project Business Event List

The *Project Scope Blitz* is very interactive with clients and subject-matter experts. It involves extracting from them the things they believe should be within the scope of the project. Our experience is that the more senior the participants are, the better your results will be.

Before continuing, please review the earlier section on *business events*, Part 3: The Business Event. You will recall that a *business event* is a situation, condition, circumstance or external requirement. It is not a process. The process is <u>what</u> we do to supports the *business events* – not <u>how</u>.

When you start up a *Project Scope Blitz*, you can start by asking the participants about some of the things they need to have in their new business system. Their answers will not be in the form of *business events*. It's up to you, as the analyst, to distill what they say and turn it into a *business event* statement. When you do hear what they say, and you turn it into a *business event* statement, it is best to confirm with the speaker if your understanding of their requirement, as you have stated it in your *business event* statement, is correct.

Each time you identify a *business event*, it must be listed and displayed so the participants can see what you are doing, and they can read the *business event* statement as you have written it. My preferred method is to write the *business events* statements with a marker pen on *Write On – Cling On* sheets[37] which stick to the wall.

---

[37] Since not everyone has a Smart Board, *Write On – Cling Sheets*™ are white poly static sheets that come in about 3-foot squares that stick to walls – and anything else – and act like a whiteboard. You can erase what you write or draw on them with a marker, and you can move the sheets around, or roll them up. They can also be reused. A Google search will find this product for you.

You can also use higher technology, involving a projector. As *business event* statements are captured in a document, they can be projected onto a wall for everyone to see. The important point is, everyone gets to see what's being documented. In this way, they can see what you hear.

One approach that we recommend when conducting a *Project Scope Blitz*, is to create a short list of *business events* yourself, and then present these as "potential events" to your clients and subject-matter experts. It's very important to suggest them strictly as "potential events" since participants are more likely to buy-in to their own knowledge and contributions than to yours. This approach is particularly useful if you don't have much information about the project, or when the project deals with something that's new or different.

The whole idea behind this use of "potential events" is to stimulate participation by the clients and subject-matter experts that are part of your *Project Scope Blitz*. In the early part of any interactive session, people are often hesitant to say anything or to get the ball rolling. If this is the case, then it's easy for you to toss out a "potential event" and to ask participants if that *business event* is something that could be part of the scope of the project. The answer could be a blunt *"no"*, in which case you strike it from your list.

Hopefully, it will stimulate discussion and determination of the "potential event" as a real *business event*, in scope or not.

After completing a *Project Scope Blitz*, you will have a long or short list of *business events* for the project. There's no doubt you will <u>not</u> have discovered all of the required *business events*, but you will have enough to get you started.

For each *business event* in the project, you will need to plan one detailed discovery session. Your plan should provide for four (4) hours per *business event* to complete all the documentation; but the detailed discovery session itself should only have one (1) hour per *business event* of discovery time with clients and subject-matter experts, regardless of its perceived complexity or simplicity.

Detailed Discovery Sessions. A regular detailed discovery session for one *business event* should be scheduled for one (1) hour with clients and subject-matter experts.

An "average" project, we have found, is between 25-75 *business events*; "small" is less than 25 *business events*; and "large" is over 75 *business events*. Based on needing one hour of discovery time per *business events*, a "small" project needs less than 25 hours of client and SME time; an "average" project needs between 25 and 75 hours of client and SME time; and a "large" project needs over 75 hours of their time. If necessary, this can all be scheduled one hour at a time, over an extended period. For mission critical projects, detailed discovery sessions for a project can also be scheduled, one hour per *business event*, on consecutive days with all parties involved. This "complete immersion" approach is very effective (arguably the most effective approach), but also very exhausting for subject-matter experts and the business analyst. We must also consider that clients and SMEs have their own work to do, and dedicating several full days to discovery sessions is usually difficult.

Regardless of the approach you take – and I do recommend the scheduling of one-hour sessions – each *business event* needs an average of three (3) additional hours by the analyst to dig up more details with SMEs, apply Business Data Rule # 5 to extract new Objects (see Part 4.4: Business Data Rule # 5) and add them to the BUSINESS RULES TABLE, convene meetings with SMEs to determine the rules that come from the new Objects, perhaps convene additional detailed discovery sessions for *business events* that are found from the new Objects and rules; and, complete the documentation.

The detailed discovery session is a team activity, therefore typical teamwork guidelines apply. It usually takes a project team, consisting of analysts and SMEs, a couple of days of detailed discovery sessions to jell and to ramp up on foundation information.

What kind of Facility is Required?

Any room with lots of uncluttered wall space will do. The wall space is important so you can put *Write On – Cling On* sheets on them to draw the diagrams you need, so everyone who is in the room can see what has been done. While there is lots of technology that can project the diagrams onto a screen or a wall, including Smart Boards, we have found the dynamics and comfort level of participants when using *Write On – Cling On* sheets and whiteboards can't be duplicated.

Participants should be seated comfortably with desk or table space.

Who should Participate?

A detailed discovery session should include a number of key people. Each discovery session should include clients and subject-matter experts who are crucial to the success of the project, including senior managers, other business partners with a stake in the project, project 'primes' and any other persons who have a good understanding of the project's objectives, business rationale, and re-engineering vision.

A business and its systems can only be as good as the dedication and participation shown by its owners and stakeholders. All participants in a detailed discovery session must bring an open mind. These discovery sessions enable participants to "liberate the mind" and potentially discover business re-engineering opportunities, including immediate opportunities for improvement[38]. These IOI's, often uncovered in discovery sessions, can be invaluable to an agile organization.

Participants in detailed discovery sessions should include the following:

Discovery Session Leader – The Pilot. The "Pilot" is a business system analyst who leads and facilitates discovery sessions. We use the term "Pilot" because he or she must lead the session, keep it on course, and take it to its desired destination without problems.

---

[38] An 'Immediate Opportunity for Improvement', or 'IOI', is an opportunity discovered during requirements analysis that can be acted upon almost immediately and can lead to substantial business process improvement and added value to the business.

Without a doubt, the "Pilot" is most instrumental to the success of the detailed discovery session, and the successful "Pilot" has an exceptional combination of skills.

- The "Pilot" must have excellent communication and cooperation skills.

- The "Pilot" must be able to deal with political disputes, power struggles and personality clashes, although this doesn't happen very often.

- The "Pilot" needs to be completely impartial, with no political baggage, and able to keep an open mind while managing conversations.

- The "Pilot" must be sensitive to hidden agendas and be able to redirect them constructively.

- The "Pilot" must be able to bridge communication gaps – technical, linguistic and cultural.

- The "Pilot" must be comfortable speaking to and managing a group of people that often includes senior executives.

- The "Pilot" must encourage quiet group members to contribute their thoughts, and manage positively strong personalities that sometimes dominate sessions.

Achieving all of this is not for the faint-of-heart. Therefore, the "Pilot" must have the respect of those who participate in discovery sessions. That respect is earned through a series of successful discovery sessions, but it also comes from general comportment, dress, civility, respect for participants, and being non-judgmental of contributions.

Our experience is that when a requirements discovery session fails, it is almost always because of the session leader or facilitator.

One of the reasons for session failure is when an organization wants to train a large number of people as "Pilots", but they lack sufficient recognition of the value of experience. Some managers (thankfully, not too many) believe they can assign a new "Pilot" to a project immediately after a candidate has finished an analysis course. Unfortunately, the result of trying to get everyone up to speed immediately, without the blessings and pain of experience, is that almost no one gets there. This, in turn, can lead to unskilled "Pilots" and weak results. Weak results can lead to backsliding to the endless search for an analysis methodology "that works". Of course, the methodology works just fine; problems are usually the result of "Pilot" error.

It is my opinion that an organization that intends to use this approach to business system analysis should train, and support, a small core group of expert "Pilot" practitioners. These "Pilots" should conduct as many discovery sessions throughout the year as possible. Our experience is that it takes about four projects for a new "Pilot" to become reasonably proficient. And it quickly gets better after that.

Expert Scribe – The Co-Pilot. The "co-pilot" must truly be *expert*. The "co-pilot" can't just be the next available body. They must be fully trained in business requirements analysis and how a discovery session is run. They must know what they are hearing when they hear it; such as Objects, data attributes and business rules. And they must have the knowledge and ability to back up the "Pilot", if required. We call this person a 'co-pilot' for just that reason.

The primary role of the "co-pilot" is to record what is said and done in the detailed discovery session. As such, this person will actively participate to make sure everything that's said and done is clear and concise.

Sometimes a "Pilot" is their own "co-pilot"; i.e., they wear a different hat at different times. However, if a "Pilot" is supported by someone else as "co-pilot", the time it takes to complete all the requirements documentation for the project is about half of what's needed if the "Pilot" works alone as both "Pilot" and "co-pilot".

An Expert Coach. For the first four projects we recommend that an analyst be supported by an expert coach: Someone who is expert at this approach to business systems analysis. Having a coach who is experienced with this approach will lead to mastery of the methods and project success much faster, and with fewer challenges. This is a common practice in almost all professions and trades. It is time that we assured our own success by applying this best practice.

Executive Sponsors and Project Primes. If you want the project to succeed, make sure an executive sponsor or a fully empowered project prime participate in the *Project Scope Blitz*. The absence of these people sends the message that the project isn't important enough for participation by other business partners and subject-matter experts.

Subject-Matter Experts and other Business Partners. Get them involved as much as possible and as quickly as possible. Involve the client directly, as well as the subject-matter experts. Involve as many of the key people from the affected business areas and department as quickly as you can. They should have a deep interest and enthusiasm for the success of the project. They should be the decision-makers, as well as the subject-matter experts (and these may be the same people). Their knowledge of the business and their vision is instrumental to the success of the sessions.

8.3 Key Success Factors

There are many success factors that are unique to each particular discovery session. However, there are some generally accepted success factors that apply to just about any kind of interactive session:

- Be sure that the project's executive sponsors and key stakeholders attend and actively participate in the initial *Project Scope Blitz*.

- Issue the **Project Business Event List** to everyone who participated in the *Project Scope Blitz* as soon as possible after the session is done. It should go out no later than a day after the session.

- Set realistic expectations for the work to be done in the detailed discovery sessions, and a realistic schedule. In terms of the time required, plan on one (1) hour per *business event*, with clients and SMEs participating, and an additional three (3) hours per *business events* to complete the analysis and documentation. That will be fast, and realistic.[39]

- Be very visible by conducting discovery sessions with all the people required to be involved in a *business event*. Avoid one-person interviews. They are inefficient, take much too long, and hide your visibility. Visibility demonstrates that you are not only gathering the requirements, but you are *seen* to be gathering the requirements.

- If the project becomes a software acquisition or development project, make sure the software engineers (the programmers, database designers and system designers) know how to read the BUSINESS REQUIREMENTS DOCUMENT and, if custom building the software, how to turn it into a solution design.

- Do a lot of discovery sessions, every chance you get; but perfect practice – with a coach and mentor for "Pilots" and "co-pilots" – works better than practice without guidance by an expert. Having a coach experienced in this kind of business system analysis will lead to mastery of the methods much faster, and project success with fewer challenges.

Other general success factors include:

- Actively encourage everyone to participate. Instead of being just a facilitator, be a proactive "Pilot" and leader.

- Have well established and agreed upon objectives for each discovery session. Explain to participants how a discovery session will generally only deal with the *business event* scheduled and the business process, Objects, data, and business rules needed to support it. Explain how you may find new, previously undiscovered *business events*, but these will not be dealt with in the discovery session. New *events* discovered will be added to the **Project Business Event (Parking Lot)** and will be done at some later time in the schedule.

- Be unbiased and neutral about the business requirement. As a business system analyst it is your responsibility to determine what the client needs to support the business. It is not the business analyst's function to assess the correctness or value of the client's requirements. While you may suggest a path (by using questions rather than answers), it is the client's responsibility to determine the business processes and data that add value to the business.

- "Keep it as simple as possible, but no simpler."[40]

- Keep focused on the objectives – stay with the subject *business event*, and don't jump to other unplanned subjects. Use the **Project Business Event List (Parking Lot)** for

---

[39] You may not actually need the addition three hours for every *business event*. For some, you'll be able to clean it up and get it ready for distribution in less than 30 minutes, but for others it could take 6 or even 12 hours, depending on what you discover in your post-discovery session assessment. The three hours is an average over all the *events*. Therefore, if you have 30 events, you'll need 30 one-hour discovery sessions with SMEs, and a total of 90 additional hours of finishing work.

[40] With thanks to Albert Einstein.

other *business events* that come up in discussion, or as a result of the Business Rules Table.

- Lead the discovery process ... facilitate the requirements.

- Complete the Business Rules Table, and its questions, immediately after finishing the **Business-Process Diagram** that supports a *business event*.

- Use the client's terminology – no technobabble.

- Don't judge the client's questions and answers. If you didn't understand what they said, or if it just sounded strange, ask them to help you understand their question or answer.

- Never fear that your questions will sound strange or uninformed. I've found that this is actually a good thing, even when I have to pretend to understand less than I actually do. People love to tell you about what they do and their responsibilities. They also love to tell you what they know. And that's what discovery sessions are all about – getting the expert knowledge from the subject-matter experts.

- Challenge the SME's thinking, not the SME. Sounds good, but how do you do that? The first step is to never ask *"Why?"* when they give you an answer. "Why?" is not a good question to ask adults. It in effect asks them to justify or rationalize their answer, and they are not there to do that. If a senior sales manager says, *"We want a report on widgets sold in the northwest region"*, and you're not quite certain what this means, it's not a good idea to ask that manager *"Why?"* The answer you get is probably not what you're looking for. Instead, replace your desire to ask "Why?" with the following question: *"John, if we have the report on widget sales in the northwest region, what will that enable us to do that we have to be able to do?"* ... or, from another perspective, *"John, if we don't have the report on widget sales in the northwest region, what will that prevent us from doing that we must be able to do?"* You'll get a real answer with either of these questions (which are just two sides of the same coin). The answer you get will be the real *business event* that you're looking for.

- Be clear and understandable. Don't mumble. Use complete sentences consisting of both nouns and verbs, at least most of the time. Don't use techno-babble or terms the subject-matter experts are not familiar with. Avoid using acronyms unless they are common to your industry (which means many others besides yourself must know the acronym).

- Make people feel good. The better they feel, the more readily they will participate in future discovery sessions. Be good finding.

- Smile. A lot. People respond a whole lot better to smiles, especially if the subject is serious and sometimes complicated.

- Have fun. Use your good sense of humor. If this is sometimes difficult for you, work on developing a sense of humor.

- Listen... listen... and listen some more. What people say and what they mean are sometimes a little different. Keep really focused on what they mean. When you're not sure, ask them to *"help me understand that better"*.

- If you are asked a question, you must <u>always</u> respond to the participant's answer in some manner.

These are some of the key success factors. Undoubtedly, there are many others that apply equally well.

8.4 Tips and Techniques for Discovery Sessions

About The Discovery Sessions

★ When starting a requirements discovery session, remember to ground the participants in the fact that you will be focusing on the **'WHAT'**, not the **'HOW'**. Keep reminding them of this if they drift into how things should be done (solution design) or other solution discussions.

★ Remember the basic principle of *"Partition the effort to minimize complexity"*. If the business process is becoming too complex, it's probably because the subject-matter experts are attempting to have one process support several *business events*. While this is natural, try to keep it as simple as possible. Simple works. Don't try to make it more complex. Go with it until you know better. Don't speculate about what you don't know.

★ Optics is important in discovery sessions. Print legibly on the whiteboards or *Write On – Cling On* sheets, and use red and blue as alternating colors when going through the process. It helps visual recognition of material for your subject-matter experts, the "co-pilot", and you, the "Pilot". Stay away from the other colors, since most of them can't be seen very well from even a few feet away.

★ At the completion of each **Business Process Diagram**, walk through (or talk through) the process as a wrap-up, so your SMEs can confirm its substance once again. It also enables your "co-pilot" to validate that the narrative has been recorded accurately.

★ As the "Pilot", periodically check to ensure that the "co-pilot" is keeping up to you. Before a detailed discovery session, work out signals between the two of you so the "co-pilot" can indicate a need to catch up before moving forward.

★ As the "Pilot", listen for the "co-pilot's" fingers hitting the keyboard. If there is dead silence, take a break from the discovery session and speak with your "co-pilot" to determine if everything is OK – that the "co-pilot" is actually capturing the information as it arises during the discovery session. Also listen for the pace of keying; i.e., is the "co-pilot" still keying something while you are ready to move ahead to the next topic. Or, has keying stopped and it appears the "co-pilot" is also ready to move on. This is particularly an issue when going through the 'BRT Questions' in the BUSINESS RULES TABLE.

★ Tracking requirements in a system can be done by identifying attributes in Objects that define a particular status (e.g., open, closed, approved, rejected, etc.).

Attributing a *date/time* data item to each different status will provide a complete record of an instance of an Object as it changes state in a system.

★ Remember that an "inventory" is really a list of many instances of a particular Object, each having its own unique identifier (key). If you are looking at inventory management *business events*, consider having a status attribute on the Object (e.g., sold, available, returned, etc.) with an associated *date/time*. This will easily provide the information needed to create reports, issue product reorders, etc.

About The Business Process Diagrams

★ A data flow line that goes <u>from</u> an Object <u>into</u> a **Business Process Diagram** represents **finding** information (data items) about that source Object in order to satisfy the requirements of a task in the process.

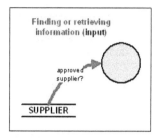

Fig. 8-2: Data flow as input to a process

★ A data flow line that goes <u>into</u> an Object <u>from</u> the process represents **recording** or **remembering** information (data items) about that Object. This satisfies the requirement in the process to update or record changes to individual data items, or to create a new instance of an Object.

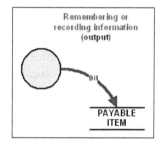

Fig. 8-3: Data flow as output from a process

★ Avoid using the words "update" and "modify" on data flow dialogues. Use pointer words like "**record**" and "**remember**". If you need to add extra emphasis to the data flow, you can also identify the name of the data item in the data dialogue.

★ A double-headed arrow between the process and an Object (i.e., an arrow on each end) represents a 'Query/Response' task action – a dialogue. This is nothing more than personal style and preference.

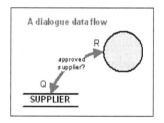

Fig. 8-4: A dialogue data flow

★ Always ensure that the name of the *business event* that's the subject of the **Business Process Diagram** is identified on the top of the diagram. If you find the conversation with your SMEs drifting, point to the *business event* name with the question, "*Is this conversation about this business event, or another one?*" This refocuses the discussion, and may even lead to the identification of a new *business event* that was missing from the original list.

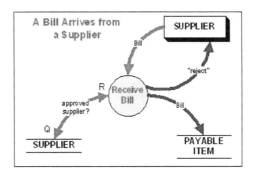

Fig. 8-5: Always identify event statements(s) at the top of a process diagram

A business process does <u>not</u> always have a **Terminator** as a 'stimulus' to start the process, or end it. Stimuli for initiating the process can come from an Object (e.g., a data attribute), or can be a specific time or date that kicks off the process.

About The Objects

★ Following the 5 Business Data Rules (Part 4.4: Summary of the Business Data Rules) is extremely important for clarity of the finished business requirements. In particular, watch out for multi-value data items ('mv') as they may indicate the need to create a new Object that is 'characteristic' of the original Object.

★ Always remember to get your SMEs to provide a concise definition of an Object. It ensures everyone has the same understanding of what the Object represents. Interestingly, Object definitions expand considerably during most detailed discovery sessions, so don't be happy with the first definition you encounter. It will probably change as you progress with the discovery sessions.

★ Always think of Objects in the singular. It helps ground people in understanding the purpose of the business process without getting distracted by number of instances, time, etc. Also, we (people) are not very good at thinking through multiplicity. Stick to the singular.

★ Always name an Object in the singular, even though it represents all possible occurrences of the Object, including its history. Your diagrams represent the business view of the information, not a database design view.

★ If a multi-value ("mv") data item is identified in an Object, but there is no immediate need during a discovery session to break it out into its own Object, do so after the discovery session if it improves the detail of the analysis. If this results in a new Object, you will have to revisit the questions it will generate through the BUSINESS RULES TABLE, and the answers it will produce.

About The Business Rules Table

✳ When writing the business rules that come from the BUSINESS RULES TABLE and form part of an Object, is important to ensure that a descriptive verb is used to express the business rule properly. It is likely that you can use the verb you used to name the **Business Process Diagram**, but this doesn't always work. Try to choose a verb structure that represents the context of the **Business Process Diagram**. In a worst-case scenario, when you just can't figure out the right verb structure, use 'have' or 'be' as a standby.

✳ Sometimes, the answer to the first placeholder 'BRT Questions' is, *"We don't really care"* or *"We don't have an interest in that"*. In this case, put an "N/A" (not applicable) in the intersection cell of the two Objects that were queried. The fact that there may not be any interest in a specific anchor Object having a relationship with another specific Object in the circumstance identified (the *business event* you're working on), does not mean there won't be an interest in them under another circumstance.

About The 'Co-Pilot"

The "co-pilot" is as important to the success of the discovery session as the "Pilot". They have different but equally important roles. The following notes are for "co-pilots" who work with "Pilots" by documenting everything as it happens during a detailed discovery session.[41]

During the Discovery Session

• **Have the "Pilot" explain your role.**

Initially, as a "co-pilot", people will wonder why you are there and what you are recording. Will their words be held against them? Are you a spy? Clarify that you are there to ensure that the information discovered during this session is appropriately documented. Let participants know that a BUSINESS REQUIREMENTS DOCUMENT will be produced as soon as possible after all the discovery sessions are done. If the BUSINESS REQUIREMENTS DOCUMENT, or some part of it will be distributed, let them know that too.

• **Listen, listen, and listen some more.**

Often, there will be more than one conversation taking place. The challenge is to figure out which is the key one. Try to stay focused on the same dialogue as the "Pilot" is engaged in. Because the "Pilot" will likely be actively listening to a specific discussion, encourage others to speak up (at the right time) if you are aware of other side discussions taking place.

• **Seek clarification.**

If there is something you don't understand, ask for clarification. Most people in the room don't expect you to be an expert in the business at hand – that's their job. Your role is to ensure that the facts, as well as the thoughts and concerns of the

---

[41] Not all projects have both a Pilot and Co-pilot. Some projects have a Pilot only, who also fills the role of Co-pilot. This would be one of those famous "team of one" projects.

SMEs get appropriately documented. Consequently, if you do not understand, or if the discussion has gone off in several directions, it is absolutely appropriate to ask participants to repeat their words to ensure that the discussion is accurately documented.

However, as the expert "co-pilot", there is an expectation that you will have some innate ability to hear all, understand all, and document all. Sometimes you may find that it is more appropriate to follow up with specific individuals off line. Your good judgment is necessary.

- **Read back complex narratives or business rules for confirmation.**

  If a particularly complex business process has been under discussion for some time, it may be appropriate to request a break so that you can consolidate your notes. If you do, after the break read back the updated version of the narrative or the business rules.

- **Define all acronyms.**

  If acronyms are used in the discovery session (and they almost always are), make a note of them and follow up with individuals off line to ensure complete understanding. Ensure that full definitions of these terms are included at least once in the document. If appropriate, consider adding a glossary of acronyms as an appendix.

- **If participants wish to see what you're doing, share it with them on breaks.**

  Remember, the document you are preparing belongs to everyone in the room. It is the consolidation of all their thoughts, ideas and experience. If they want to grab a glimpse on a break, share it with them. This is an excellent opportunity to check with individuals one-on-one to validate specific comments in the document. This will also enhance their confidence that their words are being recorded appropriately and that a great deal of work is being done by you, the scribing "co-pilot", as well as by the people in the room.

- **Leave the diagrams for later.**

  A **Business Process Diagram** will likely change as you progress through the Discovery session. The diagrams are usually on whiteboards or on *Write On – Cling On* sheets on the wall. Use the diagrams to get the process narratives correct during the session. Once the process definition and diagram are stable, add the diagram to your documentation.

Outside the Discovery Session

- **Add the diagrams to your documentation.**
  - Copy the diagrams from the whiteboards or *Write on – Cling On* sheets on the walls to your documentation during the consolidation period at the end of the day, when there are no clients or subject-matter experts around. Since diagrams can change during a discovery session as you get more information, there will

be no time for you to capture the diagrams (perhaps more than once) during the session.

- **Create a backup of the diagrams.**
  - Before you move any of the diagrams on *Write On – Cling On* sheets, create backup copies by using your trusty digital camera or iPhone. Take photos of all the diagrams. For any specific **Business Process Diagram**, you may want to take more than one photo, as it can change as a result of discoveries in different sessions.

- **Confirm the content.**
  - Do the narratives make sense?
  - Do the definitions (Objects and data) make sense?
  - Do the relationships defined in the business rules make sense?
  - Do you have at least one example for every "*never*" answer from the 'BRT Questions'?
  - Have you checked all Objects in the Object-Task Table?

Other thoughts

- Where appropriate, give key subject-matter experts an opportunity to "see" an early version of the documentation for a specific **Business Process Diagram** (which may support one or more *business events*). This gives them a sense of how much work is actually getting done. Visibility is one of the keys to success.

- When reviewing specific documentation with a subject-matter expert, be prepared for some "wordsmithing". This is why you are reviewing it – to ensure that the way the information is documented is how they want it. "Wordsmithing" is a step in the ownership process.

- As discussed earlier, consider posting individual processes and their supporting information as part of an internal Wiki. The business processes should represent what the organization wants, without detailing how it will be delivered, and it should be a living document. As a Wiki, it can be used by the client community as a teaching or training tool, and it can easily be maintained by the client community that owns the business processes.

- Accept the applause.

Tips and Techniques for Co-Pilots

Topic	Tip / Technique
Listening	During the detailed discovery session, concentrate on listening to what is being said. Business Process Diagrams and Object data attributes can be captured at the end of the day – they'll still be on the *Write On – Cling On* sheets when all the subject-matter experts have left. Also, most narratives can be constructed from a good diagram quite easily. Look to the data flows to find the tasks. There is a lot said during the session, by the "Pilot" and by the SMEs themselves that does not appear on the diagram but needs to be captured in your narratives. Concentrate on combining what you see on the diagrams (the task nodes) with what you've heard, and you should be able to build a process narrative that accurately describes the process taking place.
Judgment	A large part of being an expert "co-pilot" is being able to determine what needs to be captured, and to distinguish the needed data from other information that arises during the discussion. Many times in a discovery session a SME will get caught up in an explanation that contains a lot of information which is not really applicable to the immediate work you are doing. You are not there to capture full descriptions of the job functions of everybody in the room. You only want to capture information that belongs to the project's business requirements. Any extraneous information captured means there is that much more for the readers of the document to wade through to get to the real requirements. However, it is not your job to cut somebody off and tell them that the information they are providing, while it might be important, is not useful in the document. Leave managing the room up to the "Pilot", who will step in if the discussion is getting off track.
Verification	Don't be afraid to interrupt, stop the discussion, and insure that what you've captured is what has been said. The information that you are capturing must represent what was said – you are building the definitive record of the business requirements. If you're not sure, double-check with the people that know best – the subject-matter experts. Be sure to discuss your 'interruption option' with the "Pilot" before the discovery session starts. Agree on the best way to verify your information where required, and try to stick to that method. Don't step on any toes. However, do not interrupt the discussion to add your own two cents worth regarding the business process. As the "co-pilot" you are not one of the subject-matter experts – that's why they are in the room.

	If you have a vested interest in the outcome of the session, do not agree to be the "co-pilot". If you're talking, you can't be listening or recording, and you'll very quickly find that you're falling behind in the capture of information. Your writing will also be biased, even if it is unintentional.
Teamwork	You and the "Pilot" are a team. Do your best to use your knowledge of this approach to business system analysis to know the direction in which the discussion could be heading, so you're not caught by surprise. Be ready to read back anything you've captured, at any time. If you have any questions about what is drawn or annotated on a *Write On – Cling On* sheet, ask the "Pilot" right away.
The Business Rules Table	Capturing the business rules through the BUSINESS RULES TABLE can be the fastest moving part of the discovery session, and this makes it difficult for the "co-pilot". Don't be afraid to interrupt the session, politely, and insure you've got the right information captured – the notation of cardinality will be there (on the *Write On – Cling On* sheets or whiteboards) at the end of the day, but the verbs used to structure the questions and examples that are used aren't captured anywhere except by you. To reconstruct these after the sessions can be very challenging. Keep track of the verb structure used for each intersection cell, or you will have a lot of trouble documenting the rules later.
Technical Details	The business requirements concern the "<u>what</u>" and not the "<u>how</u>". It is not a technical specification. It is a business specification. That being said, there are times during discovery sessions when there are things mentioned that might not be considered to be business requirements, but might be information that's needed to populate the database once it is complete. Example: An Object called GAS TANK has been defined, with attributes such as *height*, *width*, *depth*, *location*, *weight*, *date entered into inventory*, and *capacity*. One of the SMEs mentions, *"Well, none of our tanks can hold more than <x amount>. Ever."* Although this is a piece of technical data (which is certainly implementation dependent, since it could change in the future), it could save some time at a later point in the project if this fact is noted now, and it won't take long to record it as part of the business requirements. The way to get around the "physical" nature of this data is to just enter it as a note in the description of the attribute (*capacity*, in this example).
Five Phrases	You have learned five phrases or words that will help you in building your process narratives: 1. **"For each …"** 2. **"Periodically …"** 3. **"Determine …"** 4. **"Remember (or record) …"** 5. **"Find (or identify) …"**

Don't limit yourself to these particular phrases when building your narratives, but they may come in very handy if you find you can't think of how to word what you've just heard.

In addition to the word "Find" another word that might be helpful is "Identify". For example, when making a sale you want to remember who made the sale, but you don't need any sales person information and you don't need to record anything about the salesperson. In this case, you might say, *"Identify the* **SALESPERSON** *who made the sale."*

The real key to being a successful expert "co-pilot" is to practice what you've learned. You'll find that the more you scribe, the better you'll be, and the easier it is to hear everything that's being said. You might even find, with lots of practice, that you can listen to two (or even three) conversations at the same time and pick out what's important in each of them. (Ideally, there should only ever be one conversation taking place in the room at the same time, but we all know that this isn't reality.)

Lastly, know the methodology you're learning. Not just learn it, but know it. Internalize it. Because if you know how all of the information that you're hearing in a discovery session fits together, you'll spend much less time thinking about where to put what you've heard – and you'll miss less. Session participants will be absolutely amazed by how you can capture so much information, and that you can so accurately describe their business processes.

9. The System Requirements Specification
– The Bridge from Business Requirements to Code

Contents

This section has nothing to do with the practice of business system requirements, agile or otherwise. However, we need to discuss what happens to the BUSINESS REQUIREMENTS DOCUMENT. If business requirements are documented in such a way that it satisfies only the needs of the business people, we have then failed to communicate effectively with the technical team. Remember that the technical team – the software engineers – are also part of the project team. And this is where they come in.

The SYSTEM REQUIREMENTS SPECIFICATION is an expansion of the BUSINESS REQUIREMENTS DOCUMENT. To describe the system solution design, details must be added to the specification that explains the business requirements. The SYSTEM REQUIREMENTS SPECIFICATION identifies the technology platforms, hardware and software, screens and document design, database requirements, interface requirements, essential performance criteria, and the checks and balances needed in the implemented system. In other words, it defines the "how" of the business requirements.

If the software for the project is being acquired as commercial-off-the-shelf (COTS) software, we do not need to expand the business requirements. In this case, much of the solution design doesn't have to be done, since the software vendor will present their own solution, mostly. This may also be true if you plan on outsourcing the system design to a consulting company. However, we do need to expand the business requirements if we are going to custom build the software internally or if we outsource it to a consulting firm for software engineering only (i.e., we do the system design; they do the code and implementation).

To custom build, we must first complete the prescription for the database design, based on the business requirements.

9.1 The Rx for Database Design

Each of the BUSINESS RULES TABLES that was done with the **Business Process Diagrams** is a prescription for access to information based on the needs of the business. In addition to being the source of 'BRT Questions', the BUSINESS RULES TABLE is also a table that answers the question, *"... can we get there from here?"*.

From a database design perspective, when all the BUSINESS RULES TABLES are combined into a single composite table, and Objects are defined and attributed with data required to support the business, and all data are attributed to Objects based on the 5 Rules of Business Data[42], then we have the beginnings of a Conceptual Data Model – all done with transparency during business systems analysis.

A normalized[43] Conceptual Data Model accomplishes a number of things:

- Provides the prescription for physical database design.

- Provides a stable data model that represents the essential structure of the information required by the business, independent of system design.

- Allows for easy assessment of changes in data structure and access based on changes in business needs.

- Ensures a correct, flexible, consistent and easily understood model of the organization's information structure.

- Enables effective communication between clients, subject-matter experts, systems management, consultants, database designers, and software engineers.[44]

- Enables possible integration of several Conceptual Data Models across the enterprise, or across different business areas.

The Conceptual Data Model is a view of the "bigger picture" – in the form of a composite diagram[45] – and tells the software engineers how Objects of related information are logically joined, and how to get from one Object to another to find related information.

In the example on the next page, we show where the Conceptual Data Model comes from, and how the notation in the BUSINESS RULES TABLE converts into a diagram. The only thing that remains is to resolve the many-to-many relationships between Objects.

---

[42] See Part 4.4: The 5 Rules of Business Data.

[43] "Normalization" is the process of removing all forms of redundant data attributes from Objects, including data items hiding under different names (aliases).

[44] Clients, subject-matter experts, non-technical staff and even IT management can refer to the BUSINESS RULES TABLE or the plain-language business rules written under each Object, while technical staff and database designers can refer to the Conceptual Data Model.

[45] See the earlier discussion of the "bigger picture"; Part 7.3, Are Composite Diagrams Still OK?

So, where does the Conceptual Data Model come from?

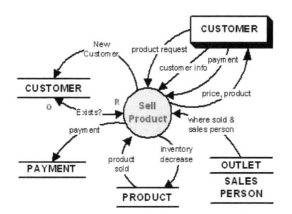

Fig. 9-1: Business Process Diagram for "Sell Product"

The above diagrams result in a BUSINESS RULES TABLE, as below.

	BRT	Salesperson	Customer	Outlet	Product	Payment
1	Salesperson		N,0	1,N	N	N
1	Customer	1,N,0		1,N	1,N,0	1,N,0
1	Outlet	N	N		N	N
1	Product	1,N,0	1,N,0	1,N		1,N,0
1	Payment	1,N	1	1	1,N	

This BRT, in turn, leads to an Object model, as below, using Chen Notation.

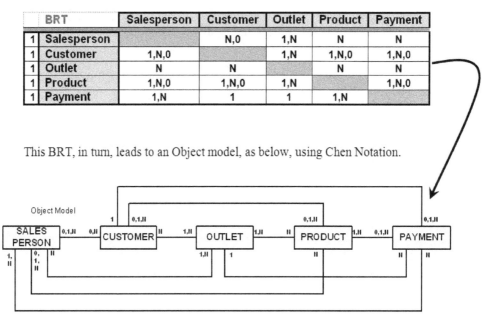

Fig. 9-2: Business Rules Table with corresponding ER diagram using Chen Notation

The preceding diagram uses Chen notation (0,1,N)[46], which is pretty well universally understood by database professionals. Many software tools, however, use Bachman Notation[47] (the "crowsfoot" notation) which is only understood by technical folks and others who don't understand the meaning of 0, 1 and N. The diagram below shows how Bachman Notation illustrates the same thing as the preceding diagram.

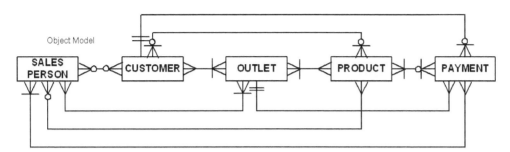

Fig. 9-3: Object diagram with Crow's Foot Notation

To move toward a database solution, database analysts or designers must accomplish all of the following, or our efforts will be wasted. They can use the information that's part of the BUSINESS REQUIREMENTS DOCUMENT to accomplish all of this.

- Using the individual BUSINESS RULES TABLES, the database analyst should create a single consolidate BUSINESS RULES TABLE.

- From the single consolidate BUSINESS RULES TABLE, create a composite Object diagram, as illustrated in Figs. 9-1 and 9-2, using Chen or Bachman or other suitable notation.

- Using the Object definitions already completed, make sure that every Object has a unique identifier (primary key).

- Using the composite BUSINESS RULES TABLE, make sure every Object that intersects with another Object in the table has a foreign key joining it to the intersecting Object; and that any foreign key is multi-valued ("mv") if the cardinality in the intersecting cell contains an "N".

- Resolve the many-to-many (*n-ary*) relationships between Objects in the resulting Object model (see Figs. 9-1 and 9-2).

- Locate and resolve individual multi-valued data items ("mv") that are dependent on multi-valued Objects.

---

[46] Dr. Peter Chen published (in March 1976) his article *The Entity-Relationship Model – Toward a Unified View of Data* (ACM Transactions on Database Systems). He followed this with *The Entity-Relationship Model: A Basis for the Enterprise View of Data* (1977 National Computer Conference).

[47] Charles W. Bachman is the prolific author of over 30 technical papers and articles, and scores of lectures on database issues over a 40 year period. His entire inventory of lectures, correspondence and project notes were given to the Charles Babbage Institute in 1996.

- Document the known <u>business rules</u> of the individual data attributes (e.g., allowable values, data type, security, business constraints, etc.).

- Integrate the resulting project-based Object model with other existing Object models, resolving overlaps, omissions and inconsistencies (e.g., different Object or data names, and conflicting rules).

The fact that database professionals can directly use the business requirements means they will take less time understanding database design requirements for the project.

Converting the BUSINESS RULES TABLES and Object definitions into a Conceptual Data Model is not usually the responsibility of business system analysts. This is normally done by database analysts or designers. So why would they want to do this? There are several reasons, some of which we dealt with earlier.

The Conceptual Data Model[48] – as well as being a prescription for access to data based on business requirements – is also a picture that answers the question, *"Can we get there from here?"* The answer to this question is always the database designer's primary concern. While it is also true that the cells of the BUSINESS RULES TABLE can answer this question, most technical database professionals are simply more comfortable with the kind of diagram below to illustrate the Conceptual data model.

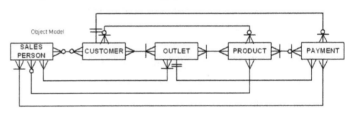

Fig. 9-4: Object diagram with Crow's Foot Notation

Another clear purpose of the Conceptual data model is to arrive at a database design that meets the needs of the business. But, with the objective of processing efficiency, this may be more challenging than just implementing the pure business view. In other words, there may be some 'denormalization' of data needed[49].

---

[48] The Conceptual Data Model, to be complete, must consist of the Object Model (see Fig. 9-4), Object definitions, data attributes belonging to Objects, primary identifiers for each Object, and foreign keys; must be normalized, and must have many-to-many relationships resolved.

[49] **Denormalization** is the process of adding controlled redundancies to the design of a database to improve efficiency. In a true relational model (a "true normal form") there can be no **totals** or **status flags**. A total is the sum of other fields or records; therefore a total represents a duplication of data that already exists. Accordingly, a **total** would violate Business Data Rule # 1 (*"Attribute the data item to the Object it describes best, <u>and to no other object</u>"*). Denormalization – which should only be done at design time when all the facts about accesses, volumes and throughput rates are known – recognizes that it is sometimes better to build in "controlled redundancy" such as a **total** to eliminate the need to find all the records.

The same applies to a **status flag**. We usually use **status flags** to substitute for something else. Anything that "substitutes for something else" is redundant, also violating Business Data Rule # 1. Since the business analyst knows nothing about what would constitute good database design (yet), they should not build in any bias based on convention. Later, when all the facts are in, the database design specialist can, if needed, 'denormalize' the records by putting in **status flags**. Then again, maybe not, if it doesn't make for good design.

Also, a consolidated Object Model will make it evident which Objects are the "busiest" and therefore the most likely to need ongoing maintenance. "Busiest" means most relationships to other Objects. The Object that has a relationship with the greatest number of other Objects is the "busiest".

Such extended relationships with other Objects also usually means that the "busy" Object participates in many *business events*. Regardless of the amount of data warehoused, it is likely that a "busy" Object will be the most often accessed under different circumstances (or in different *business events*) – to create, view, change and eventually to retire or archive the Object. By definition, this means such Objects are more prone to necessary maintenance.

Ultimately, based on a composite BUSINESS RULES TABLE, Object definitions, data attributes and *keys*, the database design specialist can create the Conceptual Data Model to illustrate the *access to information* required by the business.

9.2 How to Find and Allocate Foreign Keys

A 'foreign key' is an Object's unique identifier contained within another Object. The foreign key provides the ability to find information from other related Objects to support the information needs of a specified business process. A foreign key is essentially an index or a pointer that joins one Object to other related Objects.

The "joining" of objects in this manner eliminates the need for data repetition or redundancy. Foreign keys can be single-valued (i.e., point to one occurrence of another Object); or they can be multi-valued (i.e., point to several instances of another Object, using the notation "mv"). The ratio of occurrences ('cardinality') between Objects is determined from the BUSINESS RULES TABLE, which in turn specifies the foreign keys needed for the Conceptual Data Model.

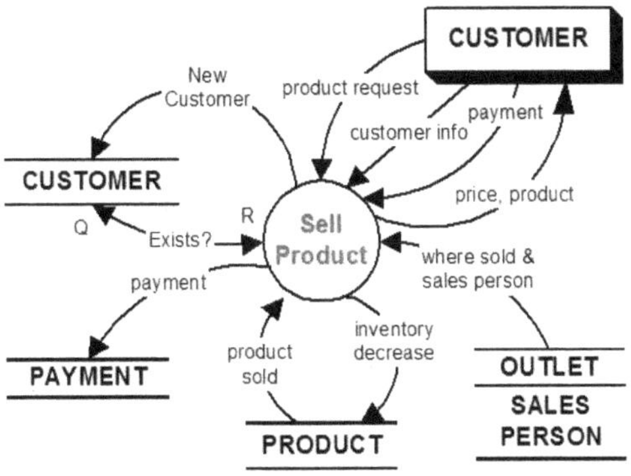

Fig. 9-5: Business process with related Objects

It is implicit in each diagram – such as the one on the right – that a "relationship" exists between each (or most) of the Objects in the diagram. To locate the related Objects and data requires that each Object will have a unique identifier and that their respective unique identifiers connect all related Objects. The specific relationships ('cardinality' or 'ratio of occurrences') are determined when the BUSINESS RULES TABLE is created.

BRT	Salesperson	Customer	Outlet	Product	Payment
1 Salesperson		N,0	1,N	N	N
1 Customer	1,N, 0		1,N	1,N,0	1,N,0
1 Outlet	N	N		N	N
1 Product	1,N,0	1,N,0	1,N		1,N,0
1 Payment	1,N	1	1	1,N	

Fig. 9-6: Business Rules Table with relationships between Objects identified

If a value appears in a cell in the BRT, then there must be a relationship between the anchor and intersecting Objects. If "**N**" appears, there must be more than one instance of the intersecting Object that is joined to a single instance of the anchor Object; therefore we put "**mv**" behind the foreign key.

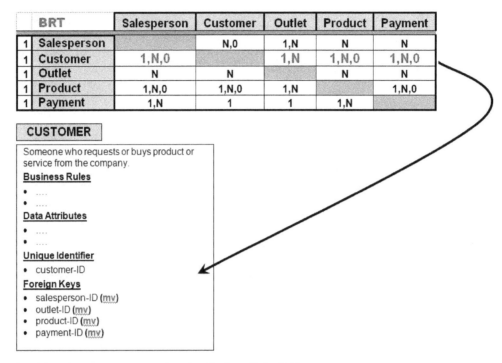

BRT	Salesperson	Customer	Outlet	Product	Payment
1 Salesperson		N,0	1,N	N	N
1 Customer	1,N,0		1,N	1,N,0	1,N,0
1 Outlet	N	N		N	N
1 Product	1,N,0	1,N,0	1,N		1,N,0
1 Payment	1,N	1	1	1,N	

CUSTOMER

Someone who requests or buys product or service from the company.
Business Rules
•   ....
•   ....
Data Attributes
•   ....
•   ....
Unique Identifier
• customer-ID
Foreign Keys
• salesperson-ID (mv)
• outlet-ID (mv)
• product-ID (mv)
• payment-ID (mv)

Fig. 9-7: Object with Foreign Keys based on Business Rules Table

The subject of this book is business system analysis, not database design. Accordingly, business systems analysts do not normally determine the physical key or its properties. That's the job of the database design specialist. Therefore, all keys, when identified as part of the Object definition, are given the name of the Object with "ID" added as a suffix (such as **customer-ID**). If another name is needed (it's not) then the database designers can change it later.

9.3 Today's Software Engineering Challenges

Database design, program design and code generation (software engineering) are not the problem today, especially with access to good tools. Software development can be rapid and effective with Object-based programming tools and relational database structures.

Today's top challenges – as always – are:

- **Determining** complete and accurate business requirements – quickly.
- **Identifying** the technologies that will enable the business requirements.
- **Integrating** several technologies, often in new and different ways.

We have already dealt with the first point – complete and accurate business requirement, fast. But the business requirements must migrate to a technology architecture and solution design. The question becomes, how do we do that, using the business requirements as the foundation?

There is simply no silver bullet to solve system design issues. How we design a system – what we make it look like, and how we make it perform – is still a matter of knowledge, imagination and skill. And perhaps imagination is the most important of this trio. One thing for sure is that we must imagine how something can be done before we can go about designing it (which is akin to inventing a solution). It's not possible to design a solution or a way of doing things that we know little about. For example, imagine wanting to implement some of your organization's business applications using Enterprise Cloud Computing. But you could not entertain that thought if you had little knowledge about how Cloud computing worked; and you couldn't imagine it if you didn't create a mental picture of how it might work.

I'm not going to say much about "system design", since that isn't the subject of this book, except for a few words about the transition from the BUSINESS REQUIREMENTS DOCUMENT to a solution design. Suffice it to say that today's programmers truly are software engineers. They are also 'imagineers' who must create interactive components all the way through to the implementation of a system – but based entirely on the business requirements.

9.4 Software Development without Risk

At the beginning of time, when wheels were square, a system designer would create a document (well, sometimes) and write a narrative for it in something like pseudocode until it was the size of a Victorian novel. Then the system designer would toss this large and wonderful document over the wall to the programmers. The programmers would dutifully produce the code based on the inherent design and structured logic of what they got. Many are still doing this today.

The only problem with this approach for the programmers was that the system design wasn't theirs. The specification (which was really more like a generalization) contained the programming logic and design of the analyst/designer rather than the person who would work on developing the software. Even if there might have been different or better ways of designing systems, programmers rarely had the opportunity to find out. They obediently regurgitated the software design they were given. This is very similar to the way a letter, back in the day, used to be dictated to a secretary. As a result, the secretary became very good at typing what was dictated, but didn't have much opportunity to practice the skill of writing the letters in the first place. The same applied to programmers.

Developing software directly from the elements of the BUSINESS REQUIREMENTS DOCUMENT enables a professional programmer today to develop his or her system design skills, as well as facilitating faster delivery of code, with very little risk. Programmers with less experience can be guided to become more experienced professionals, while we focus the design effort and contain the risk to one business process, or group of related processes, at a time. This opportunity to practice with guidance and focus on individual business processes leads to much higher quality – of delivered systems *and* system professionals.

Let's look at the elements needed for system design that have already been gathered during the business requirements analysis. We'll use the process **"Pay a Supplier"** as an example. These are the five basic elements we've already gathered.

1. **Interface requirements** (with a person, an organization or another system).
2. **Software and peopleware tasks** (functional decomposition).
3. **Data for each task.**
4. **Data accesses.**
5. **Test cases for business rules.**

Let's address each of these six items.

1. **Interface requirements** (with a person, an organization or another system, internally or externally).

    Requirements for interfaces with the outside world have already been identified as part of the **"Pay Supplier" Business Process Diagram**. Since we already know the primary interface is with suppliers, what the software engineering team has to decide is … how should we send payments to them? What technology will we employ? Snail-mail? Electronic funds transfer? Whatever is decided affects the design of the system and must be documented.

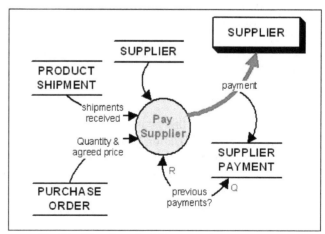

Fig. 9-8: "Pay Supplier" Business Process Diagram
identifies external interface.

2. Software and peopleware tasks.

This also has already been done and is contained in the descriptive narrative of what the process does. You will recall that we went through a process of functional decomposition earlier to be able to write the narrative.

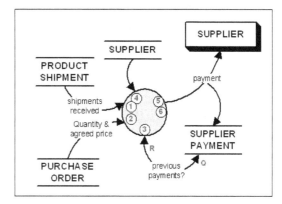

Fig. 9-9: "Pay Supplier" Business Process Diagram identifies software tasks.

The narrative that accompanies the **"Pay Supplier"** process is based on identifying the tasks that make up the process. Most tasks identified by this kind of functional decomposition turn into software tasks. With the development tools currently available, software engineers should be able to work with this directly without much refinement. Since so much has already been determined during the front-end business analysis, this truly fosters an "agile" development environment.

While I'm of the mind that software engineers can work very effectively from these process diagrams and narratives (along with Object data attributes and behavioral business rules), there are other schools of thought that suggest an expanded and more formal technical 'Use Case' should be developed at this point.

Point Form Style

1. Find **product shipments** not completely paid.

2. Determine the amount owed, based on the amount of **product** received and the agreed price.

3. Deduct any previous **payments** made against the same **purchase order**.

4. Find the **supplier's** location and preferred method of payment.

5. Pay the **supplier**.

6. Record the **payment**.

Fig. 9-10: Point form narrative based on tasks

3. Data for each task.

Data attributes for each of the Objects that support the **"Pay Supplier"** process should have been identified when the business requirements were being done. What now remains is to look at the data attributes for each Object in the process and determine the specific data that's need for the individual software tasks (identified above).

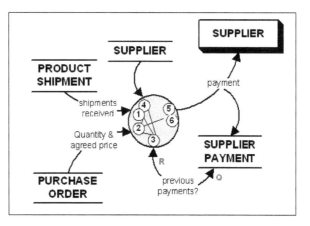

Fig. 9-11: "Pay Supplier" Business Process Diagram with data specific to the process

The fact that we have Objects with all their data attributes is not entirely useful from a software development perspective. All of the data that defines an Object will not usually be needed for a single specific process, such as **"Pay Supplier"**, nor will all the Object's data be needed to satisfy a specific task. The data we have attributed so far to an Object represents everything that's needed to support all the business processes it participates in. Accordingly, each participating Object's data should be deconstructed to identify (a) the data needed to support each individual process, and (b) the data items needed to support a specific task.

Business analysts can help this process by identifying each Object's data that's needed for a specific process; but leave task data decomposition to the software engineers.

4. **Data accesses.**

This, too, was done when we completed our analysis of business requirements. Below is the BUSINESS RULES TABLE for the **"Pay Supplier"** process. The use of the 'BRT Questions' was instrumental in determining business rules. Database design specialist can now turn this table into an Object Model, and then a Conceptual Data Model.

	BRT	Supplier	Supplier Payment	Purchase Order	Product Shipment
1	Supplier	---	1, N, 0	1, N, 0	1, N, 0
1	Supplier Payment	1	---	1, N	1, N
1	Purchase Order	1	1, N, 0	---	1, N, 0
1	Product Shipment	1	1, N	1, N	---

Fig. 9-12: Business Rules Table for "Pay Supplier" Business Process
Diagram with data specific to the process

In the **Business Process Diagram** below you'll notice the relationship between Objects is evident when we look closely at the tasks required. These relationships necessitate *foreign keys* in the Objects that participate in the process, so these Objects can join to other Objects to fulfill the data needs specific to the process. This in turn enables us to find a **SUPPLIER** record for a specific **PURCHASE ORDER**, or a set of **SUPPLIER PAYMENTs** for a specific **SUPPLIER** and **PURCHASE ORDER**. Each of the required *foreign keys* is documented in the Objects that participate in the process.

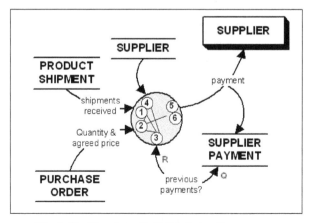

Fig. 9-13: "Pay Supplier" Business Process
Diagram with data specific to the process

5. **Tests cases for business rules.**

As the software is developed we will also need tests that address functionality. Most functionality is based on what Objects are allowed to do, or not to do, under specific circumstances (*business events*). How do we build these tests? All business rules specific to an Object are documented under that Object. These rules came from the BUSINESS RULES TABLE.

Tests can be set up for each of the business rules for an Object (see the business rules example on the right, Fig. 9-14). All business rules tests go directly to functionality. Therefore, testing the business rules of all the Objects in a project results in a complete functional test. Life becomes a lot easier in terms of writing test cases, since these test cases have already been uncovered when doing the business analysis for the project.

SUPPLIER

Business Rules

- We can receive one or more **PAYABLE ITEM**s from a **SUPPLIER**.

- We may never receive a **PAYABLE ITEM** from a **SUPPLIER** (e.g., may go out of business before we order a product; may not have been able to fill the only order from us).

- We can pay one or more **PAYABLE ITEM**s for a **SUPPLIER**.

- We may never have a **PAYABLE ITEM** to pay for a **SUPPLIER** (e.g., may go out of business before we order a product; may not have been able to fill the only order from us).

- We can issue one or more **PAYMENT**s to a **SUPPLIER**.

- We may never issue a **PAYMENT** to a **SUPPLIER** (e.g., we just didn't order anything from them).

Fig. 9-14: "SUPPLIER" Object with Business Rules

There are clearly many other things to consider when engineering the software, but much information has already been gathered during the business requirements analysis.

9.5 How to Build in Controls – Checks and Balances

I have carefully avoided reference to controls and various checks and balances up to now. That's because one of the essentials of getting a high quality business document done quickly (without technological bias) is to avoid thinking about *__how__* something should be done, and to focus strictly on *__what__* is required. All controls applied to a business process are based on specific ways of doing things – by machine or by human, real time or not, centralized or distributed. Controls, by their very nature, are essentially implementation dependent and therefore physical. Therefore, they are to be built in during solution design, not during business requirements analysis.

Any controls specified prior to a project's solution design can only be speculation. Below is a list of the general control issues that should be addressed on every project, once the software engineering team takes the project forward, whether by software acquisition or a custom-built solution.

These questions must be asked in relation to each and every business process done for the project. While some of these questions may not be relevant to some processes on a specific project, each must still be asked. Since the questions are generic, software engineers will have to use their imagination in some cases and make them specific to the project.

How do the software engineers make these general questions specific to a project? Now it's their turn to work with project subject-matter experts, and they should be able to answer the question *"Where is this documented?"* for each process in the project.

1. Is data capture and its identification completed?

2. Is control established close to the transaction source and carried through the entire system or business area?

3. Does input bear evidence of authorization?

4. Are error prevention and detection procedures in place at all input stages?

5. Has completeness and accuracy of all data input been assured?

6. Are procedures for early detection of hardware, software or peopleware malfunction in place?

7. Are there methods in place to measure successful processing (adding, removing, changing, and retiring)?

8. Are there appropriate uses of edits?

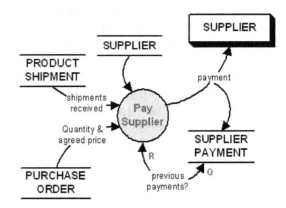

1. Find **product shipments** not completely paid.

2. Determine the amount owed, based on the amount of **product** received and the agreed price.

3. Deduct any previous **payments** made against the same **purchase order**.

4. Find the **supplier**'s location and preferred method of payment.

5. Pay the **supplier**.

6. Record the **payment**.

Fig. 9-15: "Pay Supplier" process and narrative.

9. Are there appropriate checking, distribution and reconciliation procedures for information output and display?

10. Are there appropriate error correction procedures?

11. Are there procedures for forward and backward tracing and identification of data?

Do the software engineers have to ask every question of every process? No, they only need to ask the questions that apply to a process. In other words, for any given process, many of the 11 preceding questions simply don't apply; therefore, don't ask them.

The principles of good checks and balances also require that most processes have one or more **control tasks**, each of which must be added to the process narratives.

Checks and balances also come in the flavor of **control data attributes** that must be added to Objects for the purpose of audit or management trails. These control data attributes all result from control tasks within processes.

Control processes, tasks, and data attributes should be reviewed in detail with the correct subject matter-experts.

10. End Thoughts – What Does "Agile" Really Mean?

Contents

The keys to success with this approach to business requirements analysis includes many other best practices that have not been explored in this book. They are better left to other volumes, since this book is just about this particular approach to business systems analysis. However, I do want to conclude with a few comments on areas that participants in our workshops have brought out.

10.1 How to Source a 3rd Party Solution

Sourcing commercial off-the-shelf ("COTS") software can be a very painful and difficult exercise. It seems that most vendors have just one reply to questions about functionality and compatibility: *"Yes, our solution can do that!"*

When an organization issues an RFI, RFP or RFQ to a vendor, its first objective should be to eliminate those vendors that can't support their business requirements. Generalized statements outlining the business requirements won't accomplish this. In my experience, an effective way of clearing out the wannabees from the professionals is to give vendors a reasonably detailed statement of business requirements, which they can then assess against their own software product. This enables them to make specific reference to your requirements in addition to doing their usual selling job.

We have found the following approach to acquiring a COTS solution to be effective.

1. Identify a list of vendors who claim to have a software solution suitable to your business requirements (your 'long list', perhaps 6 to 10 vendors).

2. Conduct a ½-day or 1-day *Project Scope Blitz* to identify the *business events* the new COTS system must handle.

Fig. 10-1: Abbreviated Business Event list from Project Scope Blitz

3. Prepare a <u>Request for Information</u> ('RFI') consisting of the following:

(a) System Objectives (general introduction and overview).

(b) Client Community Summary (who will use the system, which departments or groups, and where).

(c) System Interfaces (required interfaces to your existing systems).

(d) Hardware Interfaces (required interfaces to your existing technology and networks)

(e) Software Interfaces (required compatibility with your existing software)

(f) Communications Interfaces (required interfaces to your existing communications networks)

(g) Other Interfaces (anything not mentioned above)

(h) Audit, Control & Security Requirements (statements of required control and security levels)

(i) Performance Criteria (minimum acceptable performance levels)

(j) System Required Business Events (from the <u>Business Event list</u> developed in your *Project Scope Blitz* – this specifies required functionality)

Issue the RFI to the long list of vendors (6 to 10) and request their response by a specified deadline. Ask that their response specifically address each of the items listed – items (b) through (i) – and ask how their solution meets your specific environmental requirements.

Request that they also specifically address each of the *business events* on your list – item (j) – stating whether their solution handles each *business events* or not, but without details. Explain that short-listed vendors will have an opportunity to do detailed presentations.

Their responses should be written and emailed to you. Only short-listed vendors should be permitted to demonstrate their solution.

Ask them to include a cost overview (at a high level), including potential conversion costs for existing data, all hardware and software acquisition or lease costs, and the cost of training on the new system; as well as a potential installation schedule, conversion and full training of personnel, with a final 'up-and-running' target date. (This sounds like a lot of work for a vendor, but for the investment required by the buyer, it is a reasonable effort on their part.)

4. From the responses, shorten the list of vendors to two or three only. Notify those that have been successfully short-listed, and let them know about the next steps.

5. Ask each of the 2 or 3 short-listed vendors to demonstrate their system's functionality, based only on each *business event* stipulated in the original RFI.

6. After the event-specific demonstrations, select a vendor, negotiate terms, and acquire or lease the selected COTS solution, if one of them meets your needs.

These steps and the requirement for vendors to demonstrate their solutions based on individual *business events* helps to keep them focused on the facts, and prevents the usual "dog and pony" show that's intended to solicit an emotional response to their proposal. This approach tells the vendors that you know exactly what you want, and that you have analyzed your requirements very carefully.

10.2 Keep a Master Business Events List

There are a limited number of *business events* in the world, and – yes – it is possible to collect your own list suitable to your organization and industry. Our organization has collected thousands of different and unique *business events* from all kinds of different projects. This kind of list helps business analysts to conduct a comprehensive *Project Scope Blitz* with clients and – usually in less than a day – determine the size, ownership and duration of the requirements analysis for any project. By extracting project *business events* from a Master Business Events List, an analyst will be able to quickly preview them with clients, as part of the *Project Scope Blitz*, which will lead to a complete project-specific list even faster. Any organization, public or private, can accomplish this if the following is done:

- Collect and keep a Master Business Events List of all the *business events* you define for your organization, as you apply these methods on different projects. Categorize the *business events* by business area.

- For each new project, determine what *business events* on your Master Business Events List might be reusable on the new project. Do this as follows:

1. Make a copy of your Master Business Events List.
2. Remove all those *business events* that clearly do not apply.
3. Change the **nouns** in each *business event* statement to be the most likely nouns that will appear in the new project.
4. Select the *business events* that look like they will fit the new project.

Use this list of likely *business events* as input to your first step – the *Project Scope Blitz*. This gives you a good head start and saves a lot of time.

10.3 Apply Weinberg's 'Lump Law'

Partition the effort to minimize complexity. Break the project up into small, understandable and manageable pieces. Don't try to lump everything under one big, all-inclusive *business event*. Develop one business process at a time. Partition groups of data into small, meaningful Objects. Focus on the individual questions from the BUSINESS RULES TABLE. Find one Object and ask one question at a time.

10.4 How to Fail without Really Trying Hard

There are lots of ways to really fail without too much effort. There are also lots of ways to win, which we have already discussed at length. Here's a short list of ways to get it dead wrong.

■ Avoid the direct involvement of clients and subject-matter experts. (They really do have answers; we just have to ask them the right questions.)

■ Guess at what the client might want. (Ask them, they really do have the answers.)

■ Imagine that the client or SME doesn't know their business. (They do, you just have to ask them the questions right.)

■ Worry about implementation issues too soon. (Figure out *what* before *how*.)

10.5 What Does an 'Agile' Environment Really Mean?

An "agile" project or agile environment is really a frame of mind, rather than a process. It's a paradigm or mental model of how we can approach our work. It's certainly not a methodology. An agile environment simply means, allow project teams to adapt working practices according to the needs of the individual project. The emphasis must be on delivering business value early, and then to continually improve it. "Delivering business value early" does not just refer to implementing software; it means to deliver value in how you interact with your business partners, clients and subject-matter experts … and how you are seen to do so.

It also means don't do anything you don't have to do and try to think outside the box to minimize doing things in a certain way just because they have always been done that way. But, to accomplish this you also have to recognize that (a) you are doing something that you may not need to do; and (b) what you're doing is only being done that way because it has always been done that way. In other words, you have to be aware of the conflict, which is easier said than done. If you're not an expert in the conventional approach, then how would you know if a different approach is better? What's your benchmark? What do you compare to?

"Agile" doesn't mean doing something differently just because you can do it differently. "Agile" doesn't mean doing less of the project, just to beat the clock. "Agile" means knowing which best practices really are "best" rather than conventional. There are lots of so-called best practices heralded by maintainers of the *status quo*. Bear in mind that "best practices" have usually been around a long time for them to be accepted as best practices by the community.

Also, "agile" does not mean chaos on the project team. It means finding the straightest road to the planned destination, and then taking that road even when others think you should take the most circuitous and bureaucratic route possible.

Dr. Christian Mann[50] said it very well when he wrote, *"Don't produce a document when you don't know what it's for ... Don't duplicate [information] ... Don't produce anything you don't need later ... [Always] produce what the customer wants."* This is the essence of an agile environment. But it only addresses documentation. There's more.

"Agile" also means learning new methods and techniques, not blindly sticking with methods that haven't changed in years, and without any indication things are getting better. It also means to not avoid doing what's required (some of the administrative things) just because it seems faster that way. Times change; methods change.

The Agile Manifesto[51] stipulates the following as core values:

- **Individuals and interactions** over processes and tools. (I completely agree.)
- **Working software** over comprehensive documentation. (This doesn't need to be a trade-off. I believe you can have both, really fast.)
- **Customer collaboration** over contract negotiation. (I agree.)
- **Responding to change** over following a plan. (100% in agreement.)

Granted, some individuals and organizations have taken this too literally (which is always a danger when something is labeled a "manifesto"), which has led to challenged projects because of lack of professional discipline. There's more to a project than fast code. But when you read the Agile Manifesto completely you quickly discover that it is sound, well reasoned, and embodies core principles that make good sense.

Above all, if you want to foster an agile environment, involve your clients and subject-matter experts in requirements discovery, and involve them a lot.

Your business requirements documentation should be in business language, and as brief as possible. And a client should not be expected to learn the technology you're using.

Recognize that you serve your client – whether that client is part of an internal group or a customer outside your organization – and you need their help and active participation to understand their requirements.

---

[50] Dr. Christian Mann is a member of the Scrum Alliance, a philosopher and an IT consultant based in Germany.

[51] The complete Agile Alliance Manifesto can be found at www.AgileAlliance.org

Recognize that requirements will change as your client understands better the information they want and can have. It's not a bad thing to "change your mind" when you have more information. As the famous British economist John Maynard Keynes once said, *"When the facts change, I change my opinion. What do you do?"*[52] The issue is how to deal with those changes, since history tells us that change is good. This is what learning is all about, so when a client or subject-matter expert changes their mind, don't think *"not on my project."* This is actually a move in the right direction.

I believe very strongly that requirements analysis should be focused on individual *business events*, and their supporting processes, rather than trying to write a novel about how a system should work. By focusing on the individual *business event* and its supporting processes and data, you can respond very quickly to any change that is needed. It minimizes the complexity of changing page after page in a serial novel. In event-based analysis, as I've described in this book, there is no redundancy; therefore, there is no domino effect[53] in the documentation. It allows the business analyst to respond rapidly, while it gives the client or subject-matter expert the confidence to contribute without fear of criticism of "constantly changing their mind". Also, the direct 'BRT Questions' keeps them highly focused, and they won't wander all over the scope of the requirements.

In my opinion, "agile" means being fast and responsive, but without chaos and risk. An event-based approach to business requirements analysis is extremely fast, and without risk. The alternative – conventional system analysis that usually takes a long time – often leads to abbreviated requirements analysis (*"we finished when we ran out of time"*), which in turn leads to incomplete work down the line, and perhaps costly rework later on.

Some people refer to this event-based analysis approach as a "methodology". Well, so be it. I prefer to call it a paradigm; a constructive framework.[54] While Thomas Kuhn gave paradigm its contemporary meaning, I have tried to develop this event-based analysis paradigm on his definition:

- *what* is to be observed and scrutinized
- the kind of *questions* that are supposed to be asked and probed for answers in relation to this subject
- *how* these questions are to be structured
- *how* the results of scientific investigations should be interpreted

In the end, quality of work is always directly related to education, professional development training, experience, and the quality of the methods used and thinking applied.

---

[52] Quoted in **The Economist**, 24 October 1998, page 57.

[53] A cumulative effect produced when one condition sets off a chain of similar events.

[54] Thomas Kuhn, in his controversial book *"The Structure of Scientific Revolutions"* used the term "paradigm shift". He also argued that rival paradigms are incommensurable – that is, it is not possible to understand one paradigm through the conceptual framework and terminology of another rival paradigm. I would certainly agree with that.

Use good methods and clarity of thinking. Use modern methods. Practice using these good methods and thinking. It gets better.

Keep studying. There is always more to learn.

11. Appendix – List of Terms

Agile Environment: An "agile" business analysis environment simply means, try to think outside the box to <u>minimize doing things in a certain way just because they have always been done that way</u>. "Agile" does not mean chaos on the project team. It means finding the straightest road to your destination, and then taking that road even when others think you should take the most circuitous and bureaucratic route possible.

AJAD: (Automated Joint Application Development) A JAD session is very similar to a requirements discovery session, as described in these pages. An AJAD session is an automated JAD session, conducted with the use of automation tools. Often, the most productive tool can be a simple word processor to record the information identified during a JAD or discovery session. Sometimes, tools are used to capture process and data models in real time. However, some software tools can be sufficiently complex that they can slow down the JAD discovery process and become the bottleneck. However, many organizations have found great success in conducting automated requirements discovery sessions using tools as simple as a word processor. See also **'JAD'**.

Anchor Object: An Object is an 'anchor' or 'cardinal' Object when it is used in the BUSINESS RULES TABLE to describe its relationship with other Objects and to define its business policies. It is the stable 'anchor' that is the subject of any question that is asked about its relationship with other participating Objects. This approach stipulates that every Object in a relationship is equally important (which certainly eliminates the high subjectivity of figuring out which one is *most important,* which is required by some methodologies) and therefore must be queried about its relationship with other Objects in a relationship. Since it takes two to make a relationship, each of the two Objects (from their own perspective) are the most important. Accordingly, every Object is the 'anchor' to a question. See also **'Object'**.

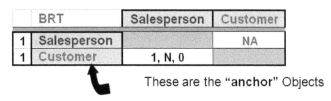

These are the "anchor" Objects

Associative Object: An associative Object is an Object identified and created to remember essential information required in response to the occurrence of a *business event*. While it has all the attributes of any other kind of Object, it is also (a) dependent on some of the other Objects that participate in the same relationship; and (b) is created from the data that arises out of the process which supports the underlying relationship, since this new data can not be found (by way of a *foreign key*) in any of the other Objects that participate in the same relationship. See also **'Object'**.

BRD: See **'Business Requirements Document'**.

Business Event: A **business event** is an essential business circumstance, condition, situation, state or external requirement that exists which the target business area must respond to or deal with in order to carry on operations to successfully support its key business objectives, goals, mission, direction and vision.

Business Interfaces Diagram: Also known as a 'Context Diagram' in some circles, this is a single process diagram representing a composite of all the *business events* and business processes that make up the whole project or target system. The Business Interfaces Diagram illustrates what the target system communicates with other businesses, organizations, systems, or entities outside its own boundary. It is the highest, most abstract view of the system.

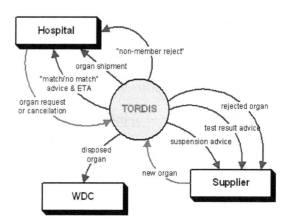

Business Process Diagram: This is an illustration of retrieval of data, the movement of data, and the recording of required data in a business process. A single Business Process Diagram can support one or more *business events*. Each diagram must also have a narrative written in plain language to describe it. Objects that appear in a diagram must also be defined, with their data attributes, as well as the business rules that govern the behavior and existence of the Objects.

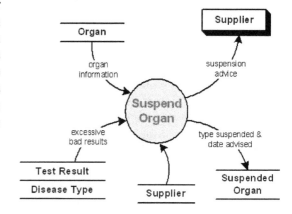

Business Requirements Document: The Business Requirement Document is all the documentation needed to represent all the business needs for a particular business area, project or system. It consists of diagrams showing all the required business processes, including descriptive narratives, Object definitions, data items that belong to Objects, and the business rules that govern the behavior and existence of the Objects. This document should be as free of technological bias as possible; i.e., it should document what is needed but not how it will be implemented.

Slaw Cable

Video-On-Demand
Business Requirements
Document

May 25

Cardinality: This is the "ratio of occurrences" between pairs of Objects; i.e., 0, 1 and N, or any combination of these. See also **'Business Rules Table'.**

<u>CASE Tool</u>: An acronym for 'Computer Assisted Software Engineering' tool.

<u>Characteristic Object</u>: When two or more *related and inseparable* data items are discovered, each having multiple values for a single instance of an Object, this data group is separated from the original Object in which it was present, to form a new and distinct Object. For example, if a **SUPPLIER** Object has several locations, then data attributes like *supplier address* and *supplier city* will be part of a multi-valued (repeating) group. This multi-valued group of data items is separated from the originating or parent Object, and named **SUPPLIER LOCATION**, and is "characteristic" of the original Object.

<u>Client</u>: A client is one of the key stakeholders on a project. The client can also be one of the project's subject-matter experts.

<u>Conceptual Data Model</u>: The Conceptual Data Model is a prescription for access to information based on the needs of the business. It is a graphic that answers the question *"... can we get there from here?"* that's asked by database designers. This diagram is created by the database analysts and designers, based on the **Business Rules Table**. To complete the Conceptual Data Model, all Objects must be attributed with data and many-to-many relationships must be resolved.

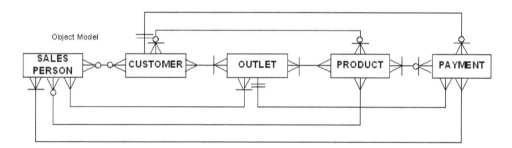

<u>Context Diagram</u>: See **'Business Interfaces Diagram'**.

<u>Data Attribute</u>: A data attribute is an element of data, which is a property of the Object to which it is attributed. A data attribute is described by a name and description, and eventually represented by a set of standard values, including sounds and images. Data attributes are required to define what must be remembered or known about each Object. See also **'Object'**.

PRODUCT

Data Attributes

- product description
- product photos & views (mv)
- examples of use (mv)
- product demonstrations (mv)
- product sounds (mv)
- reorder point
- product selling price
- volume discount available
- delivery lead time
- payment options (mv)
- product availability

Data Flow: A data flow represents the directional flow of information between a process and an Object or a Terminator.

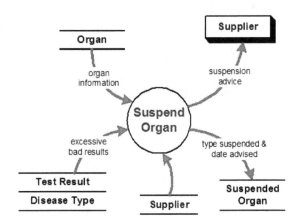

Denormalization: This is the process of adding controlled redundancies to a database design to improve efficiency. In a true relational model there can be no <u>totals</u> or <u>status flags</u>. A total is the sum of other fields or records, therefore it represents a duplication of data that already exists. A total violates Business Data Rule # 1 (*"Attribute the data item to the object it describes best, <u>and to no other object</u>"*). Denormalization – which is only done at database design time when all the facts about accesses, volumes and throughput rates are known – recognizes that it is sometimes better to build in 'controlled redundancy' such as a total to eliminate the need to read all those records. The same applies to a status flag. Status flags are often used to substitute for something else – which is clearly redundant – also violating Business Data Rule # 1. See also **'Normalization'.**

Discovery Session: See **'Requirements Discovery Session'.**

Exclusion Question (for Data): A question that identifies the consequences of excluding a data item by finding the *business event* the data item would otherwise support. See also **'Inclusion Question (for Data)'.**

Exclusion Question (for Objects): A question that identifies the consequences of excluding an Object by finding the *business event* the Object would otherwise support. See also **'Inclusion Question (for Objects)'.**

Exclusion Question (for Events): A question that identifies the consequences of excluding a *business event*. See also **'Inclusion Question (for Events)'.**

Exclusion Question (for Reports): A question that identifies the consequences of excluding a Report by finding the *business event* the Report would otherwise support. See also **'Inclusion Question (for Reports)'.**

Foreign Key: A foreign key is an Object's unique identifier contained within another Object. The foreign key provides the ability to find information from other related Objects to support the information needs of a specified business process. A foreign key is essentially an index or a pointer that 'joins' one Object to other related Objects. The 'joining' of Objects in this manner eliminates the need for redundant data repetition. A foreign key can be single-valued (i.e., point to <u>one</u> occurrence of another object); or it can be multi-valued (i.e., point to <u>several</u> instances of another Object). The ratio of occurrences (cardinality) between Objects is determined from the **Business Rules Table**.

CABLE ACCOUNT
<u>**Unique Identified**</u>
Cable Account-ID
<u>**Foreign Keys**</u>
Customer-ID (mv)
Rental-ID (mv)
Solution-ID (mv)
Promotion-ID (mv)

BRT: See **'Business Rules Table'.**

Business Rule: These are the rules that govern the behavior and existence of Objects that support the business processes. Business rules are documented as simple declaratives under each Object (to which the rule is attributed) in plain language.

SUPPLIER

Business Rules
- We can receive one or more **PAYABLE ITEM**s from a **SUPPLIER**.
- We may never receive a **PAYABLE ITEM** from a **SUPPLIER** (e.g., may go out of business before we order a product; may not have been able to fill the only order from us).

Business Rules Table: This table is a unique tool that enables the discovery of the rules that govern the behavior and existence of Objects that support the business requirements. It ensures the completeness of the business requirements by using a specific syntax to determine the questions to be asked to uncover the rules (the 'BRT Questions'). It also identifies the 'ratio of occurrences' between Objects, therefore creating a prescription for eventual database design (a Conceptual Data Model) based on the business requirements.

	BRT	Salesperson	Customer	Outlet	Product	Payment
1	Salesperson		N,0	1,N	N,0	N,0
1	Customer	1,N,0		1,N	1,N,0	1,N,0
1	Outlet	N	N		N	N
1	Product	1,N,0	1,N,0	1,N		1,N,0
1	Payment	1,N	1	1	1,N	

Inclusion Question (for Data): A question that identifies the necessity to include a data item by finding the *business event* the data items supports. See also **'Exclusion Question (for Data)'.**

Inclusion Question (for Objects): A question that identifies the necessity to include an Object by finding the *business event* the Object supports. See also '**Exclusion Question (for Objects)**'.

Inclusion Question (for Events): A question that identifies the necessity to include a *business event* by finding the consequences of including the *business event* (and therefore another *business event*). See also '**Exclusion Question (for Events)**'.

Inclusion Question (for Reports): A question that identifies the necessity to include a Report by finding the *business event* the Report supports. See also '**Exclusion Question (for Reports)**'.

JAD: (Joint Application Development) A JAD session is very similar to a requirements discovery session, as described in this book. JAD was developed by Chuck Morris of IBM Raleigh and Tony Crawford of IBM Toronto in the late 1970's. In 1980 Crawford and Morris taught JAD in Toronto and Crawford led several workshops to prove the concept. The results were good and JAD became a well accepted best practice in many companies. In time, JAD developed and gained general approval in the corporate world. Crawford defines JAD as an interactive systems design concept involving discussion groups in a workshop setting. Originally, JAD was designed to bring system developers and users of varying backgrounds and opinions together in a productive and creative environment. The meetings were a way of obtaining quality requirements and specifications. This provided a good alternative to previously traditional serial interviews by system analysts. See also '**AJAD**' and '**Requirements Discovery Session**'.

Multi-valued (Repeating) Group: See '**Characteristic Object**'.

Normalization: "Normalization" is a commonly accepted method of eliminating data redundancies. The science underlying normalization theory is quite complex and normally requires considerable study. However, only researchers and teachers need this degree of familiarity with normalization theory and all its abstractions. Business analysts need to know how to do it so good Objects can be defined to support business processes – 'good' meaning Objects that are focused, and not a mixed bag of all kinds of data about all kinds of stuff. Knowing the details of the theory does not enhance our ability to deliver a business requirement with "fully normalized" data to support it. Scores of books have been written about this subject, so you can learn as much about the underlying theory as you want by searching on the Internet or buying a few good technical books. But to get a "normalized" data set for your project simply means following the **5 Rules of Business Data**. These Rules, when followed, will deliver a view of the data that is sufficiently "normalized" with redundancies minimized.

It should be noted that the conventional view is that normalization is "done" after all the needed data has been gathered and attributed to Objects, in a step-wise progression through different levels of normalization. While this does work, it also takes a very long time to do, and is very frustrating to people who want to get on with the work.

Using the methods in the book, normalization is done immediately when specific data is discovered. The data attribution rules are applied during the process of data discovery, not afterwards. Accordingly, it's done right away as a natural and inherent part of business system analysis. See also **'Denormalization'**.

Object (in an Object-Relationship Diagram): An Object (sometimes called an *entity*) is a person, place or thing that the target business area needs to know or remember something about. An Object is a noun, but it is distinct from other nouns that are data attributes because a <u>business</u> Object (1) consists of two or more data attributes to give it 'substance'; (2) is <u>essential</u> to the successful operation of the target business area to meet client objectives (i.e., the Object *must* be present); and (3) is defined by its business rules and data attributes. All <u>business</u> Objects must consist of two or more data attributes, but these objects can be 'normalized' to just a single data attribute when finalizing the physical database design.

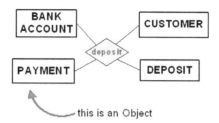

ACCOUNTING SYSTEM
It is Time to Deposit Customer
Payment to a Bank Account

this is an Object

PAYMENT

Definition

A financial instrument offered by a customer in exchange for the company's products.

Business Rules

- Is credited to one sales person only (i.e., there are no split commissions)
- Is from one customer only
- Can only be received in one outlet
- Must be for one or many products (i.e., future payments and credits are not accepted)
- Must be for one or more sales transactions (i.e., payments against future transactions are not accepted)

Data Attributes

- payment date
- method of payment
- amount of payment
- type of card
- card expiry date

Object (in a Business-Process Diagram): Objects that appear in Business Process Diagrams are the exact same Objects as defined in an Object Relationship Diagram. Objects that are present in a process diagram were often called "data stores" in their earlier incarnation. See also **'Business Process Diagram'**.

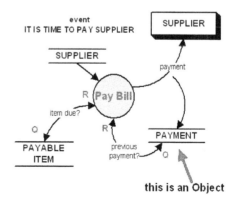

this is an Object

Object-Relationship Diagram: This is a picture of the information that we need to know about (retrieve) or remember (record), in a specific context. It shows how groups of related information (Objects) are joined together, and the circumstance (i.e., the *business event*) under which they are associated with other groups of data (Objects).

This type of diagram can be one of the components of the business requirements, if the new system is research-based or data warehouse oriented rather than process-based. These diagrams do not show the flow of data in a process, except for the verb in the diamond (the relationship) that joins the Objects together.

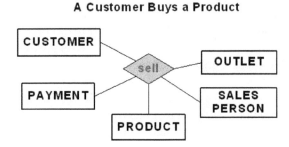

Process Narrative: A Business Process Diagram must always have a narrative written in plain language to describe it. The narrative can be written in several styles, the most common being 'Point Form Style' and the 'Structured Narrative Style'.

Point Form Style

For each request for a product from the customer:

- Find out if the customer exists in our system.
- Find the product sold.
- If it is available, give it to the customer with the price.
- Accept the payment from the customer.
- Remember the payment.
- Remember the salesperson who served the customer, and in which outlet.
- Reduce inventory by the quantity of product sold.
- If it is a new customer, get the customer information from the customer.
- Remember the new customer information.

Structured Narrative Style

For each request for a product from the customer, find the product. If it is available give it to the customer with the cost. Accept the payment from the customer. Remember the payment and the sales transaction, including the sales person who served the customer, and in which outlet. Reduce inventory by the quantity of the product sold. If it is a new customer, remember the customer.

Ratio of Occurrences: See 'Cardinality'.

Requirements Discovery Session: An interactive meeting of project clients and subject-matter experts, led by an expert "Pilot" and possibly supported by an expert "co-pilot", with the purpose of discovering business requirements. See also 'JAD'.

SME: See also 'Subject-Matter Expert'.

Subject-Matter Expert: An individual who may or may not be the client. Subject-matter experts are individuals who have all the required knowledge about the business areas and information that's involved in the targeted processes. A subject-matter expert should never be a surrogate client who does not work hands-on in the business area for which they are expert.

Subtype Object: A "subtype Object" (a.k.a. 'subclass') is a type of Object which has only those data attributes that are specific to a particular view of the Object (i.e., the subtype). Data attributed to one subtype Object cannot be attributed to any other Object. Data which is common to more than one subtype is attributed to the Object associated with the subtype, which is called a supertype Object. Each subtype Object must be associated with only one supertype Object. See also **'Supertype Object'** and **'Object'.**

Supertype Object: A "supertype Object" (a.k.a. 'superclass') is an Object that has several different views of the information it represents, with each distinct view known as a subtype Object. Each subtype of a supertype Object has unique and distinct data attributes. Supertype Objects contain only the data attributes that are common to all its subtypes. See also **'Subtype Object'** and **'Object'.**

System Requirements Document: This is an expansion of the business requirements, including the solution design and implementation details. In addition to everything in the Business Requirements Document, it may include a Conceptual Data Model as a prescription for database design. The business functions may also have additional information, based on solution design, including expanded Use Cases.

Terminator: A Terminator is an external entity over which the business process it communicates with has no control. The Terminator can be outside the organization, or inside, but it is always external to the process that communicates with it. It acts as a source of input information, or a destination of information from the business process, but the processes and data inside a terminator are outside the scope of the target system. Many (but not all) terminators are also Objects, since we usually have to remember something about them.

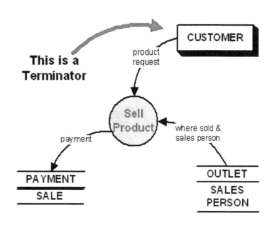

Unique Identifier: A primary identifier or *key* is a unique identifier of a specific instance of an Object. The unique identifier should never contain data to be used in a process. It is simply a locator address. See also **'Object'.**

About the Author

Trond Frantzen has over 30 years of experience as a management consultant, team leader and business analyst specializing in mission-critical, strategic and "challenged" projects. He is the author of several books on modern, agile approaches to business requirements analysis, and developer of the "PowerStart Analysis Approach", which is used by many organizations.

Trond is well known as a business and IT "requirements analysis" authority. He has broad experience in financial services and insurance, government services, manufacturing, retail, aerospace, telecommunications, distribution and consulting services. His expertise includes business & system requirements analysis, project rescue and metrics (measurement and estimation). He has delivered Business Requirements Analysis courses and seminars to over 35,000 people.

Trond's strengths are his skills in simplifying complex issues, business process re-engineering, and strategic thinking and imagination.

Trond was born in Norway, raised in Toronto, graduated from Concordia University, and lives in Calgary. His passion is investing in the success of others – people, organizations and his community.

You can reach him at trond.frantzen@powerstartgroup.com

www.ingramcontent.com/pod-product-compliance
Lightning Source LLC
Chambersburg PA
CBHW060556060326
40690CB00017B/3730